Golfing in Oregon

The *Complete* guide to Oregon's golf facilities

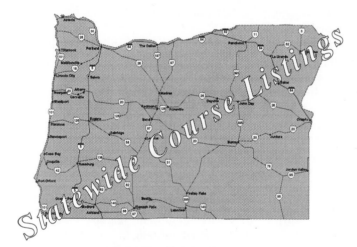

Statewide Course Listings

Eighth Edition
by
Daniel MacMillan

Published by:

M A C Productions

Golf Guides Since 1986

Carnation, Washington

Waiver on Accuracy
We have gone to great lengths to provide the golfer with an up-to-date, accurate and comprehensive guide to golfing facilities in the state of Oregon; nevertheless, we all slice it out of bounds from time to time. Each course reserves the right to change their prices and policies at any time and we will not be held liable for any inaccuracies presented in this book.

Library of Congress Cataloging-in-Publication Data
MacMillan, Daniel E.
Golfing in Oregon; The complete guide to Oregon's Golf facilities
(eighth edition)
1. Golf course guide-Oregon state
2. Travel-golf-related in Oregon state

Printed in Canada

Cover photos appear courtesy of:
Broken Top Club (front), Bend, OR
Broken Top Club (back), Bend, OR

First Edition, April 1990	Second Edition, January 1992
Third Edition, March 1993	Fourth Edition, March 1994
Fifth Edition, March 1995	Sixth Edition, March 1996
Seventh Edition, April 1996	Eighth Edition, March 1998

ISBN 1-878591-23-1, $9.95

Published by:
MAC Productions
P.O. Box 655
Carnation, Washington 98014 USA
Phone: (425) 880-4411
FAX: (425) 880-4450
e-mail address: waorgolf@concentric.net

Preface

In this the eighth edition of **"Golfing in Oregon"** I hope it will be the most complete golf guide in the state published to date. The size is designed with the idea that the book will more easily fit in your glove box or golf bag. We have also provided small map inserts along with the driving directions to help you get to the golf facilities. As always you will find new courses, par 3's, and ranges just opened or due to open later in the season. Layouts, prices and yardage have been revised to reflect any changes that have occurred since last year. I hope you enjoy the book, see you on the links!

Acknowledgements

A special thanks to all the pros, owners and course managers who have been so helpful in providing us access to their courses and current information. Thanks to the Oregon Department of Transportation for the endless supply of maps needed in doing this project.

Jeff Shelley for his help and personal support on these projects. Without Jeffs help these projects would not have got out on time. Thanks Jeff!!!

Thanks to Bob Valentine and his personal touch on these projects over the years, Thanks Robert!!!

This book would not have been possible without the tremendous support of my entire family and my friends. I thank each and every one of them for the special interest they have shown in the golf books.

To my children Joshua Daniel, Sarah Gene and the new addition Christian Rogers for showing me what really is important in life.

Thanks to my loving wife Kristi Gene. Words cannot express the love and support she has given me on this project. I feel blessed to have a wife whom provided a loving, caring, Christ like atmosphere in which to produce this book in. Thanks Kristi Gene. Most importantly my Lord Jesus, for his gentle hand and firm grip with my life and this company.

Daniel

Golf Courses (continued)

Driving Ranges

Golf Courses of the Pacific N.W.
Fairgreens Media, INC 216

MAC Productions Titles:
*Golf Courses of the
Pacific Northwest
Golfing in Washington
Golfing in Oregon
Golfing in Idaho & Montana
The Birdie Book*
Order Form..............................217

Daniel MacMillan has been an avid golfer for the past 14 years. He enjoys
researching and playing the various golf courses of the Pacific Northwest
(if it were only that easy!!). *Golfing in Washington* was the brainchild of
Daniel and his previous partner Mark Fouty who, one day while playing a
round at Snohomish Golf Course, discussed finding a guide to use themselves.
When no such guide was available this one was written. The book has taken on
many stages. It was originally called *Golfing in Western Washington*, which
encompassed only the more populous half of the state. In 1988 it expanded to
Golfing in Washington (now in it's 13th edition). Meanwhile Mark pursued a
career in New York so Daniel bought out Mark's share of the company. The
company has therefore become a real family operation. Daniel drags his wife
Kristi and their three children throughout the Pacific Northwest seeking information on new courses and facilities for upcoming publications. We hope all the
thousands of miles and endless phone calls have paid off. This guide is designed
to have all the information a golfer wants and needs to know about playing a
course, and as a golfer Daniel has done just that.

Golfing in Oregon is the second book published by MAC Productions
and written by Daniel. Now in its 8th edition it also is published on
an annual basis. This book too has taken many forms it was originally called
Golfing in Oregon & Idaho. In 1992 the book was changed to reflect the
new format and now only includes the state of Oregon.

Golfing in Idaho & Montana is the third book published by MAC
Productions and written by Daniel. The first edition of this book was called
Golfing In Idaho and was published in 1994. The new book which came
out in spring of 1996 includes the great state of Montana and is called *Golfing
In Idaho & Montana* look for it in a pro shop or book store near you.

The Birdie Book is another one of MAC Productions titles that is a cooperative
effort with newly formed Dornoch Publishing. It is a coupon book that offers
the golfer nearly $2,200.00 worth of savings at many of Washington's finest
golf facilities and learning centers. Hopefully in the future *The Birdie Book* will
feature Oregon's finest golf courses and will cover the entire northwest region.

New territories are always being explored for writing golf course guides such
as this. It takes many man hours and attention to detail to produce books of
this nature. From start to finish a new book takes about two years to produce.
Currently five more are in the works with many more in the initial planning
stage. Look for the new publications at a pro shop or book store near you.
Daniel's hope is that you will find this to be the best golf guide of its kind on
the shelf.

Map 1

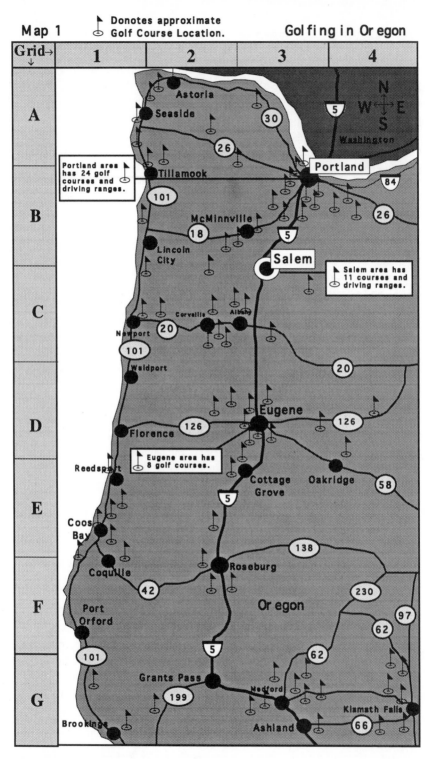

Donotes approximate
Golf Course Location.

Golfing in Oregon

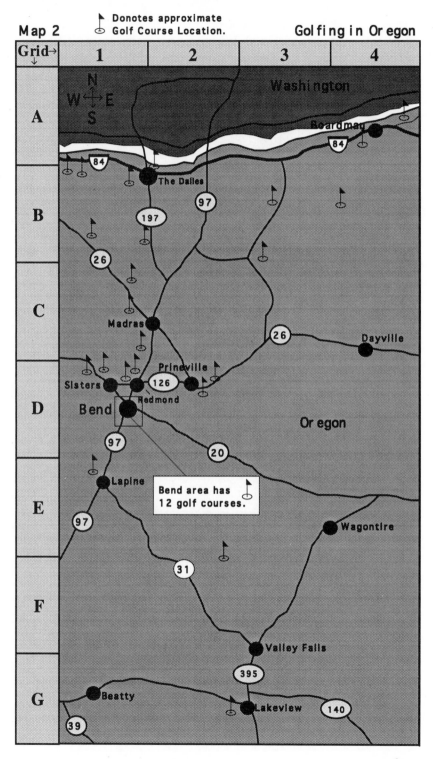

Map 2

Donotes approximate
Golf Course Location.

Golfing in Oregon

Grid→ 1 2 3 4

A

Washington

N
W E
S

Boardman

84

84

The Dalles

B

197

97

26

C

Madras

26

Dayville

Sisters

Prineville

D

Bend

126

Redmond

Or egon

97

20

E

Lapine

Bend area has
12 golf courses.

97

Wagontire

31

F

Valley Falls

395

G

Beatty

Lakeview

140

39

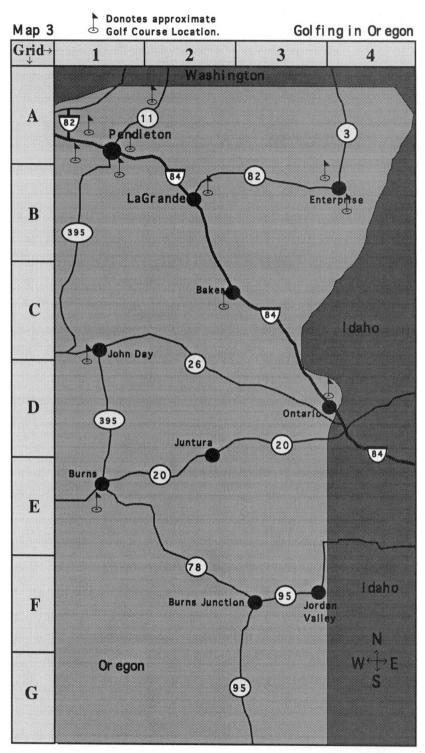

Map 3

Donotes approximate
Golf Course Location.

Grid→

1 2 3 4

Washington

A

82 11 Pendleton 3

84 82

B LaGrande Enterprise

395

Baker

C 84 Idaho

John Day 26

D 395 Ontario

Juntura 20

Burns 20 84

E

78

F Burns Junction 95 Jordan Idaho
Valley

N
W E
S

Oregon

G 95

Abbreviations, Explanatory notes and Disclaimers

Executive Course-An executive golf course is usually longer than a typical par 3 short course but shorter than a regulation course.

Private Course- A golf course that is not open to public play.

Semi-private- golf courses that are closed to the public at certain times during the week. Best to call ahead to reserve tee-times.

Tees: **T**-Tour; **C**-Championship; **M**-Men; **F**-Forward; **W**-Women. **W/D**-Weekday; **W/E**-Weekend.

N/A-Not available.

Course rating-This rates the degree of difficulty of course in the NorthWest and refers to the average number of shots per round a scratch golfer ought to shoot. It is figured by rating teams who factor in terrain, length and hazards of each course. The higher the rating the more difficult the course. Course ratings appear courtesy of the *Pacific Northwest Golf Association* and the *Oregon Golf Association.*

Slope-This is similar to the course rating but it considers other factors as well. The slope rating takes into consideration the playing difficulty of a course for handicaps above scratch. The higher the number, the more difficult the golf course. Slope ratings courtesy of the *Pacific Northwest Golf Association* and the *Oregon Golf Association.*

Greens fee- prices are subject to change at any time. Because a number of Eastern Oregon courses close for the winter, the prices may reflect those of last year. When two prices are given, the first refers to the 18 hole fee, the second to the 9 hole fee. "Reciprocates" refers to the practice of private courses allowing members of other private courses to play their courses. However, because some courses only reciprocate with a limited number of other courses, it's best to call first.

Trail fee- the fee a course charges an individual to use their own power cart on the course.

Reservation policy- This refers to the maximum number of days the course allows reservations to made in advance under normal circumstances.

Winter condition- Dry, damp, wet refers to the club pro's opinion of the course's condition in rainy conditions.

Terrain- flat, flat some hills, relatively hilly, very hilly.

Tees- Grass or mats are the alternatives.

Spikes- many of the area golf courses are going to a soft spike policy during the peak golfing season. Be sure to check each course prior to play as the policies vary a great deal from course to course.

Course layouts/yardage- My intent is to show tees in relation to greens, obvious hazards and other holes. Some hazards may not be adequately represented, nor are trees shown. Use these layouts as a reference at the kind of golf course you are planning to visit. The more the hazards the more difficult the golf course will play.

Agate Beach Golf Course (public, 9 hole course)
4100 North Coast Highway; Newport, OR 97365
Phone: (541) 265-7331. Fax: none. Internet: none.
Pro: Terry R. Martin, PGA. Superintendent: Terry R. Martin.
Rating/Slope: M 65.8/109;W 68.7/109. **Course record:** 62.
Green fees: $24/$12 all week long; M/C, VISA.
Power cart: $22/$11. **Pull cart:** $2. **Trail fee:** $3/$6 for personal carts.
Reservation policy: yes, please call up to 7 days in advance for tee-times
Winter condition: the course is open all year long, very dry and drains well.
Terrain: flat, some slight hills. **Tees:** grass. **Spikes:** metal spikes permitted.
Services: club rentals, lessons, restaurant, beer, wine, pro shop, driving range.
Comments: Well maintained course with medium sized greens that are
fronted by few hazards. Fairways are fairly wide with large landing areas.
This track has excellent drainage for winter and off season play. This easy to
walk, picturesque golf course is a favorite for weekenders and vacationers on
the Oregon Coast. Be sure to call ahead for tee times during the summer.

Directions: the golf course is located at
the north end of Newport Oregon on the
east side of Hwy 101, one mile north of
the Fred Meyer shopping center. Look
for signs marking the way to the course.

Course Yardage & Par:
M-3002 yards, par 36.
W-2894 yards, par 38.

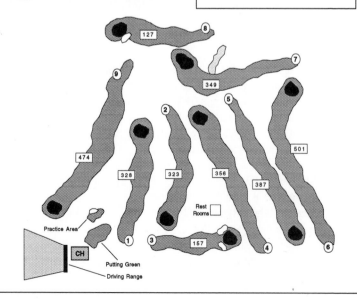

Alderbrook Golf Course (public, 18 hole course)
7300 Alderbrook Road; Tillamook, OR 97141
Phone: (503) 842-6413. Fax: (503) 842-4596. Internet: none.
Owner: Neil Abrahamson. Pro: Steve Wilkes, PGA.
Rating/Slope: M 66.8/105; W 70/109. **Course record:** 62.
Green fees: $20/$12 all week long; Jr rates; M/C, VISA.
Power cart: $20/12. **Pull cart:** $2. **Trail fee:** $10 per day.
Reservation policy: call ahead for weekend tee times. May thru October only.
Winter condition: golf course is open all year long, weather permitting.
Terrain: flat, some hills. **Tees:** grass. **Spikes:** metal spikes permitted.
Services: club rentals, snack bar, beer, wine, pro shop, putting green.
Comments: mature trees line the fairways of this excellent par 69 layout. A creek comes into play on several holes throughout the course and is a major factor off the tee or on your approach shots. Greens are forgiving with few hazards fronting them. Excellent golf course to play while visiting the scenic and beautiful Oregon Coast.

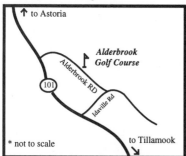

Directions: the golf course is located 4 miles north of Tillamook off of Hwy 101. Proceed 4 miles north on Hwy 101 and go east on Alderbrook Road (just north of the cheese factory). When you come to a fork in the road stay left. The golf course will be on your right, 1.9 miles ahead. Look for a sign marking your way to the golf course.

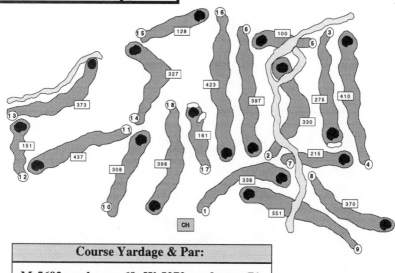

Course Yardage & Par:
M-5692 yards, par 69; W-5272 yards, par 71.

Alpine Meadows Golf Course (public, 9 hole course)
P.O. Box 238; Golf Course Road; Enterprise, OR 97828
Phone: (541) 426-3246. Fax: none. Internet: none.
Manager/Pro: Jim Chestnut. Superintendent: none.
Rating/Slope: M 66.8/113;W 69.9/116. **Course record:** 65.
Green fees: $15/$9 all week long; no special rates; no credit cards.
Power cart: $20/$10. **Pull cart:** $3/$1.50. **Trail fee:** $5 for personal carts.
Reservation policy: advance reservations are not needed or required.
Winter condition: the golf course is closed from October 15th to April 1st.
Terrain: flat, some hills. **Tees:** all grass. **Spikes:** metal spikes permitted.
Services: club rentals, lessons, snack bar, lounge, beer, wine, liquor, pro shop,
putting & chipping greens. **Comments:** Beautiful setting in the Wallowa
Mountains. Greens are large and kept in excellent condition throughout the
peak season. Dual tee's are available for those wanting to play a full 18.

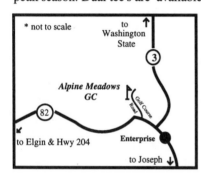

Directions: from Hwy 82 turn north
on Golf Course Road (the road between
the Safeway store and Carmie's).
Proceed to the golf course, which will
be on your left hand side. The golf
course is located on the west end of the
city. Look for signs marking your turn
to the golf course.

Course Yardage & Par:
M-3033 yards, par 36.
W-2806 yards, par 38.
Dual tees for 18 holes:
M-6060 yards, par 72.
W-5620 yards, par 75.

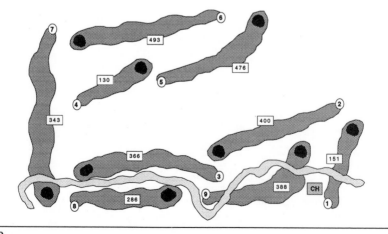

Applegate Golf (public, 9 hole course)
7350 New Hope Road; Grants Pass, OR 97527
Phone: (541) 955-0480. Fax: none. Internet: none.
Managers: John Briggs & Nancy Sweeny.
Rating/Slope: M 65.8/104;W 64.8/101. **Course record:** 32.
Green fees: $15/$10 all week long; winter, Jr. & Sr. rates; M/C, VISA, AMEX.
Power cart: not available. **Pull cart:** $2/$1. **Trail fee:** not allowed.
Reservation policy: advance reservations are not needed or required.
Winter condition: the golf course is open all year round weather permitting.
Terrain: flat, some hills. **Tees:** all grass. **Spikes:** metal spikes permitted.
Services: club rentals, lessons, snack bar, lounge, beer, wine, pro shop.
Comments: new golf course that opened in mid 1996 that features fairly flat
terrain and tree lined fairways. Water is a major factor coming into play on over
half the the holes at Applegate. Fairways are medium wide giving the golfer
some room off the tee. Greens are moderate with few slopes to them. The course
has a very friendly atmosphere and feel. Great course to have your tournament.

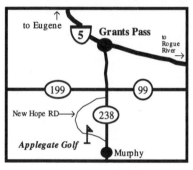

Directions: from I-5 N&S exit at
Grants Pass to Highway 238 and head
southbound toward Murphy Oregon.
When you reach New Hope Road turn
westbound and proceed 1.2 miles to the
golf course. Your turn is 6.8 miles from
Grants Pass. Look for signs.

Course Yardage & Par:
M-2677 yards, par 36.
W-2478 yards, par 36.

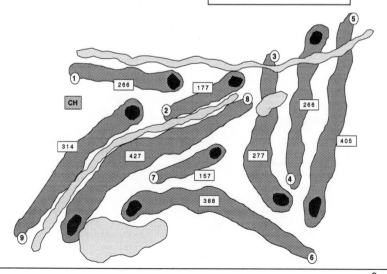

Arrowhead Golf Club (private, 18 hole course)
28301 South Highway 213; Molalla, OR 97038
Phone: (503) 655-1441, (503) 829-8080. Fax: (503) 829-8367.
Director of Golf: Joe Clarizio. Pro: Rob Gibbons, PGA.
Rating/Slope: C 69.9/125; M 68.6/122;W 69.4/116. **Course record:** 67.
Green fees: private club, members & guests of members only; reciprocates.
Power cart: private club. **Pull cart:** private club. **Trail fee:** private club.
Reservation policy: call up to one week in advance for members only.
Winter condition: the golf course is open all year long weather permitting.
Terrain: flat, easy walking. **Tees:** grass. **Spikes:** metal spikes permitted.
Services: club rentals, lessons, snack bar, restaurant, lounge, beer, liquor,
pro shop, lockers, driving range, putting & chipping greens, practice bunker.
Comments: Situated along the banks of the Molalla River. A peaceful country
club atmosphere. The driving range is open to the public for your practice
needs. Good private facility with large, well conditioned greens and fairways.

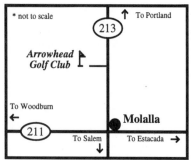

Directions: from I-205 N&S take exit
#10 (Hwy 213) to Molalla, Oregon.
From here proceed southbound on Hwy
213 for 14 miles. The golf course will
be located on your right hand side when
traveling southbound on Highway 213.
Look for a sign indicating your turn.

Course Yardage & Par:
C-6324 yards, par 71.
M-6050 yards, par 71.
W-5293 yards, par 73.

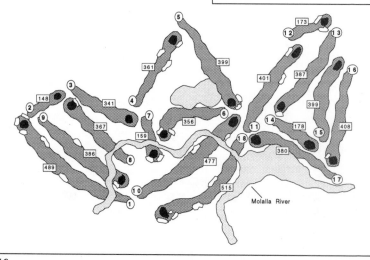

Molalla River

Aspen Lakes Golf Club (public, 27 hole course)

17204 Highway 126; Sisters, OR 97759
Phone: (541) 549-4653 or toll free 1-800-866-3981. Fax: none.
Director of Golf: James Spadoni. Superintendent: none.
Rating/Slope: C 73.8/132; M 71.4/127; W 74.6/133. **Course record:** 68.
Green fees: $35/$25 all week long; M/C, VISA, AMEX.
Power cart: $25/$14. **Pull cart:** $3/$2. **Trail fee:** to be determined.
Reservation policy: please call up to 1 week in advance for tee times.
Winter condition: the golf course is closed during the winter months.
Terrain: flat, some hills. **Tees:** all grass. **Spikes:** metal spikes permitted.
Services: club rentals, lessons, putting green, pro shop, driving range.
Comments: this 27 hole Bill Overdorf design is a real challeng at every turn.
Ponds are everywhere leaving the golfer many hazards from the tee. This golf
course is very mature for being such a new track. Towering pines lin almost all
the fairways and are a major factor in your course management. Great course.

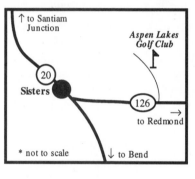

Directions: from Hwy 20 east and west turn eastbound on Hwy 126 heading towards Redmond Oregon. The course is located approximately 3.7 miles ahead on your left hand side if you are coming from Sisters. Look for a sign posted at your turn.

Course Yardage & Par:

T-7000 yards, par 72.
C-6540 yards, par 72.
M-6100 yards, par 72
W-5400 yards, par 72.

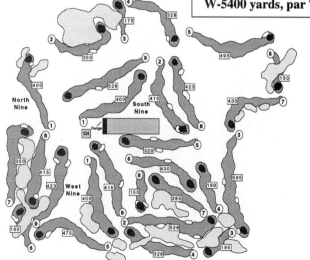

Astoria Golf & Country Club (private, 18 hole course)
Route 1, Box 536; Highway 101; Warrenton, OR 97146
Phone: (503) 861-2545. Fax: (503) 738-8359. Internet: www.astgolf@pacifier.com .
Pro: Mike Gove, PGA. Superintendent: John Whisler.
Rating/Slope: C 71.0/120; M 70.4/118;W 74.4/125. **Course record:** 63.
Green fees: private club, members and guests of members only, reciprocates.
Power cart: private club, members & guests of members only.
Pull cart: private club, members only. **Trail fee:** personal carts are not allowed.
Reservation policy: please call ahead for golf course availablity.
Winter condition: the golf course is open all year long, weather permitting.
Terrain: relatively hilly. **Tees:** all grass. **Spikes:** metal spikes permitted.
Services: club rentals, lessons, restaurant, lounge, beer, wine, liquor, pro shop,
lockers, showers, driving range, putting & chipping greens, club memberships.
Comments: Beautiful older course that was built in 1924. The track is situated
on the stunning Oregon Coast. Greens are large, well bunkered with few
undulations. Fairways are wide & rolling giving the golfer a large landing areas.

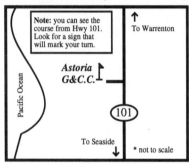

Directions: from Hwy 101 the course
is located at the south end of Warrenton Oregon. From Hwy 101 on the
west side of the Hwy look for a blue &
white sign marking the entrance to the
golf course. **Note:** the golf course can
be seen from Hwy 101.

Course Yardage & Par:
C-6488 yards, par 72.
M-6380 yards, par 72.
W-5893 yards, par 74.

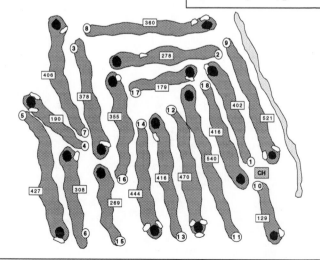

Auburn Center Golf Club (public, 9 hole course)

5220 Center Street NE; Salem, OR 97301
Phone: (503) 363-4404. Fax: none. Internet: none.
Managers: Gregg & Cindy Smith.
Rating/Slope: the golf course is not rated. **Course record:** 27.
Green fees: $10/$6 all week long; Jr. and Sr. rates; no credit cards.
Power cart: no power carts are available for use. **Pull cart:** $1.50.
Trail fee: personal carts are not allowed on the golf course at anytime.
Reservation policy: advance reservations are not needed or required.
Winter condition: wet conditions. The golf course is open all year long.
Terrain: flat, easy walking. **Tees:** grass. **Spikes:** metal spikes permitted.
Services: club rentals, snack bar, beverages, miniature golf, game room,
putting & chipping green. **Comments:** Flat golf course, that is very easy to
walk. Course is excellent for the beginner and senior golfer.

Directions: from I-5 S, take Market St.
exit #256 and go east to Lancaster Dr.
Go south (right) on Lancaster Dr. to
Center St. and turn left. The course is
located 1.1 miles ahead on Center St.
The course will be on your right side.
I-5N take Mission St exit #253 and go
east on Mission St. (N Santiam Hwy)
to Lancaster Dr. and go north on
Lancaster Dr. to Center St. Turn right
on Center St. and follow to course.

Course Yardage & Par:
M-1338 yards, par 29; W-1338 yards, par 29.
M-2708 yards, par 59; W-2708 yards, par 59.

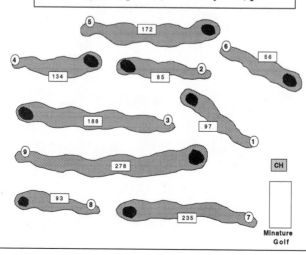

Awbrey Glen Golf Club (private, limited outside play)
2500 N.W. Awbrey Glen Drive; Bend, OR 97701
Phone: (541) 388-8526. Fax: none. Internet: none.
Pro: Steve Gillespie, PGA. Director of Golf: Mark Amberson, PGA.
Rating/Slope: T 72.8/130; C 70.3/124; M 67.9/124; W 70.0/125.
Green fees: private club. Limited outside play. Call 7 days ahead for T-times $50.
Power cart: $26. **Pull cart:** N/A. **Trail fee:** no personal carts are allowed.
Reservation policy: limited outside play call 7 Days in for tee-times.
Winter condition: the golf course is closed during the winter months.
Terrain: flat, rolling hills. **Tees:** all grass. **Spikes:** metal spikes permitted.
Services: lessons, snack bar, beer, wine, lockers, pro shop, restaurant, lounge, driving range, chipping green, 5 hole par 3 learning center golf course.
Comments: this spectacular Bunny Mason design features the finest learning centers in the NW. The double ended range is surrounded by a 5 hole par 3 course. This course, if you are able is a must play. Call for outside play policies.

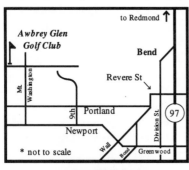

Directions: from Hwy 97 (3rd St.), turn west on Greenwood (turns to Newport), continue on Shevlin Park Road. Proceed to Mt. Washington Drive and turn right. Proceed to Awbrey Glen Drive and turn left. Proceed to the golf course.

Course Yardage & Par:
"Awbrey Loop" 598 yards, par 15.

Course Yardage & Par:
Tour: 7005 yards, par 72.
Championship: 6557 yards, par 72.
Members: 6163 yards, par 72.
Challenge: 5396 yards, par 72.

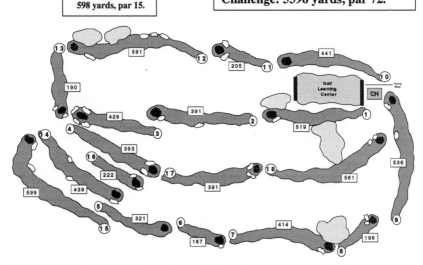

Baker Golf Club (public, 9 hole course)
2801 Indiana Avenue; Baker City, OR 97814
Phone: (541) 523-2358. **Fax:** none. **Internet:** none.
Pro: Ron Blankenship. **Superintendent:** Bill Woodcock.
Rating/Slope: M 68.7/103; W 70.0/109. **Course record:** 62.
Green fees: $16/$10 all week long; Jr. rates; M/C, VISA.
Power cart: $18/$9. **Pull cart:** $2/$1. **Trail fee:** no charge for personal carts.
Reservation policy: please call ahead on Saturdays after 10am for tee-times.
Winter condition: course is closed from November from15th to March 1st.
Terrain: flat, some hills. **Tees:** all grass. **Spikes:** metal spikes permitted.
Services: club rentals, lessons, lounge, beer, wine, liquor, beverages, pro shop.
Comments: the golf course is relatively short with wide open fairways, small greens and rolling terrain. Picturesque setting with mountain views from many of the teeing areas. The course has dual tees for those wanting to play a full 18.

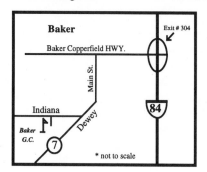

<u>Directions:</u> off of I-84 exit at City Center (Elm Street) #304. Follow Hwy 7 towards Sumpter. Turn right on Indiana Avenue, (look for a sign that is posted). The course is located at the top of the hill on your left hand side.

Course Yardage & Par:
M-3018 yards, par 35.
W-2926 yards, par 38.
<u>Dual tees for 18 holes:</u>
M-6116 yards, par 70.
W-5932 yards, par 70.

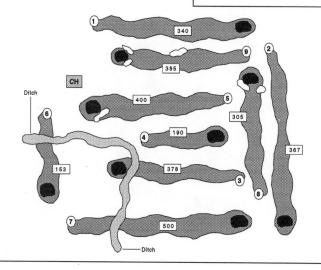

Bandon Face Rock Golf Course (public, 9 hole course)
3235 Beach Loop Drive; Bandon, OR 97411
Phone: (541) 347-3818. Fax: (541) 347-4781. Internet: none.
Manager: Jerried Brown. Superintendent: none.
Rating/Slope: M 59.64/99 W 59.9/102. **Course record:** 26.
Green fees: W/D $14/$9; W/E $15/$10; VISA, M/C.
Power cart: $18/$10. **Pull cart:** $2. **Trail fee:** $5 for personal carts.
Reservation policy: advance reservations are not needed or required for times.
Winter condition: the golf course is open all year long. Dry conditions.
Terrain: flat, easy walking course. **Tees:** grass. **Spikes:** metal spikes permitted.
Services: club rentals, lessons, snack bar, pop, small pro shop, putting area.
Comments: this 9 hole course winds along the scenic Johnson Creek. The golf
course is located next to the ocean in a valley protected from the wind. Excellent
walking golf course for the senior or first time golfer. Good public golf course.

Directions: Course located in the south
end of Bandon. From Hwy 101, go west
on Sea Bird Drive to Beach Loop Road.
At Beach Loop Drive turn left and travel
.2 miles to the golf course which will be
on your left. The golf course is located
behind the Inn at Face Rock Motel.
Look for signs the way is well marked.

Course Yardage & Par:
M-2096 yards, par 32.
W-1915 yards, par 32.
Dual tees for 18 holes:
M-4308 yards, par 64.
W-4011 yards, par 64.

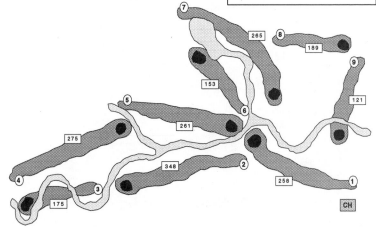

Battle Creek Golf Course (public, 18 hole course)
6161 Commercial Street SE; Salem, OR 97306
Phone: (503) 585-1402. Fax: (503) 399-7752. Internet: none.
Pro: C. Lynn Baxter, PGA. Superintendent: not available.
Rating/Slope: C 68.8/117; M 65.7/110; W 68.5/113. **Course record: 64.**
Green fees: W/D $23/$13; W/E $25/$15; M/C, VISA are welcome.
Power cart: $20/$10. **Pull cart:** $2. **Trail fee:** $10 for personal carts.
Reservation policy: yes, call ahead 7 days for Saturday and Sundays only.
Winter condition: the golf course is open all year long, weather permitting.
Terrain: very flat. **Tees:** all grass tees. **Spikes:** metal spikes permitted.
Services: club rentals, lessons, caddy shack, restaurant, lounge, beer, wine,
liquor, beverages, large pro shop, lockers, putting & chipping greens.
Comments: Challenging course with small, well bunkered elevated greens.
Good drainage makes this golf course very playable in the winter months.
Excellent course that can play much more difficult than the yardage indicates.

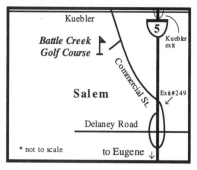

Directions: I-5S. Take Kuebler exit. Keep right to Commercial St. Take a left on Commercial follow for 1 mile to the course on your right. I-5N take Salem exit #249. Follow road for approximately 1 mile. The golf course will be located on your left hand side. Course is located at the south end of Salem. Look for signs that are posted at your turns.

Course Yardage & Par:
C-6015 yards, par 72. M-5395 yards, par 72. W-4945 yards, par 72.

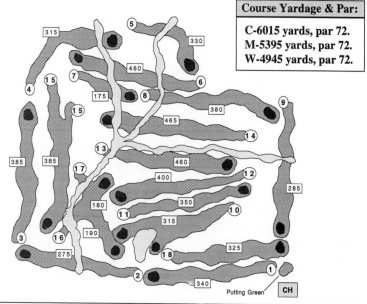

Bay Breeze Golf & Driving Range (public, 9 hole par 3)
2325 Latimer Road; Tillamook, OR 97141
Phone: (503) 842-1166. **Fax: none. Internet: none.**
Instructor: Mike Lehman. **Superintendent: none.**
Rating/Slope: the golf course is not rated. **Course record:** 24.
Green fees: $6 all week long; credit cards are accepted.
Power cart: power carts are not available. **Pull cart:** $1.
Reservation policy: reservations are not required or needed for play.
Winter condition: the course is closed from November 1st to February 15th.
Terrain: very flat. **Tees:** all grass. **Spikes:** metal spikes permitted.
Services: club rentals, pro shop, deli, covered driving range, putting green.
Comments: this short par 3 golf course features two lake holes and large bent grass greens with generous landing areas. The facility will features a covered driving range and putting course for those weekenders on the Oregon Coast.

Directions: the golf course is located on Highway 101 directly across from the Tillamook Cheese factory on the east side of the Highway. Look for signs marking your turn to the parking lot.

Course Yardage & Par:
M-1061 yards, par 27.
W-853 yards, par 27.

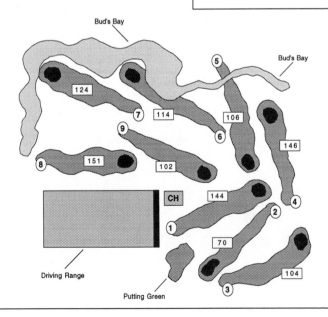

Bayou Golf Club (public, 9 hole course & 9 hole par 3 course)

9301 SW Bayou Drive; McMinnville, OR 97128
Phone: (503) 472-4651. **Fax:** none. **Internet:** none.
Pro: Sarah Bakefelt. **Superintendent:** Jerry Claussen.
Rating/Slope: C 70.2/118; M 68.6/116;W 67.6/109. **Course record:** 64.
Green fees: $20/$12 all week long; Jr. and Sr. rates, no credit cards.
Green fees for the Short 9: $10/$5 all week long; Jr./Sr. rates; no credit cards.
Power cart: $20/$12. **Pull cart:** $3/$2. **Trail fee:** $10/$6.
Reservation policy: yes, call ahead for Saturday, Sunday and Holidays only.
Winter condition: open all year weather permitting. Fair conditions.
Terrain: gentle rolling hills. **Tees:** all grass. **Spikes:** metal spikes permitted.
Services: club rentals, lessons, snack bar, beer, wine, pro shop, driving range, putting & chipping greens. **Comments:** Course was built in 1964. Riverside setting with water hazards coming into play on all 9 holes. Good test of golf.

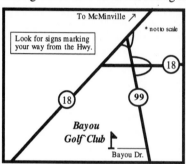

Look for signs marking your way from the Hwy.

To McMinnville ↗

* not to scale

Bayou Golf Club

Bayou Dr.

Directions: the golf course located is 1.25 miles southwest of McMinnville Oregon on Hwy 99W. Look for a large sign on the Hwy. If on Hwy 18 watch for signs for Hwy 99W southbound and follow to the golf course which will be on your right hand side.

Course Yardage & Par:

C-3154 yards, par 36.
M-3016 yards, par 36.
W-2576 yards, par 36.

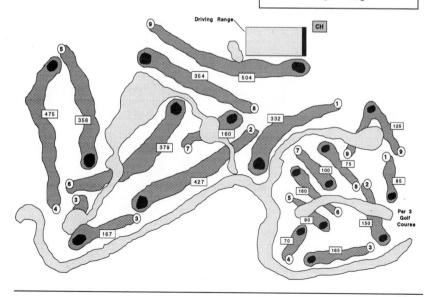

Bear Creek Family Golf Center (public, 9 hole course)
2355 South Pacific Highway; Medford, OR 97501
Phone: (541) 773-1822. **Fax:** (541) 773-8945. **Internet:** none.
Owner: Marla Corbin. **Superintendent:** none.
Rating/Slope: M 56.6/84; W 58.0/82. **Course record:** 28.
Green fees: W/D $12/$7; W/E $13/$8; M/C, VISA, DISCOVER
Power cart: none available. **Pull cart:** $1.25. **Trail fee:** not allowed.
Reservation policy: advance tee-time reservations are not needed or required.
Winter condition: the golf course is open all year long, weather permitting.
Terrain: flat, some hills. **Tees:** grass. **Spikes:** metal spikes permitted.
Services: club rentals, lessons, snack bar, beer, wine, beverages, pro shop,
covered driving range, putting green & chipping area, 18 hole miniature course.
Comments: Very popular golf complex. Facility is kept in excellent shape
during the peak season. Great golf course to take the family or first time golfer
to. Water is a major factor on half the holes so be sure to bring plenty of balls.

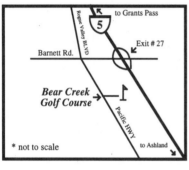

Directions: from I-5 northbound &
southbound use exit #27 to Barnett Road
Proceed to Highway 99 (Pacific Hwy).
Turn southbound on Pacific Highway
and proceed for 3/4 of a mile to the golf
course. The golf course will be located
on your left hand side. The course has
great freeway access. Look for signs
marking your way.

Course Yardage & Par:
M-1501 yards, par 29.
W-1501 yards, par 30.

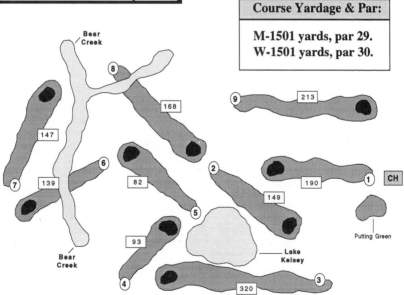

Bend Golf & Country Club (private, 18 hole course)
20399 Murphy Road; Bend, OR 97702
Phone: (541) 382-7437. **Fax:** none. **Internet:** none.
Pro: Thomas R. Tirrill, PGA. **Superintendent:** Tom Zoller.
Rating/Slope: C 73.8/132; M 71.4/127; W 74.6/133. **Course record:** 68.
Green fees: private club, members & guests only, reciprocates ; M/C, VISA.
Power cart: private club. **Pull cart:** private club. **Trail fee:** not allowed.
Reservation policy: private golf club members & guests of members only.
Winter condition: the golf course is closed in winter from November to thaw.
Terrain: flat, some hills. **Tees:** all grass. **Spikes:** metal spikes permitted.
Services: club rentals, lessons, snack bar, lounge, beer, wine, liquor, pro shop,
lockers, showers, driving range, putting & chipping greens, club memberships.
Comments: the golf course was redesigned in 1992 by Bill Robinson. The
redesign consisted of new greens, mounding along with some rebuilt bunkers.
Addition of 3 new water hazards has enhanced what was already a great course.
Tree lined fairways along with mountain views abound on this private track.

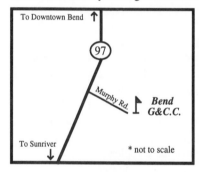

Directions: from Highway 97 turn on
Murphy Rd. and proceed eastbound.
Follow Murphy Rd. for 3/4 of a mile to
Country Club Dr. The golf course will
be just ahead on your right hand side.

Course Yardage & Par:
C-6851 yards, par 72.
M-6441 yards, par 72.
W-6004 yards, par 75.

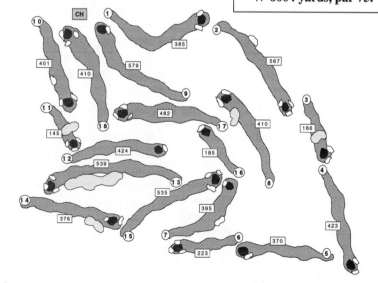

Black Butte Ranch (semi-private resort) Big Meadow (18 holes)

P.O. Box 8000; Highway 20; Sisters, OR 97759
Phone: (541) 595-1500 or call toll free: 1-800-399-2322.
Director of Golf: JD Mowlds, PGA. Superintendent: Guss Johnson.
Rating/Slope: C 72.0/127; M 70.0/124; W 70.5/115. **Course record:** 65.
Green fees: $55/$33 all week long; off season rates; M/C, VISA, AMEX.
Power cart: $28/$17. **Pull cart:** $4/$2. **Trail fee:** personal carts not allowed.
Reservation policy: General public: please call up tp 7 days in advance for your tee-times. Ranch Guests: may call up to 14 or 7 days in advance depending on date (odd or even). Call well in advance for tee- times during the peak season.
Winter condition: the golf course is closed from late October to mid March.
Terrain: flat, some hills. **Tees:** grass tees. **Spikes:** metal not spikes permitted.
Services: club rentals, lessons, snack bar, beer, wine, pro shop, driving range.
Comments: excellent facility that is worth a special trip. Big Meadow course is of traditional design featuring tree-lined fairways, well bunkered greens and varied terrain. Great views of the Cascade Mountain Range and forests abound from nearly every hole on the course. This course is a must play for any golfer.

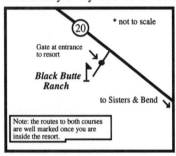

Directions: the golf course is located 7 miles west of Sisters Oregon on Hwy 20. The turn for the Black Butte Ranch is well marked. Once inside the complex the route to the golf course has plenty of signs to mark your way. Look for the signs that say Hawks Beard it runs throughout the complex.

Black Butte Ranch (semi-private resort) Glaze Meadow (18 holes)

P.O. Box 8000; Highway 20; Sisters, OR 97759
Phone: (541) 595-1500 or call toll free: 1-800-399-2322.
Director of Golf: JD Mowlds, PGA. Superintendent: Guss Johnson.
Rating/Slope: C 71.5/128; M 69.9/124;W 72.1/120. **Course record:** 65.
Green fees: $55/$33 all week long; off season rates; M/C, VISA, AMEX.
Power cart: $28/$17. **Pull cart:** $4/$2. **Trail fee:** personal carts not allowed.
Reservation policy: General public: please call up tp 7 days in advance for your tee-times. Ranch Guests: may call up to 14 or 7 days in advance depending on date (odd or even). Call well in advance for tee- times during the peak season.
Winter condition: the golf course is closed from late October to mid March.
Terrain: flat, some hills. **Tees:** grass tees. **Spikes:** metal not spikes permitted.
Services: club rentals, lessons, snack bar, beer, wine, pro shop, driving range.
Comments: excellent facility. Glaze Meadow is a great shot makers course. The fairways are narrow in spots leaving the golfer many lay up shots from the tee. Greens are large and well bunkered on nearly every hole. This is one of my most favorite golf courses in the state. Be sure to bring the entire family. Great golf.

Big Meadow Golf Course

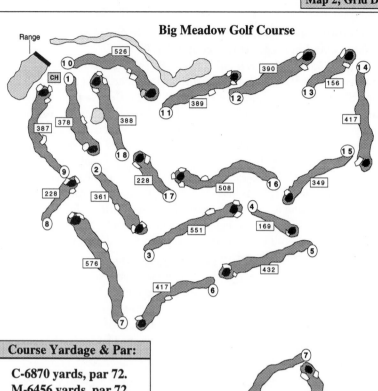

Course Yardage & Par:

C-6870 yards, par 72.
M-6456 yards, par 72.
W-5678 yards, par 72.
Big Meadow

Glaze Meadow Golf Course

Course Yardage & Par:

C-6574 yards, par 72.
M-6273 yards, par 72.
W-5610 yards, par 72.
Glaze Meadow

Broadmoor Golf Course (public, 18 hole course)
3509 NE Columbia Boulevard; Portland, OR 97211
Phone: (503) 281-1337. **Fax:** (503) 288-9578. **Internet:** none.
Pro: Scott Krieger, PGA. **Superintendent:** Joe Goodling.
Rating/Slope: C 70.2/122; M 68.4/116; W 73.5/118. **Course record:** 63.
Green fees: W/D $20/$10; W/E $22/$11; M/C, VISA for merchandise only.
Power cart: $22/$11. **Pull cart:** $2. **Trail fee:** personal carts are not allowed.
Reservation policy: yes, call Monday for the following week and weekend.
Winter condition: the golf course is open all year long, weather permitting.
Terrain: flat, some hills. **Tees:** all grass tees. **Spikes:** metal spikes permitted.
Services: club rentals, lessons, restaurant, beer, wine, beverages, pro shop,
driving range, putting & chipping greens. **Comments:** Beautiful tree lined
course with water and sand coming into play on several holes. One of Portland's
most popular public golf courses that can get very busy during the peak season.

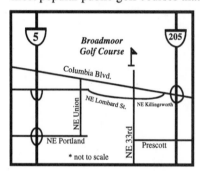

Directions: from I-5 N&S take the Columbia Street exit and proceed eastbound for 1 mile to NE 33rd. Turn left to the golf course. From I-205 N&S take the Columbia Street exit and proceed westbound for 2 miles to the course on your left. Look for signs.

Course Yardage & Par:
C-6498 yards, par 72.
M-5966 yards, par 72.
W-5384 yards, par 74.

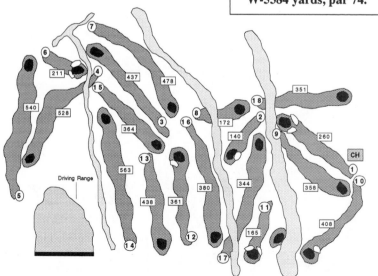

Broken Top Club (private, 18 hole course)
62000 Broken Top Drive; Bend OR 97702
Phone: (541) 383-0868. **Fax:** (541) 383-1963. **Internet:** none.
Pro: Andy Heinly, PGA. **Superintendent:** Ken Zack.
Rating/Slope: C 73.5/131; M 70.6/126; F 67.4/118; W 69.4/123.
Green fees: private club, members only; pro reciprocation on a limited basis.
Power cart: private club. **Pull cart:** yes. **Trail fee:** personal carts not allowed.
Reservation policy: private club, members and guests of members only.
Winter condition: as dictated by weather. Closed generally during the winter.
Terrain: flat, some hills. **Tees:** all bent grass . **Spikes:** metal spikes permitted.
Services: full service country club, driving range, putting & chipping greens.
Comments: this Tom Weiskopf, Jay Moorish designed golf course opened in July of 1993. The par 4, 364 yard, 11th is the course's signature hole. The course features classic championship design that plays over 7100 yards from the back.

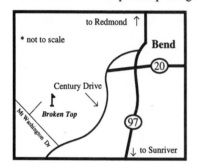

Directions: from Hwy 97 south entering Bend. Look for signs (Mt. Bachelor Ski area). **1st sign:** Hwy 97 & Division Street (follow Division). **2nd sign:** Division & Colorado (follow Colorado). **3rd sign:** Colorado & Century Dr. (follow Century Dr.) Turn right on Mt. Washington. Turn left at Broken Top Dr. (3rd left).

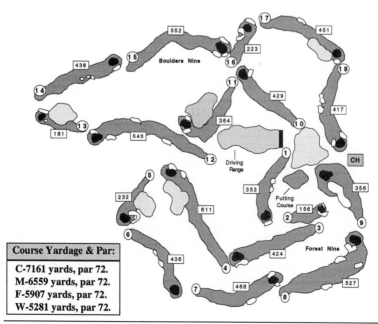

Course Yardage & Par:

C-7161 yards, par 72.
M-6559 yards, par 72.
F-5907 yards, par 72.
W-5281 yards, par 72.

Cedar Bend Golf Club (public, 9 hole course)
34391 Squaw Valley Road; Gold Beach, OR 97444
Phone: (541) 247-6911. **Fax:** (541) 247-5608. **Internet: none.**
Manager: Kathy Allison. Superintendent: none.
Rating/Slope: C N/A; M 67.6/115; W 70.8/122. **Course record:** 67.
Green fees: $18/$13 all week long; Jr. and Sr. rates; M/C, VISA.
Power cart: $18/$12. **Pull cart:** $2/$1. **Trail fee:** $5 for personal carts.
Reservation policy: yes, call in advance for tee times. A must in the summer.
Winter condition: the golf course is open all year long, damp conditions.
Terrain: flat (easy walking). **Tees:** grass. **Spikes:** metal spikes permitted.
Services: club rentals, lessons, snack bar, lounge, beer, wine, liquor, pro shop,
putting & chipping greens, driving range. **Comments:** Streams, lush fairways
and well kept greens add to your game at this course. Good public course that is
located in a great part of Oregon. The golf course is flat and very easy to walk.

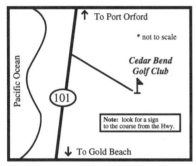

Directions: the golf course is located 12 miles north of Gold Beach and 14 miles south of Port Orford. **Note:** look for a sign on Hwy 101 for your turn to the golf course which is located 3 miles inland.

Course Yardage & Par:
C-3156 yards, par 36.
M-2872 yards, par 36.
W-2536 yards, par 37.
<u>Dual tees for 18 holes:</u>
C-6288 yards, par 72.
M-5892 yards, par 72.
W-5231 yards, par 74.

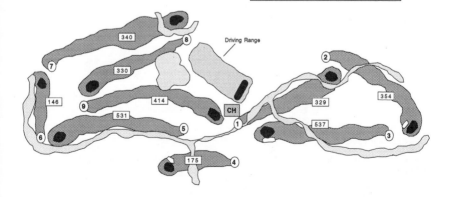

Cedar Links Golf Club (public, 18 hole course)

3155 Cedar Links Drive; Medford, OR 97504
Phone: (541) 773-4373. **Fax:** (541) 776-0974. **Internet: none.**
Pro: Scott Lusk, PGA. Superintendent: Lance Zimmerman.
Rating/Slope: C 68.9/114; M 67.9/110; W 69.4/112. **Course record:** 63.
Green fees: W/D $22/$12; W/E $24/$14; M/C, VISA, DISCOVER.
Power cart: $20/$10. **Pull cart:** $3/$2. **Trail fee:** personal carts not allowed.
Reservation policy: yes, please call up to 7 days in advance for tee-times.
Winter condition: the course is open all year long weather permitting, dry.
Terrain: flat, some hills. **Tees:** all grass. **Spikes:** metal spikes permitted.
Services: club rentals, lessons, snack bar, restaurant, lounge, beer, wine, beverages, pro shop, putting & chipping greens, excellent driving range.
Comments: Family owned public golf course in the foothills of Medford. The golf course sports several water holes and well bunkered, tricky greens. Fairways have generous landing areas and are kept in excellent condition.

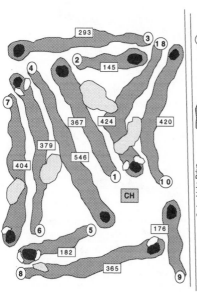

Directions: from I-5 N&S take Hwy 62 (Crater Lake Highway) exit #30 and go north. Turn right on Delta Waters Road. Proceed to Springbrook and turn right. At Cedar Links Drive, turn left to golf course which is located on your left hand side. Look for signs to the course.

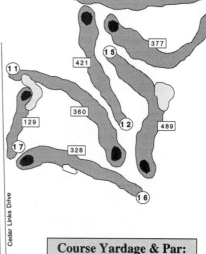

Course Yardage & Par:
C-6215 yards, par 70.
M-5908 yards, par 70.
W-5160 yards, par 71.

Charbonneau Golf & Country Club (public, 27 holes)
32020 Charbonneau Drive; Wilsonville, OR 97070
Phone: (503) 694-1246. Fax: (503) 694-2323. Internet: none.
Pro: Bob McCallister, PGA. Superintendent: Mary Arock.
Rating/Slope: C 60.6/94; M 59.8/92; W 61.9/94. **Course record: 54.**
Green fees: W/D $23/$13; W/E $25/$13; winter rates; M/C, VISA.
Power cart: $20/$10. **Pull cart:** $3/$2. **Trail fee:** not allowed.
Reservation policy: yes, call one week in advance for tee-time reservations.
Winter condition: the golf course is open all year long with dry conditions.
Terrain: flat, some slight hills. **Tees:** grass. **Spikes:** metal spikes permitted.
Services: club rentals, lessons, restaurant, lounge, beer, wine, pro shop, putting
& chipping greens, driving range. **Comments:** Beautiful executive course
layout that gives all golfers a challenge. The golf course can always be found in
great shape. Be sure to make Charonneau G.& C. C. part of any golf vacation.

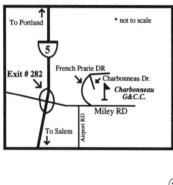

Directions: from I-5 North & South take
the Charbonneau exit #282. Go east for
approximately one mile to Charbonneau
Village and proceed to the golf course.
Look for signs along your route.

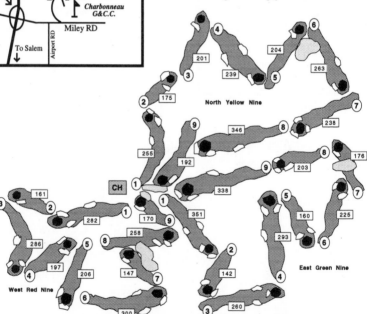

Course Yardage & Par:
North Yellow Nine: C-2172 yards, par 31; M-2026, par 31; W-1802, par 31.
East Green Nine: C-2180 yards, par 31; M-2111, par 31; W-1943, par 31.
West Red Nine: C-2047 yards, par 31; M-1936, par 31; W-1780, par 31.

The Children's Course (public, 9 hole course)

19825 River Road; Gladstone, OR 97027
Phone: (503) 722-1530. **Fax:** (503) 722-1757. **Internet: none.**
Pro: Phil Bostwick. Superintendent: Jack Dunn.
Rating/Slope: the golf course is not rated. **Course record:** 25.
Green fees: Weekdays $7; Weekends $8; Sr./Jr. rates $5.
Power cart: not available. **Pull cart:** $2. **Trail fee:** personal carts not allowed.
Reservation policy: please call in advance for your tee-times. No time limit.
Winter condition: the course is open all year long, weather permitting.
Terrain: flat (easy walking). **Tees:** all grass. **Spikes:** metal spikes permitted.
Services: club rentals, small pro shop, beverages, putting & chipping greens.
Comments: Short executive course that will challenge your short game.
Excellent walking golf course. The golf course is located next to the Willamette
River in a beautiful part of Oregon. Public tee times are available. The one of a
kind course offers a full schedule of junior clinics, camps and tournaments.

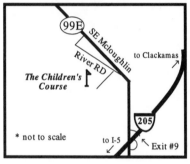

Directions: from I-205 take exit #9
onto Hwy 99E to Gladstone. proceed
for .7 mi across bridge to light where
you veer left onto River Road. Follow
River Road to the entrance immediately
on your left hand side. Look for signs
marking your way to the golf course.

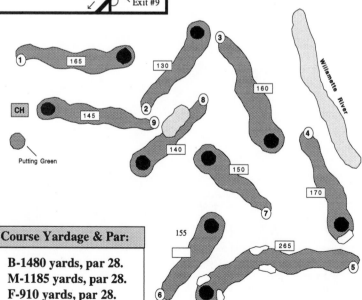

Course Yardage & Par:

B-1480 yards, par 28.
M-1185 yards, par 28.
F-910 yards, par 28.

Christmas Valley Golf Course (public, 9 hole course)
Physical address: #1 Christmas Tree Lane; Christmas Valley, OR 97641
Mailing address: P. O. Box 181; Christmas Valley, OR 97641
Phone: (541) 576-2216. **Fax:** none. **Internet:** none.
Rating/Slope: the golf course is not rated. **Course record:** 34.
Green fees: $15/$10 all week long; M/C, VISA.
Power cart: $10. **Pull cart:** $2. **Trail fee:** personal carts are allowed.
Reservation policy: advance tee times are not needed. First come first served.
Winter condition: the golf course is open all year long with dry conditions.
Terrain: flat (easy walking). **Tees:** all grass. **Spikes:** metal spikes permitted.
Services: club rentals, snack bar, restaurant, lounge, beer, wine, liquor, putting
& chipping greens, lodge. **Comments:** this medium length golf course is chall
-enging to all level of golfers. Hazards such as sand and pot bunkers, water and
sagebrush abound if you stray from the fairway. Fair public golf course.

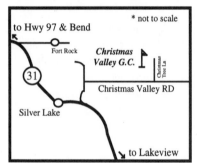

Directions: from Hwy 97 take Hwy 31 to Fort Rock/Christmas Valley exit. Take Co. Road 5-10 to Co. Road 5-14. 5-14 will become Christmas Valley Rd. at Christmas Valley. Follow this road to the golf course. **Note:** Look for signs marking your way to the golf course.

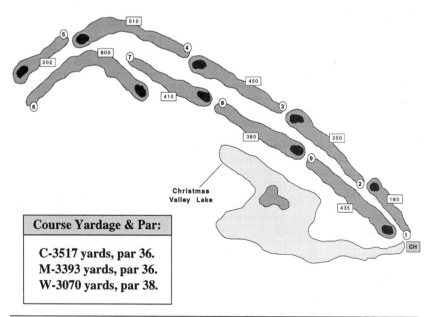

Course Yardage & Par:

C-3517 yards, par 36.
M-3393 yards, par 36.
W-3070 yards, par 38.

Circle Bar Golf Club (public, 9 hole course)

48447 West Oak Road; P. O. Box 214; Oakridge, OR 97463
Phone: (541) 782-3541. Fax: none. Internet: none.
Manager: Deanna Wellman. Superintendent: none.
Rating/Slope: M 71.8/123; W 73.0/118. **Course record:** 33.
Green fees: W/D $13/$8; W/E $16/$10; no credit cards.
Power cart: $15/$8. **Pull cart:** $3/$2. **Trail fee:** $6 for personal carts.
Reservation policy: yes, a must in summer, please call ahead for a tee time.
Winter condition: open, wet, club house closed from November to March.
Terrain: relatively hilly. **Tees:** grass. **Spikes:** metal spikes permitted.
Services: club rentals, snack bar, beer, wine, pro shop, putting green, chipping green, banquet facilities. **Comments:** club memberships are available for those wanting to join the club. Water comes into play on over half the holes. Dual tees are available for those wanting to play a full 18. If you are looking for a course for a quick 9 holes that is off the beaten track, try Circle Bar Golf Club.

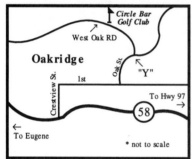

Directions: from Hwy 58 turn north on Crestview Street go across the train tracks to 1st. Turn right on 1st Street and proceed to Oak Street, turn left. Follow Oak Street to the "Y" in the road and turn left. This is West Oak Road. Follow this to the golf course. **Note:** Make sure you follow the signs marking your way.

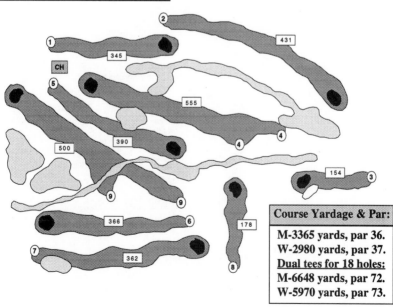

Course Yardage & Par:
M-3365 yards, par 36.
W-2980 yards, par 37.
<u>Dual tees for 18 holes:</u>
M-6648 yards, par 72.
W-5970 yards, par 73.

Claremont Golf Club (public, 9 hole course)
15955 NW West Union Road; Portland, OR 97229
Phone: (503) 690-4589. Fax: (503) 617-9433. Internet: none.
Pro: Steve Morrison. Superintendent: Steve Bizon
Rating/Slope: C 68.2/117; M 67.2/109; W 69.8/117. **Record:** 31 (9 holes).
Green fees: W/D $22/$12; W/E $26/$14; Sr. rates (M-F $7); M/C, VISA.
Power cart: $12 (9 holes). **Pull cart:** $2. **Trail fee:** personal carts not allowed.
Reservation policy: yes, please call 1 week in advance for your tee times.
Winter condition: open all year long weather permitting, course drains well.
Terrain: flat (easy walking). **Tees:** all grass. **Spikes:** metal spikes permitted.
Services: club rentals, pro shop. **Comments:** excellent walking golf course.
One of the finest 9 hole golf courses to emerge in the Portland area. Water
comes into play on several holes and can make this course play difficult.

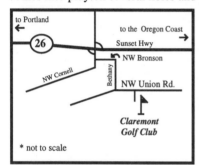

Directions: from Highway 26 (Sunset
Highway) take the Cornell/Bethany
exit and turn right at the 2nd stoplight
(Bethany Blvd.) Proceed to NW West
Union Road and turn left. The golf
course is located at the top of the hill
on the right hand side.

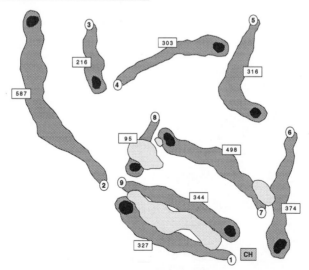

Course Yardage & Par:	Dual Tees 18 holes:
C-3060 yards, par 36.	6120 yards, par 72.
M-2961 yards, par 36.	5922 yards, par 72.
W-2692 yards, par 36.	5384 yards, par 72.

The Club at Sutherlin (public, 18 hole course)
1919 Recreation Lane; Sutherlin, OR 97479
Phone: (541) 459-4422. **Fax:** (541) 459-5071. **Internet: none.**
Pro: N/A. Superintendent: Mark Givons.
Rating/Slope: C 70.3/121; M 69.2/119; W 71.5/122. **Course record:** 64.
Green fees: $18/$12 all week long; winter & Sr. rates; M/C, VISA.
Power cart: $18/$9. **Pull cart:** none. **Trail fee:** $5 for personal carts.
Reservation policy: yes, call 1 week in advance for your tee-time reservation.
Winter condition: the golf course is open all year long, weather permitting.
Terrain: flat, rolling hills. **Tees:** grass. **Spikes:** metal spikes permitted.
Services: club rentals, lessons, snack bar, restaurant, lounge, beer, wine,
pro shop, driving range, putting & chipping green. **Comments:** the course has
had extensive upgrades in the last few years to provide an outstanding golfing
experience. Tree-lined fairways alternates with open links style design. RV
parking available for those wanting to stay the night. Friendly, well kept track.

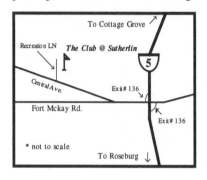

Directions: from I-5 N&S take exit #136 (Sutherlin). Upon exiting the freeway go west approximately .75 miles down the road. When you come to the sign take a right and follow to the golf course. The golf course is located near the freeway.

Course Yardage & Par:
C-6325 yards, par 72.
M-6084 yards, par 72.
W-5636 yards, par 72.

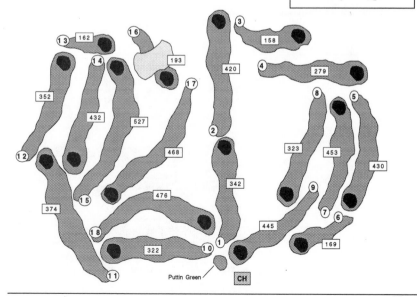

Coburg Hills Golf Course (public, 18 hole course)

P.O. Box 7881; Van Duyn Road; Eugene, OR 97401
Phone: (541) 334-1777. Fax: none. Internet: none.
Manager: Mike Haggerty. Superintendent: N/A.
Rating/Slope: the golf course has yet to be rated. **Course record:** N/A.
Green fees: W/D $28/$15; W/E $32/$16; M/C, VISA.
Power cart: $24. **Pull cart:** $4. **Trail fee:** to be determined.
Reservation policy: to be determined upon opening of the golf course.
Winter condition: the golf course is open all year long. Drains well.
Terrain: flat, some hills. **Tees:** all grass. **Spikes:** metal spikes permitted.
Services: club rentals, lessons, lounge, restaurant, snack bar, beer, wine, liquor, pro shop, driving range, putting green. **Comments:** this 18 hole course is set in the foothills of the surrounding countryside. The course plays through beautiful stands of Douglas Fir and Oregon Oak. Great views of the Willamette Valley abound from nearly every tee. The fairways have a sand base for better winter condition. Great course to play during poor weather. Look for this course to open 9 holes in September with the additional 9 opening in December 1999.

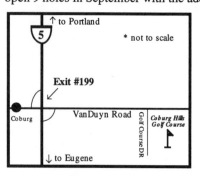

Directions: from I-5 N&S take the Coburg exit. Proceed eastbound off the exit on Van Duyn Road. Proceed to Golf Course Drive where you will turn south. Drive approximately 1 mile to the clubhouse. Look for signs to the marking your way to the golf course.

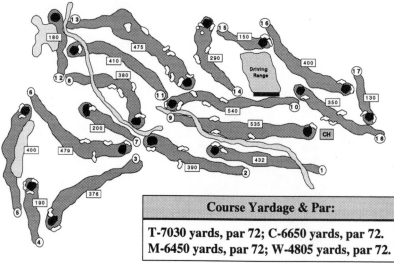

Course Yardage & Par:
T-7030 yards, par 72; C-6650 yards, par 72.
M-6450 yards, par 72; W-4805 yards, par 72.

Colonial Valley Golf Course (public, 9 hole course)
75 Nelson Way; Grants Pass, OR 97526
Phone: (541) 479-5568. **Fax:** none. **Internet:** none.
Pro: Randy Blankenship. **Superintendent:** none.
Rating/Slope: M 29/126; W 31/no rating. **Course record:** 28.
Green fees: $9 for nine holes, $5 for replay; no credit cards.
Power cart: none available. **Pull cart:** $1. **Trail fee:** $5 for personal carts.
Reservation policy: yes, groups of 12 or more please call 1 week in advance.
Winter condition: wet, course is closed from December 15th to February 1st.
Terrain: flat (easy walking). **Tees:** all grass. **Spikes:** metal spikes permitted.
Services: club rentals, lessons, snack bar, lounge, beer, wine, small pro shop.
Comments: the staff say that this course is the "Best kept secret in Southern Oregon". The track has wide fairways with medium to large sized well bunkered greens. If you are looking for a change of pace give Colonial Valley a try.

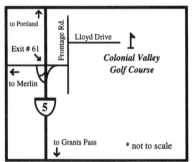

Directions: from I-5 N&S take Merlin exit #61, and go east to Frontage Road. Turn left and go north to Lloyd Drive andturn right on Lloyd Drive. Proceed 1/2 mile to the golf course on your right. **Note:** Look for signs marking your way to the golf course.

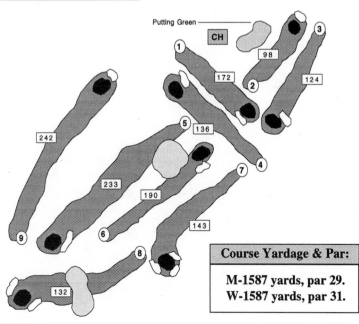

Course Yardage & Par:

M-1587 yards, par 29.
W-1587 yards, par 31.

Columbia Edgewater Country Club (private, 18 hole course)
2220 NE Marine Drive; Portland, OR 97211
Phone: (503) 285-8354. Fax: (503) 285-3977. Internet: none.
Pro: Dan Hixson, PGA. Superintendent: Bob Senseman. Record: 64.
Rating/Slope: T 72.9/131; C 71.1/128; M 69.6/124; W 73.7/129; W 71.5/125.
Green fees: private club, members and guests of members only; reciprocates.
Power cart: private club. **Pull cart:** private club. **Trail fee:** not allowed.
Reservation policy: private club members & guests only, 2 days in advance.
Winter condition: the golf course is open all year long, weather permitting.
Terrain: flat, some hills. **Tees:** grass. **Spikes:** no metal spikes in summer.
Services: lessons, snack bar, restaurant, lounge, pro shop, driving range.
Comments: old course built on rolling flood plains in 1925. Recent renovations
have been made toward the original design. Great golf course that has large
well bunkered greens. Host club of the Safeway LPGA Tour event.

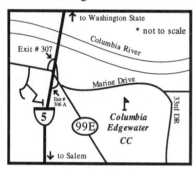

Directions: from I-5 N&S take Marine
Drive exit #306A and proceed eastbound
for .5 miles to the golf course. Look for
a sign to your turn to the golf course.

Course Yardage & Par:
T-6702 yards, par 71.
C-6342 yards, par 71.
M-6021 yards, par 71.
W-5762 yards, par 72.
W-5416 yards, par 72.

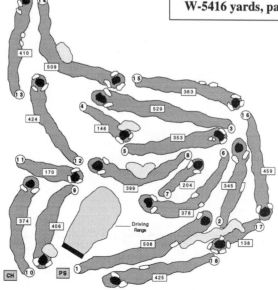

Colwood National Golf Club (public, 18 hole course)
7313 NE Columbia Boulevard; Portland, OR 97218
Phone: (503) 254-5515. Fax: (503) 255-0504. Internet: none.
Pro: Dave Miller, PGA. Superintendent: Doug Yost.
Rating/Slope: M 66.2/108; W 68.5/107. **Course record:** 63.
Green fees: W/D $18/$10; W/E $20/$11; Jr. rates.
Power cart: $22/$12. **Pull cart:** $3/$2. **Trail fee:** none.
Reservation policy: 1 week in advance for foursomes playing 18 holes only.
Winter condition: the golf course is open all year long with dry conditions.
Terrain: flat (easy walking). **Tees:** all grass. **Spikes:** metal spikes permitted.
Services: club rentals, lessons, restaurant, beer, wine, pop, lounge, pro shop,
putting & chipping green. **Comments:** This public golf course built in 1932 is
noted for it's excellent conditioned greens and well kept fairways. During the
summer month's it becomes very busy with play from the greater Portland area.

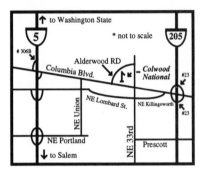

Directions: the golf course is located 1 mile east of Broadmoor off Columbia Boulevard. From I-5 northbound and southbound take NE Columbia Blvd. exit. Exit and go east for 6.7 miles. The golf course will be on your left hand side. Look for signs indicating your turns to the golf course the way is well marked.

Course Yardage & Par:
M-6277 yards, par 72.
W-5673 yards, par 77.

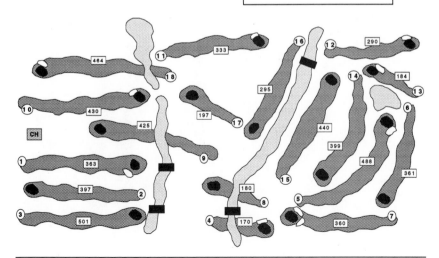

Condon Golf Course (public, 9 hole course)
North Lincoln Street; Condon, OR 97823
Phone: (541) 384-4266. Fax: none. Internet: none.
Pro: none. Manager: none.
Rating/Slope: M 68.2/105; W 70.3/109. **Course record:** 70.
Green fees: $7/$5, look for rates on the current rate sheet; no credit cards.
Power cart: not available. **Pull cart:** not available. **Trail fee:** not available.
Reservation policy: prior reservations are not needed for play.
Winter condition: the golf course is always closed during the winter months.
Terrain: flat, some slight hills. **Tees:** grass. **Spikes:** metal spikes permitted.
Services: the golf course has very limited services, putting & chipping area's.
Comments: Green fees are often paid by the honor system. Golf course is very easy to walk with some rolling hills. Greens are on the small side and can be rough in spots. This rustic golf course lies on the NW edge of the city of Condon.

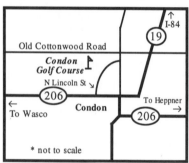

Directions: the golf course is located off of Highway 206 on North Lincoln Street in Condon. If coming from Highway 19 the golf course will be located at the north end of the city of Condon. **Note:** Be sure to look for a sign on the Highway marking the way to the golf course.

Course Yardage & Par:
M-3111 yards, par 36.
W-3111 yards, par 36.

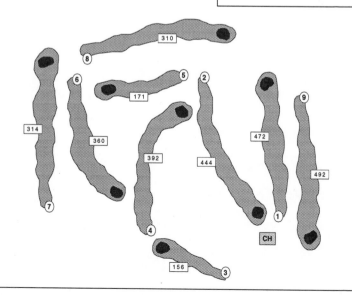

Coos Country Club (private, 18 hole course)
999 Coos City-Sumner Road; Coos Bay, OR 97420
Phone: (541) 267-7257. Fax: none. Internet: none.
Pro: Jim Bartleson, PGA. Superintendent: Dennis Olson.
Rating/Slope: M 68.6/122; W 71.3/123. **Course record:** 63.
Green fees: private club; reciprocates; credit cards for merchandise only.
Power cart: private club. **Pull cart:** private club. **Trail fee:** not allowed.
Reservation policy: private club, members & guests of members only.
Winter condition: the golf course is open all year long with wet conditions.
Terrain: flat, some hills. **Tees:** all grass. **Spikes:** metal spikes permitted.
Services: club rentals, lessons, restaurant, beer, wine, liquor, beverages,
pro shop, lockers, showers, driving range, putting green, chipping green.
Comments: The golf course is short, yet very demanding. Fairway's are narrow
with water in play everywhere. Host of the Southwest Oregon Amateur every
July 4th. Great course that is a bear. Do not let the lack of yardage fool you.
This private track is adding 9 holes that will open in April or May.

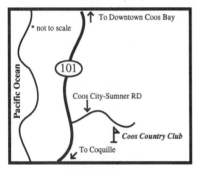

Directions: from Hwy 101 exit at Coos
City-Sumner Road. Proceed on Coos
City-Sumner Road for 1 mile to the
golf course. The golf course is located
approximately 5 miles south of the city.

Course Yardage & Par:
M-5728 yards, par 68.
W-5547 yards, par 72.

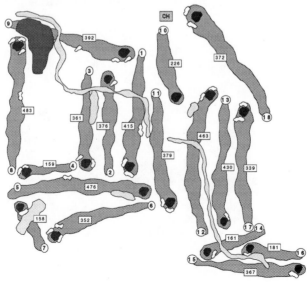

Coquille Valley Elks Golf Club (private, 9 hole course)
P. O. Box 1935; Hwy 42; Myrtle Point, OR 97458
Phone: (541) 572-5367. Fax: (541) 572-7823. Internet: none.
Manager: Don Mort. Superintendent: none.
Rating/Slope: C 63.2/103; M 62.5/101; W 66.0/103. **Course record:** 27.
Green fees: private club, members only; annual fees; non Elk guests $20.
Power cart: private club. **Pull cart:** private club. **Trail fee:** private club.
Reservation policy: private club, members only no public reservations.
Winter condition: the golf course is open all year long. Wet conditions.
Terrain: flat, some hills. **Tees:** grass. **Spikes:** metal spikes permitted.
Services: club rentals, restaurant, lounge, beer, pro shop, driving range.
Comments: course owned by the Coquille Valley Elks Lodge #1935. Home of
the State Elks tournament over Labor Day weekend. Fairly good walking course
with only one steep grade. Greens are large and flat and putt fairly well.

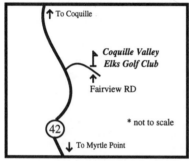

Directions: from I-5 N&S in Roseburg,
Oregon take the Coos Bay/Winston exit.
Proceed on Highway 42 for approxi-
mately 50 miles west to the golf course.
The course is located half way between
Myrtle Point and Coquille. Your turn
to the golf course will be on Fairview
Road. Look for signs indicating your
way to the golf course.

Course Yardage & Par:
M-2216 yards, par 33; W-2165 yards, par 35.

Corvallis Country Club (private, 18 hole course)

1850 SW Whiteside Drive; Corvallis, OR 97333
Phone: (541) 752-3484. Fax: (541) 752-5742. Internet: none.
Pro: Mark Tunstill, PGA. Superintendent: Doug Hubert.
Rating/Slope: C 69.0/121; M 68.0/117; W 71.1/122. **Course record:** 64.
Green fees: private; reciprocates need a membership card $45.
Power cart: private club. **Pull cart:** private club. **Trail fee:** not allowed.
Reservation policy: yes, call 6 days in advance for members and guests only.
Winter condition: the golf course is open all year long, wet conditions.
Terrain: relatively hilly. **Tees:** all grass. **Spikes:** metal spikes permitted.
Services: club rentals, lessons, snack bar, restaurant, beer, wine, liquor, pro
shop, driving range, putting/chipping greens, banquet room, club memberships.
Comments: The golf course is short, with small tricky greens. Most of the
greens are well bunkered or have water nearby. You must play a position round
of golf to score well as trees come into play from nearly every tee.

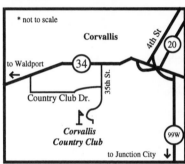

Directions: from I-5 N&S travel west
on Hwy 34 to Philomath Hwy. Turn left,
proceed to the 2nd light (35th St.), turn
left and follow the road to the clubhouse.

Course Yardage & Par:
C-6045 yards, par 71.
M-5825 yards, par 71.
W-5441 yards, par 74.

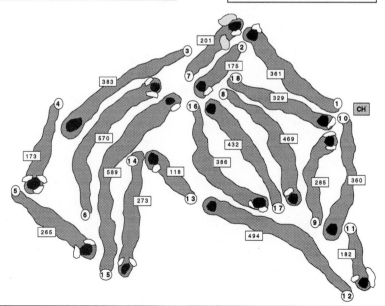

Cottonwood Lakes Golf Course & D.R. (public, 9 hole course)

3225 River Road South; Salem, OR 97302
Phone: (503) 364-3673. **Fax:** (503) 364-0730. **Internet:** none.
Pro: Jeff Mashos, PGA. **Superintendent:** Jay Kenyon.
Rating/Slope: the golf course is not rated. **Course record:** 24.
Green fees: $12/$7.50 all week long; Jr. & Sr. rates $10/$6.50.
Power cart: none available. **Pull cart:** $2. **Trail fee:** not allowed.
Reservation policy: call up to 1 week in advance. Summer is a must.
Winter condition: the golf course is open all year long with damp conditions.
Terrain: flat (easy walking). **Tees:** all grass. **Spikes:** metal spikes permitted.
Services: club rentals, lessons, snack bar, pro shop, 50 tee, covered range.
Comments: challenging par 3 golf course that will test every iron in your bag.
The length of the holes vary from short to very long. The facility is in the
process of making alot of changes. They plan to build an 18 hole putting course
that should be playable in spring of 1998. Good track that is a change of pace.

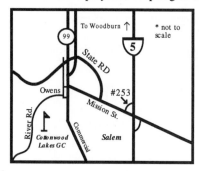

Directions: from I-5 north take Parkway
exit #248 and go north on Commercial to
Owens. Left on Owens to River Road.
Left to the golf course. From I-5 south
take exit #253 (Mission) and follow the
above directions. Look for signs.

Course Yardage & Par:
M-1250 yards, par 28.
W-1250 yards, par 29.

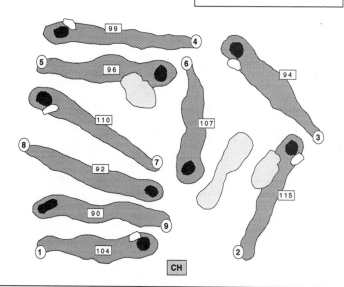

Creekside Golf Club (private, 18 hole course)
6250 Clubhouse Drive South; Salem, OR 97306
Phone: (503) 363- 4653. **Fax:** (503) 581-9008. **Internet: none.**
Pro: Tom Carey. **Manager:** Tom Ferrin. **Superintendent:** N/A.
Rating/Slope: T 73.6/131; C 71.9/128; M 69.5/120; W 70.4/122. **Record:** 64.
Green fees: private club, members and guests of members only.
Power cart: private club. **Pull cart:** private club. **Trail fee:** private club.
Reservation policy: private club, members and guests of members only.
Winter condition: the golf course is open all year long. Drains well in winter.
Terrain: flat, some hills. **Tees:** all grass. **Spikes:** metal spikes permitted.
Services: club rentals, lessons, clubhouse, restaurant, pro shop, driving range.
Comments: Course designed by Peter Jacobsen and owned and operated by American Golf Corporation. Excellent layout that will challenge you at every turn. This is a very demanding golf course from tee to green. This newer track opened for play in 1994 and is spectacular. Great private golf course.

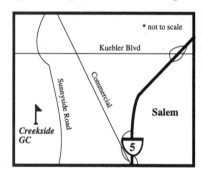

Directions: from I-5 N&S take the Kuebler exit in south Salem. Proceed westbound on Kuebler to Sunnyside Road. Turn south on Sunnyside Road for 1 mile to the golf course on the west side of the road. Look for signs.

Course Yardage & Par:
T-6887 yards, par 72.
C-6521 yards, par 72.
M-6009 yards, par 72.
W-5260 yards, par 72.

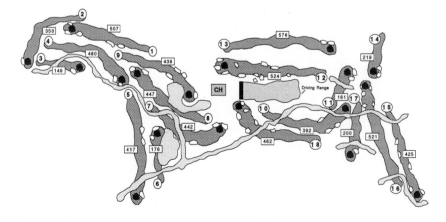

Crestview Hills Golf Course (public, 9 hole course)
1680 Crestline Drive; Waldport, OR 97394
Phone: (541) 563-3020. **Fax: none. Internet: none.**
Owners: Mark & Patricia Campbell.
Rating/Slope: M 67.6/111; W 69.5/116. **Course record:** 32.
Green fees: W/D $18/$9; W/E $20/$10; M/C, VISA.
Power cart: $18/$9. **Pull cart:** $2. **Trail fee:** $2.
Reservation policy: yes, taken 7 days in advance (suggested June to Sept.).
Winter condition: the golf course is open all year long, weather permitting.
Terrain: relatively hilly. **Tees:** all grass. **Spikes:** metal spikes permitted.
Services: club rentals, lessons, snack bar, beer, wine, pro shop, putting green.
Comments: Beautiful par 36 golf course that sits on top of a hill and is out of the coastal wind and fog. Rolling terrain will often result in some tricky lies from the fairway. Greens are on the small size and can be hard to hold in the summer. Family run course that play's much tougher than the yardage indicates.

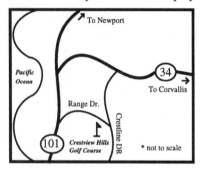

Directions: the course is located 1 mile south of Waldport Oregon. From Hwy 101 turn east on Range Drive (milepost 157) and proceed 1 mile to the course entrance on your right. Look for a sign marking your turn to the golf course. The way is well marked.

Course Yardage & Par:
C-3062 yards, par 36.
M-2881 yards, par 36.
W-2634 yards, par 36.

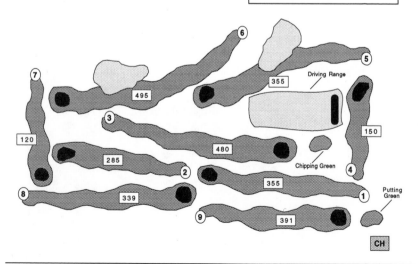

Crooked River Ranch Golf Course (public, 18 hole course)

Box 1218; 5195 Clubhouse Road; Crooked River Ranch, OR 97760
Phone: (541) 923-6343. Fax: (541) 578-0278. Internet: none.
Pro: Gary L. Popp, PGA. Superintendent: Rocky Robinson.
Rating/Slope: C 66.3/107; M 65.1/102; W 67.4/111. **Course record:** 63.
Green fees: $23/$15 everyday; winter & Jr. rates; M/C, VISA.
Power cart: $23/$15. **Pull cart:** $3/$2. **Trail fee:** $7.50 for personal carts.
Reservation policy: yes, call Tuesday noon, before the weekend for tee times.
Winter condition: the golf course is open weather permitting, dry conditions.
Terrain: flat, some hills. **Tees:** all grass. **Spikes:** metal spikes permitted.
Services: club rentals, lessons, snack bar, restaurant, lounge, beer, wine, liquor,
pro shop, driving range, putting green. **Comments:** Golf is played here all year
long when most all the other Central Oregon courses are snowed in. Scenic
golf course that has many spectacular vistas from nearly every tee. Worth a trip.

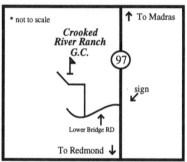

Directions: the golf course is located 7
miles from Highway 97. Turn off of
Highway 97 at the Crooked River Ranch
signs which are located on Highway 97
approximately 5 miles north of Redmond
Oregon. The way is well marked so make
sure you look for signs at your turns.

Course Yardage & Par:
C-5661 yards, par 71.
M-5355 yards, par 71.
W-5000 yards, par 71.

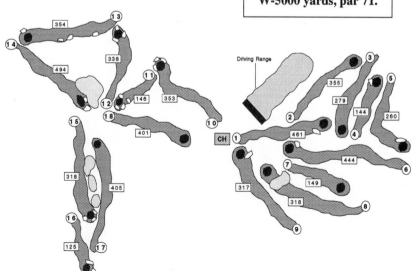

Cross Creek Golf Course (public, 9 hole course)
13935 Highway 22; Dallas, OR 97338
Phone: (503) 623-6666. Fax: none. Internet: none.
Manager: Tim Tarpley. Superintendent: none.
Rating/Slope: the golf course has yet to be rated. **Course record:** N/A.
Green fees: W/D $20/$11; W/E $22/$11; M/C, VISA.
Power cart: $18/$9. **Pull cart:** $3/$2. **Trail fee:** carts allowed but must pay.
Reservation policy: to be determined upon opening of the golf course.
Winter condition: the golf course is open all year long. Drains very well.
Terrain: flat, some hills. **Tees:** all grass. **Spikes:** metal spikes permitted.
Services: club rentals, snack bar, beer, wine, pro shop, driving range.
Comments: this 18 hole course is set in a beautiful setting of Oregon. The course features well drained soil , lots of mounding, plenty of creeks, lakes and sand bunkers. With the first 9 holes opening in spring of 1998 and the additional 9 following the next year Cross Creek will fast become great track.

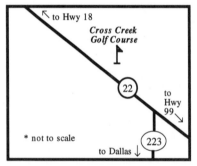

Directions: the course is located 5 miles west of Highway 99 on Highway 22.

Course Yardage & Par:
T-6830 yards, par 72.
C-6500 yards, par 72.
M-6030 yards, par 72.
W-5490 yards, par 72.

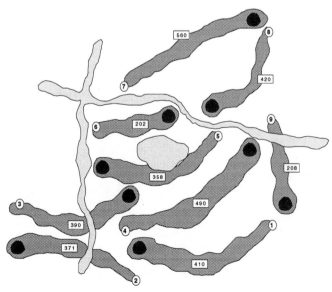

Crosswater (private with reicprocal agreement, 18 holes)

Highway 97; P.O. Box 4818; Sunriver, OR 97707
Phone: (541) 593-6196. Fax: none. Internet: none.
Pro: Brad Myrick, PGA. Superintendent: Jim Ramey.
Rating/Slope: G 75.3/136; S 74.8/134; B 73.4/129; W 71.2/125. **Record:** 67.
Green fees: member only; reciprocates with Sunriver Lodge $115; M/C, VISA.
Power cart: private club. **Pull cart:** private club. **Trail fee:** not allowed.
Reservation policy: member's can call up to 10 days in advance for times.
Winter condition: the course is closed from mid-November to mid April.
Terrain: flat, some hills. **Tees:** all grass. **Spikes:** metal spikes permitted.
Services: the course offer's the golfer a full service clubhouse and golf facility,
snack bar, club rentals, driving range, beverage service, putting/chipping greens.
Comments: this first rate facility opened in 1995 and is nothing short of
spectacular. The course is Heathland style having bentgrass throughout. If you
ever get a chance to play Crosswater be sure to take it. It will not disappoint.

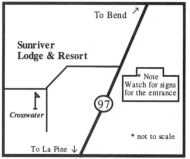

Directions: the golf course is located
approximately 15 miles south of Bend,
Oregon off of Hwy 97 in Sunriver
Oregon. Look for signs to the golf
course. The golf course is not located
in the Sunriver complex. It is located
slightly south of the Sunriver complex.
Turn into the Sunriver turn however.

Course Yardage & Par:
Gold Tees: 7693 yards, par 72. **Silver Tees: 7305 yards, par 72.** **Blue Tees: 6842 yards, par 72.** **White Tees: 6286 yards, par 72.** **Red Tees: 5389 yards, par 72.**

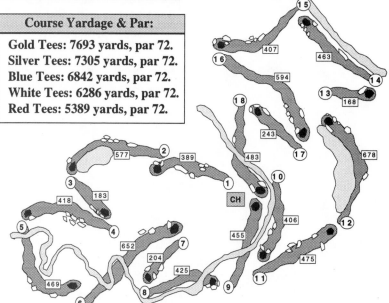

Dallas Golf Course (public, 9 hole course)

11875 Orr's Corner Road; Dallas, OR 97338
Phone: (503) 623-6832. Fax: none. Internet: none.
Pro: Brian Weaver, PGA. Superintendent: none.
Rating/Slope: M 58.2/91; W N/A. **Course record:** 55 18 holes/26 9 holes.
Green fees: $15/$9 all week long; Jr. & Sr. rates are available.
Power cart: $14/$7. **Pull cart:** $1. **Trail fee:** $7/$3.50 for personal carts.
Reservation policy: yes, please call ahead for your tee-times.
Winter condition: the golf course is open all year long. Dry, drains very well.
Terrain: flat, some hills. **Tees:** all grass tees. **Spikes:** metal spikes permitted.
Services: club rentals, lessons, pro shop, beverages, driving range, putting green.
Comments: Ponds and bunkers come into play on several of the holes. Excellent on course driving range to practice your game on. This course is well maintained and the greens are generally in excellent shape and putt very true. Good course to stop at if you are looking for a change of pace from the 6500+ yard track.

Directions: from Highway 22 exit southbound on Highway 99W for 1.7 miles to Orr's Corner Road. Turn westbound. The golf course is located 3 miles ahead on the right hand side of the road. Look for signs marking your way to the golf course. The route is well marked.

Course Yardage & Par:
M-2031 yards, par 31.
W-1891 yards, par 31.

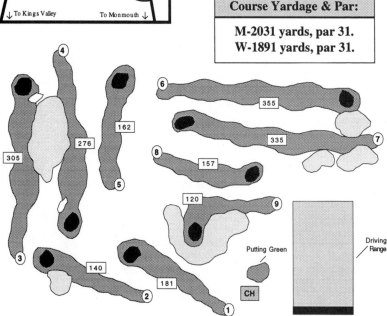

The Dalles Country Club (private, 9 hole course)

4550 Highway 30 West; The Dalles, OR 97058
Phone: (541) 296-5252. **Fax: none. Internet: none.**
Pro: Bob Sproule, PGA. **Superintendent:** Ross Randolph.
Rating/Slope: M 69.4/120; W 73.6/118. **Course record:** 61.
Green fees: private club, members or guests of a members; reciprocates.
Power cart: private club. **Pull cart:** private club. **Trail fee:** not allowed.
Reservation policy: private club, members, guests and reciprocates only.
Winter condition: the golf course is open all year long weather permitting.
Terrain: flat, some hills. **Tees:** all grass. **Spikes:** metal spikes permitted.
Services: snack bar, restaurant, lounge, beer, wine, liquor, pop, pro shop, lockers, showers, putting & chipping greens, club memberships.
Comments: this course is ranked as one of the best nine hole golf courses in the state of Oregon by the National Golf Foundation. Good course that plays much longer than the yardage would indicate. Set in a great location of Oregon.

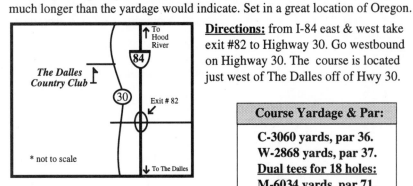

Directions: from I-84 east & west take exit #82 to Highway 30. Go westbound on Highway 30. The course is located just west of The Dalles off of Hwy 30.

Course Yardage & Par:
C-3060 yards, par 36.
W-2868 yards, par 37.
Dual tees for 18 holes:
M-6034 yards, par 71.
W-5810 yards, par 73.

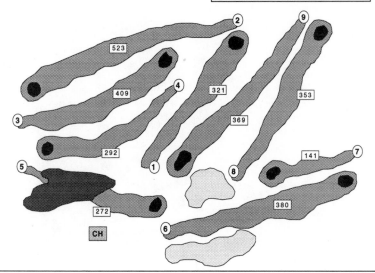

Diamond Woods Golf Course (public, 18 hole course)
96040 Territorial Road; Monroe, OR 97456
Phone: (541) 998-9707 or 800 559-GOLF. Fax:(541) 998-5272.
Managers: Jeff & Greg Doyle. Superintendent: Greg Doyle.
Rating/Slope: T 37.3/136; C 36.0/132; M 34.9/124; W 36.6/127 (9 holes).
Green fees: 28/$15; Jr. rates; play cards available; M/C, VISA.
Power cart: $22/$12. **Pull cart:** $3. **Trail fee:** not allowed.
Reservation policy: please call 7 days in advance for your tee-times.
Winter condition: the golf course is open all year long. Drains very well.
Terrain: flat, some hills. **Tees:** all grass. **Spikes:** metal spikes permitted.
Services: club rentals, snack bar, pro shop, driving range, beverage service.
Comments: The Willamette Valley's newest championship golf course promises to be a complete test of a golfer's game. The course spans over 168 acres of beautiful terrain that sports incredible views of the valley and Cascade Mountains. It is a challenging array of golf holes requiring proficiency with all clubs. Built with concept of working with the natural topography and landscapes, this is a course that all golfers enjoy.

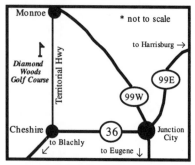

Directions: from I-5S take the Corvallis exit (Hwy 34), turn west for 10 miles. Turn south on Hwy 99, (just past the entrance to Trysting Tree GC. Follow 99, 17 miles to the town of Monroe. Course is 3 miles south of Monroe. From I-5N in Eugene take the Junction City/Santa Clara exit (Beltline W). Beltline W to Hwy 99. Turn north on Hwy 99 and travel 14 miles, (past Fiddler's Green Golf) to the traffic signal at Guaranty Chevrolet in Junction City. Turn west 4 miles to Territorial Rd. Turn north on Territorial Rd. & travel 4 miles to the course.

Course Yardage & Par:
C-6919 yards, par 72.
M-6336 yards, par 72.
W-5557 yards, par 72.

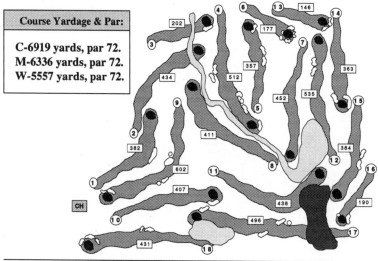

Dutcher Creek Golf Course (public, 9 hole course)
4611 Upper River Road; Grants Pass, OR 97526
Phone: (541) 474-2188. **Fax:** (541) 479-9609. **Internet:** none.
Manager/Pro: N/A. **Superintendent:** none.
Rating/Slope: C 71.2/118; M 69.9/114; W 68.6/108. **Course record:** 30.
Green fees: $22/$14 everday of the week; M/C, VISA.
Power cart: $19/$12. **Pull cart:** $1 per 9 holes. **Trail fee:** not allowed.
Reservation policy: please call one week in advance for tee-times.
Winter condition: the golf course is open all year long. Damp conditions.
Terrain: flat, some hills. **Tees:** all grass. **Spikes:** metal spikes permitted.
Services: club rentals, lessons, snack bar, beer, wine, pro shop, practice green,
practice area, driving range. **Comments:** the golf course opened for play in July
of 1994. In the picturesque Rogue Valley lies Dutcher Creek Golf Course with
Mountain views and a year-round creek. Designed in the Scottish links tradition
this course is challenging at every turn. Worth a trip if you are in the area.

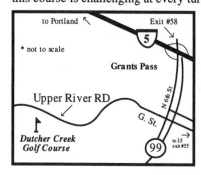

Directions: From I-5 N&S take the
Grants Pass exit and travel toward
downtown Grants Pass. Turn right on
"G" street which turns in to Upper River
Road. Continue on Upper River Road to
the golf course whichwill be on your left
(4 miles from downtown Grants Pass).

Course Yardage & Par:
C-3350 yards, par 36.
M-3135 yards, par 36.
W-2720 yards, par 36.

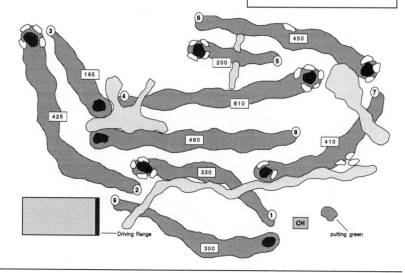

Eagle Creek Golf Course (public, 9 hole course)

25805 S.E. Dowty Road; Eagle Creek, OR 97022
Phone: (503) 235-4145. Fax: none. Internet: none.
Manager: John Bastasch. Superintendent: John Bastasch.
Rating/Slope: the golf course has not been rated yet. **Course record:** 36.
Greens fee: W/D $12/$6; W/E $16/$8; special rates.
Power cart: not available. **Pull cart:** not available. **Trail fee:** not allowed.
Reservation policy: yes, you may call anytime for advance reservations.
Winter condition: the golf course is open all year long weather permitting.
Terrain: flat (easy walking). **Tees:** all grass. **Spikes:** metal spikes permitted.
Services: construction is in progress on the clubhouse area so limited services
are available at this time. **Comments:** Challenging newer course with hundreds
of mature oak trees. Water comes into play on many holes and is a major factor.
Course will expand to 18 holes in late 1998 or 1999 depending on construction.

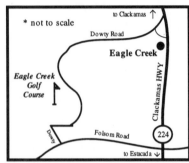

Directions: From Clackamas go
southeast to Eagle Creek, Oregon.
Travel 1.75 miles to Folsom Road.
Turn right and travel 1.1 miles to
Dowty Road. Turn right. The golf
course is located .5 miles ahead. Look
for signs marking your way to the golf
course. The route is well marked.

Course Yardage & Par:
C-3179 yards, par 35.
M-2878 yards, par 35.
W-2631 yards, par 35.

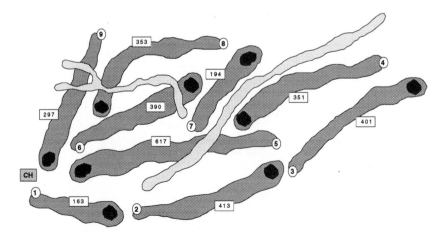

Eagle Crest Resort, Resort Course (public resort, 18 holes)

1522 Cline Falls Road; Redmond, OR 97756

Phone: (541) 923-4653. **Fax:** none. **Internet:** none.

Pro: Terry Anderson, PGA. **Superintendent:** John Thronson.

Rating/Slope: C 71.5/128; M 69.3/124; W 68.8/109. **Course record:** 65.

Green fees: $42/$25; winter rates are available; M/C, VISA, AMEX, DIS.
please call 2 weeks in advance for tee-times (bankcard guarantee is required).

Power cart: $25/$16. **Pull cart:** $2/$1. **Trail fee:** personal carts not allowed.

Reservation policy: call 1 day in advance or call Thursday before weekend.

Winter condition: the golf course is open all year long if no snow.

Terrain: flat, some hills. **Tees:** all grass. **Spikes:** metal spikes permitted.

Services: club rentals, lessons, snack bar, restaurant, lounge, beer, wine,
pro shop, driving range, putting green and chipping green, resort accomodations.

Comments: first rate facility that is kept in excellent condition. Greens are large
and well bunkered. During the summer they are firm and fast. Plan to take a trip
to central Oregon and play the Eagle Crest courses, they will not disappoint.

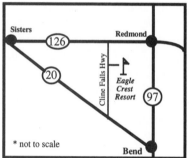

Directions: from Hwy 97 in Redmond
Oregon, travel westbound on Hwy 126
towards Sisters, Oregon. Take the first
left turn which will be Cline Falls Road,
on the south side of the bridge crossing
the Deschutes River. Travel 1/2 mile to
the resort entrance. **Note:** look for signs.

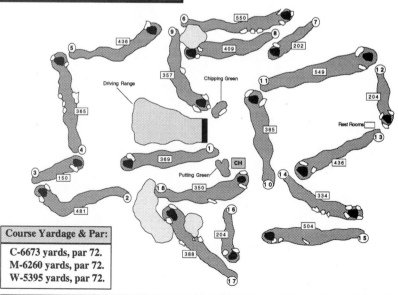

Course Yardage & Par:

C-6673 yards, par 72.
M-6260 yards, par 72.
W-5395 yards, par 72.

Eagle Crest Resort, Ridge Course (public resort, 18 holes)
1522 Cline Falls Road; Redmond, OR 97756
Phone: (541) 923-5002. Fax: none. Internet: none.
Pro: Terry Anderson, PGA. Superintendent: Bob Meyers
Rating/Slope: T 73.0/131; C 70.7/125; M 68.6/120; W 66.1/115. **Record: 65.**
Green fees: $42/$25; winter rates are available; M/C, VISA, AMEX
please call 2 weeks in advance for tee-times (bankcard guarantee is required)
Power cart: $25/$16. **Pull cart:** $2/$1. **Trail fee:** personal carts not allowed.
Reservation policy: 1 day in advance or call Thursday before the weekend.
Winter condition: the golf course is open all year long if no snow.
Terrain: flat, some hills. **Tees:** all grass. **Spikes:** metal spikes permitted.
Services: first rate services are available at Eagle Crest Resort, pro shop, pop,
driving range, putting and chipping greens, 18 hole putting golf course.
Comments: course is cut out of old growth Juniper with gently rolling terrain.
Greens are firm very fast and have some fairly dramatic slopes to them. Very
challenging golf course with 69 traps and 4 lakes. New 18 hole putting course.

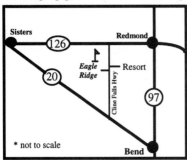

Directions: from Hwy 97 in Redmond
Oregon, travel westbound on Hwy 126
towards Sisters, Oregon. Take the first
left turn which will be Cline Falls Road,
on the south side of the bridge crossing
the Deschutes River. Travel 1/2 mile to
the resort entrance. Look for signs to the
golf course the way is well marked.

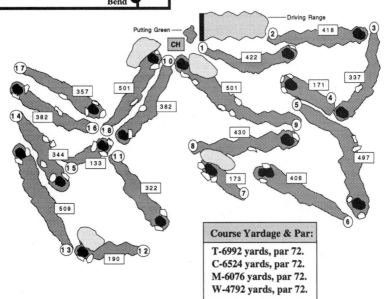

Course Yardage & Par:
T-6992 yards, par 72.
C-6524 yards, par 72.
M-6076 yards, par 72.
W-4792 yards, par 72.

Eagle Point Golf Course (public, 18 hole course)
100 Eagle Point Drive; Eagle Point, OR, 97524
Phone: (541) 826-8225. Fax: none. Internet: none.
Pro: Brian Sackett. Superintendent: N/A.
Rating/slope: T 74.3/131; C 71.7/129; M 68.7/120; F 68.9/113. **Record:** 68.
Green fees: Monday-Thursday $40; W/E & Holidays $48; M/C, VISA, AMEX.
Power cart: $20/$12. **Pull cart:** $3/$2. **Trail fee:** personal carts not allowed.
Reservation policy: 7 days in advance. Advance booking available for a fee.
Winter condition: state-of-the-art drainage system allows year round play.
Terrain: gently rolling. **Tees:** all grass. **Spikes:** metal spikes permitted.
Services: club rentals, lessons, lounge, snack bar, beer, pro shop, driving range.
Comments: ranked "3rd best new affordable public course in America for 1997"
by *Golf Digest*. Designed by the renowned **Robert Trent Jones Jr.** this gem is
exceptionally playable for the beginning golfer, with plenty of interest and challenge for the expert golfer. The best drainage system in Southern Oregon provides fantastic playing conditions all year long. Course is a must play for all.

Directions: from I-5 (Medford area) take the Crater Lake Hwy 62 exit #30. Proceed 8.5 miles to Alta Vista Drive. Travel eastbound on Alta Vista for .5 miles to the course entrance which will be on your left hand side. Note: the course is located 10 minutes from the Medford International Airport. Look for signs that are posted.

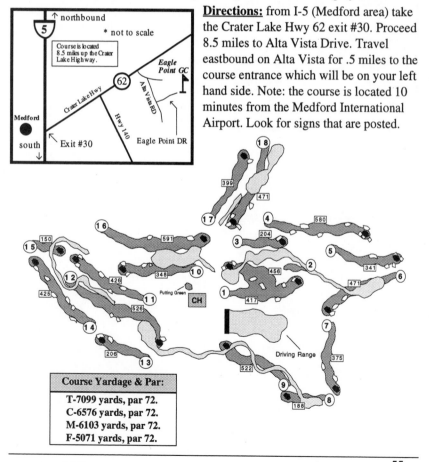

Course Yardage & Par:

T-7099 yards, par 72.
C-6576 yards, par 72.
M-6103 yards, par 72.
F-5071 yards, par 72.

Eagles on the Grgeen (private, 9 hole par 3 course)
1375 Irving Road; Eugene, OR 97404; (541) 688-9471
Pro: none. Superintendent: none.
Rating/Slope: the golf course is not rated. **Course record:** 23.
Green fees: private club, members or guests of a members only.
Power cart: none. **Pull cart:** none. **Trail fee:** not allowed.
Reservation policy: private club, members or guests of a members.
Winter condition: the golf course is open all year long weather permitting.
Terrain: flat. **Tees:** all grass. **Spikes:** metal spikes permitted.
Services: limited servies, Eagle Lodge #275 on site.
Comments: this 9 hole par 3 track is owned and operated by the Fraternal Order of Eagles Lodge #275. The track itself is very short in length but do not let the lack of yardage fool you this course is tough to break par one. Tall evergreens line the fairways leaving the golfer little room off the tee.

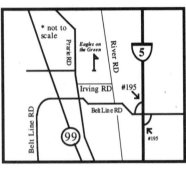

Directions: from I-5 N&S take the Beltline Road exit. Proceed westbound for 4.3 miles to Irving Road where you will turn right. The golf course is located on the right hand side of the street next to the Elks Lodge.

Course Yardage & Par:
C-1295 yards, par 27.
M-1110 yards, par 27.
W-1110 yards, par 27.

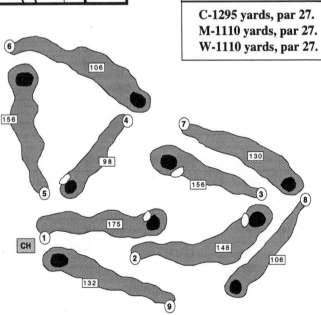

Eastmoreland Golf Course (public, 18 hole course)
2425 SE Bybee Boulevard; Portland, OR 97202
Phone: (503) 292-8570 Tee-Times. (503) 775-2900 pro shop.
Fax: (503) 774-0482. Internet: none.
Pro: Clark Cumpston, PGA. Superintendent: Steve Hoiland.
Rating/Slope: C 71.7/123; M 71.4/119; W 71.3/117. **Course record:** 63.
Green fees: W/D $19/$10; W/E $21/$11; Sr./Jr. rates $14.50; no credit cards.
Power cart: $25/$12.50. **Pull cart:** $3/$2. **Trail fee:** $4/$2 for personal carts.
Reservation policy: yes, please call 1 week in advance for tee-times.
Winter condition: the golf course is open all year long weather permitting.
Terrain: flat, some hills. **Tees:** all grass tees. **Spikes:** metal spikes permitted.
Services: club rentals, lessons, restaurant, beer, wine, pro shop, driving range.
Comments: scenic golf course rated in the top 25 public courses in *Golf Digest*.
The U.S. National Amateur Public Links Championships was held here in 1990.
The upgraded clubhouse and well managed pro shop are fantastic. If you are
looking for a great public course try Eastmoreland G.C. it will not disappoint.

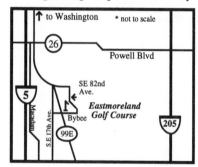

Directions: from I-5 N&S take the The
Dalles/Oregon City exit. Follow signs to
Oregon City onto Mcloughlin Blvd (99E)
southbound. Take the Eastmoreland/Reed
College exit. Turn right onto the overpass
back over Mcloughlin. The clubhouse and
parking lot are located left. Just across the
overpass. Look for signs marking your
way to the golf course.

Course Yardage & Par:
C-6508 yards, par 72.
M-6142 yards, par 72.
W-5646 yards, par 72.

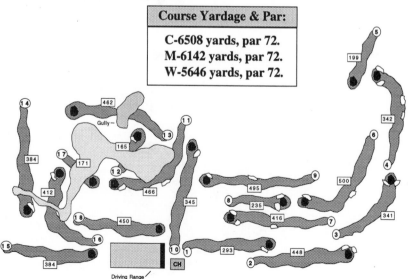

Echo Hills Golf Course (public, 9 hole course)

P.O. Box 187; 100 Golf Course Road; Echo, OR 97826
Phone: (541) 376-8244. Fax: none. Internet: none.
Manager: Randy Sperr. Superintendent: Randy Sperr.
Rating/Slope: M 68.1/113; W 68.8/117. **Course record:** 67.
Green fees: W/D $14/$8; W/E $18/$10; Sr. & Jr. and winter rates; M/C, VISA.
Power cart: $20/$10. **Pull cart:** $3/$2. **Trail fee:** $5 for personal carts.
Reservation policy: advance reservations are not needed or required.
Winter condition: the golf course is open all year long with dry conditions.
Terrain: very hilly. **Tees:** all grass. **Spikes:** metal spikes permitted.
Services: club rentals, snack bar, beer, wine, pro shop, beverages, driving range, putting & chipping greens. **Comments:** The course is well kept and very green during the peak golfing year. Hilly terrain makes this short course a challenge. The terrain will give the golfer a variety of different lies from the fairway.

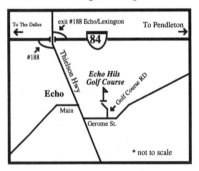

Directions: from I-84 E&W take the Echo/Lexington exit #188. Proceed for 1 mile to Gerome (Echo Schools). Golf course entrance will be ahead on your left hand side. **Note:** look for a sign marking your entrance to the course.

Course Yardage & Par:
M-2884 yards, par 36.
W-2531 yards, par 37.
Dual tees for 18 holes:
M-5867 yards, par 72.
W-5719 yards, par 74.

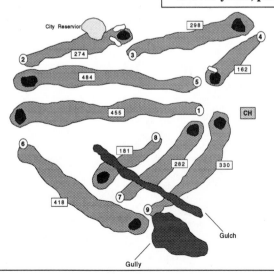

Elkhorn Valley Golf Course (public, 9 hole course)
32295 Little North Fork Road; Lyons, OR 97358
Phone: (503) 897-3368. Fax: none. Internet: none.
Manager: Elizabeth Wolf. Superintendent: none.
Rating/Slope: C 71.4/136; M 68.8/126; W 63.6/108. **Course record:** 67.
Green fees: $25/$15 all week long; M/C, VISA, DISCOVER.
Power cart: $20/$10. **Pull cart:** $2. **Trail fee:** no charge for personal carts.
Reservation policy: yes, please call anytime in advance for tee times.
Winter condition: the course is closed from November 1st to February 28th.
Terrain: flat (easy walking). **Tees:** all grass. **Spikes:** metal spikes permitted.
Services: club rentals, snack bar, beer, wine, pro shop, putting/chipping greens.
Comments: Rated by the National Golf Foundation as one of the best 9 hole
courses in the United States. Fantastic golf course that has challenging well
bunkered greens. Fairways are tight, demanding shot placement from the tee. If
you are looking for a change of pace in a great setting try Elkhorn Valley G.C.

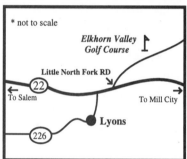

Directions: if you are coming from
Salem travel eastbound on Hwy 22
for approximately 25 miles to Lyons,
Oregon. Turn left on Little North
Fork Road. Proceed for 10 miles to the
golf course. Look for signs on the Hwy
marking your turn to the golf course.

Course Yardage & Par:

Yellow tees: 3169 yards, par 36.
Red tees: 2829 yards, par 36.
Green tees: 2445 yards, par 36.
Blue tees: 2009 yards, par 36.

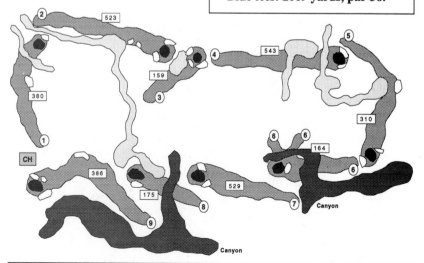

Emerald Valley Golf Club (public, 18 hole course)
83301 Dale Kuni Road; Creswell, OR 97426
Phone: (541) 895-2174. Fax: (541) 895-2812. Internet: none
Head Pro: Rob Lindsey. Superintendent: John Didier.
Rating/Slope: C 73.0/126; M 70.8/122; W 74.7/129. **Course record:** 64.
Green fees: M-Thur. $28/$15; F-Sun. $31/$17; Jr/Sr rates; M/C, VISA, AMEX.
Power cart: $20/$12. **Pull cart:** $3/$2. **Trail fee:** personal carts not allowed.
Reservation policy: yes, please call up to 1 week in advance for tee times.
Winter condition: the golf course is open all year long. Dry conditions.
Terrain: flat, some hills. **Tees:** all grass. **Spikes:** no metal spikes in summer.
Services: club rentals, lessons, snack bar, restaurant, lounge, beer, wine, liquor,
beverages, pro shop, showers, driving range, putting and chipping greens.
Comments: Beautiful championship course which is in great condition all year
round. Excellent greens that are well bunkered and fast during the peak golfing
season. Fairways are large and have wide landing area's. Excellent course.

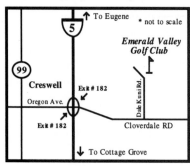

Directions: from I-5 N&S take the
Creswell exit #182 and go east for .75
miles to Dale Kuni Road Turn north
(left)on Dale Kuni Road and proceed
for .5 miles to the golf course. Look for
a sign on I-5 marking your exit.

Course Yardage & Par:
C-6873 yards, par 72.
M-6388 yards, par 72.
W-5803 yards, par 73.

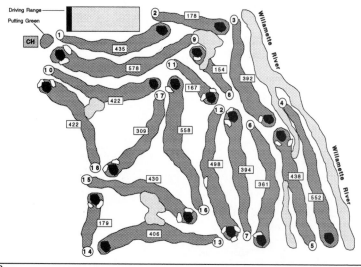

Eugene Country Club (private, 18 hole course)

255 Country Club Road; Eugene, OR 97401
Phone: (541) 344-5124. **Fax:** none. **Internet:** none.
Pro: Ron Weber, PGA. **Superintendent:** Chris Gaughn.
Rating/Slope: C 73.9/136; M 71.7/133; W 73.4/135. **Course record:** 66.
Green fees: private club, members & guests only; reciprocates; no credit cards.
Power cart: private club, members & guests of members only.
Pull cart: private club, complimentary. **Trail fee:** not allowed.
Reservation policy: private club members and guests of members only.
Winter condition: the golf course is open all year long weather permitting.
Terrain: relatively hilly. **Tees:** all grass. **Spikes:** no metal spikes permitted.
Services: full service private country club, driving range, putting green.
Comments: Eugene Country Club is one of the finest, best kept private golf
facilities in the state of Oregon. Fairways are tree-lined and narrow in spots.

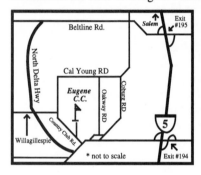

Directions: from I-5 N&S take exit
#195 and head west on Beltline Road.
From Beltline Road take the North Delta
Hwy exit and go southbound. Proceed
to Willagillespie and go east to Country
Club Road and the golf course.

Course Yardage & Par:
C-6837 yards, par 72.
M-6421 yards, par 72.
W-5805 yards, par 72.

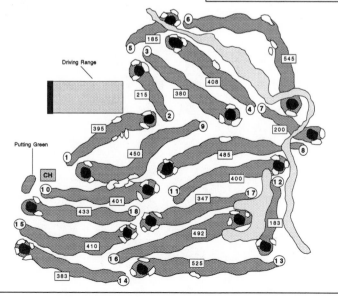

Evergreen Golf Club (public, 9 hole course)

11694 West Church Road NE; Mount Angel, OR 97362
Phone: (503) 845-9911. Fax: none. Internet: none.
Owners: Joe Druley & Maryann Mills.
Rating/Slope: M 68.6/110; W 70.8/111. **Course record:** 66.
Green fees: W/D $21/$12; W/E $22/$13; M/C, VISA,
Monday thru Friday before 2:30pm, $99 for 10 rounds of 9 hole golf.
Power cart: $20/$10. **Pull cart:** $2/$1. **Trail fee:** $3 a day.
Reservation policy: yes, please call ahead for your weekend tee-times.
Winter condition: the golf course is open all year long, weather permitting.
Terrain: rolling hills. **Tees:** all grass. **Spikes:** metal spikes permitted.
Services: club rentals, lessons, restaurant, beer, wine, liquor, pro shop.
Comments: The golf course is very easy to walk with flat terrain on most of the holes. Water is a factor on two different holes. Greens are medium in size with few hazards. Beautiful views of Mt. Hood can be seen from several holes on the course. If you are looking for a course with a friendly feel try Evergreen.

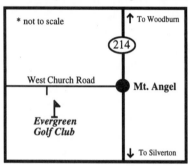

Directions: from Hwy 214 go west on West Church Road. Follow West Church Road for 1.1 miles to the golf course entrance on your left. **Note:** Look for the golf course sign on Hwy 214 that will indicate your turn.

Course Yardage & Par:
M-3021 yards, par 36.
W-2804 yards, par 37.

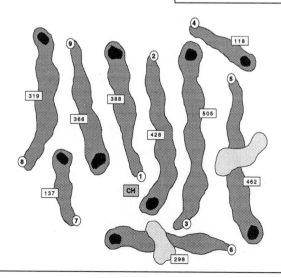

Fiddler's Green Golf Course & Driving Range (public, 18 holes)

91292 Highway 99 North; Eugene, OR 97402
Phones: (541) 689-8464 or call toll free: 1-800-999-6565
Owners: Al, Tim, Matt Whalen. Superintendent: N/A.
Rating/Slope: no golf course ratings. **Course record:** 22, 9 holes/44, 18 holes.
Green fees: $11/$6 all week long; Jr. and Sr. rates; M/C, VISA, DIS.
Power cart: not available. **Pull cart:** $1.50. **Trail fee:** not allowed.
Reservation policy: no reservations are needed for advance tee-times.
Winter condition: the golf course is open. Wet from November to March.
Terrain: flat (easy walking). **Tees:** all grass. **Spikes:** metal spikes permitted.
Services: club rentals, lessons, snack bar, beer, wine, huge pro shop, lighted & covered driving range. **Comments:** facility has one of the largest on-course pro shops in the United States. Be sure to browse and shop after golf. Excellent facility to practice your entire game. Great course for beginners and families.

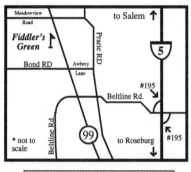

Course Yardage & Par:

M-2378 yards, par 54.
W-2378 yards, par 54.

Directions: from I-5 take the Airport exit #195 (Beltline Rd.) to Hwy 99. You will travel on Beltline for approximately 5 miles. Go north on Hwy 99 as if going to the airport. Continue on Hwy 99 past the airport to the golf course on your left. If you are north of Eugene on I-5 you can also take the Halsey exit #216. Turn west to Halsey and proceed to the flashing stop light. Turn south on Hwy 99 through Halsey, Harrisburg and Junction City. Fiddlers Green is located 4 miles south of Junction City on the west side of the Hwy. Look for signs at your turn.

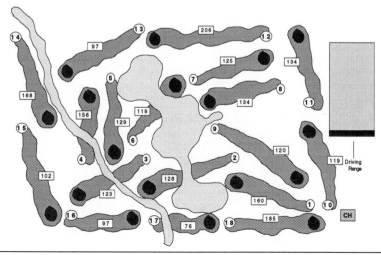

Forest Hills Country Club (semi-private, 9 hole course)
#1 Country Club Drive; Reedsport, OR 97467
Phone: (541) 271-2626. Fax: (541) 271-2626. Internet: none.
Pro: Kevin Winston, PGA. Superintendent: Rick Miska.
Rating/Slope: M 69.8/120; W 71.5/114. **Course record:** 29 (9 holes).
Green fees: $20/$12 all week long; call for winter rates; M/C, VISA.
Power cart: $18/$10. **Pull cart:** $2. **Trail fee:** $10 for personal carts.
Reservation policy: yes, encouraged during summer months and on weekends.
Winter condition: the golf course is open all year long, with damp conditions.
Terrain: flat, some hills. **Tees:** grass. **Spikes:** metal spikes permitted.
Services: club rentals, lessons, restaurant, lounge, beer, wine, liquor, pro shop,
driving range, putting/chipping green. **Comments:** Relatively flat course that
is easy to walk. Greens are large, undulating and can be extremely tough to putt.
Well taken care of facility that plays much longer than the yardage indicates.

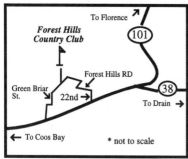

Directions: from Highway 101 turn
westbound on 22nd Street. Turn right
on Greenbriar. Turn right on Country
Club Drive and proceed to the golf
course. **Note:** Look for signs to the golf
course marking your way.

Course Yardage & Par:
M-3108 yards, par 36.
W-2774 yards, par 37.
<u>**Dual tees for 18 holes:**</u>
M-6322 yards, par 72.
W-5548 yards, par 74.

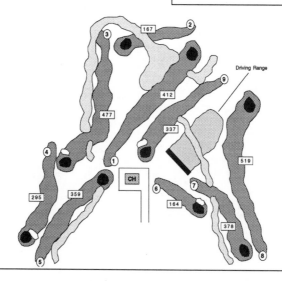

Forest Hills Golf Course (semi-private, 18 hole course)

36260 SW Tongue Lane; Cornelius, OR 97113
Phone: (503) 357-3347. Fax: none. Internet: none.
Pro: Bruce Clark, PGA. Manager: Dick Speros.
Rating/Slope: M 69.7/122; W 72.0/123. Course record: 64.
Green fees: $30/$15 all week long; M/C, VISA, AMEX.
Power cart: $20/$10. Pull cart: $2/$1. Trail fee: $10/$5.
Reservation policy: yes, call 1 week in advance for tee times.
Winter condition: the golf course is open all year long. Damp conditions.
Terrain: flat, some hills. Tees: all grass. Spikes: metal spikes permitted.
Services: club rentals, lessons, snack bar, lounge, beer, wine, liquor, beverages, pro shop, driving range, putting & chipping greens. Comments: One of the most scenic courses in the state of Oregon. Greens are large and well bunkered. Fairways are wide with generous landing area's. Great public course.

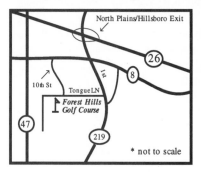

Directions: take Hwy 26 west to the Hillsboro-North Plains #57 exit. Go Back across the freeway and follow the road into Hillsboro. Proceed through Hillsboro until you are 3 miles south having made no turns. Turn right on Tongue Lane. Proceed to the golf course.

Course Yardage & Par:
M-6173 yards, par 72.
W-5673 yards, par 74.

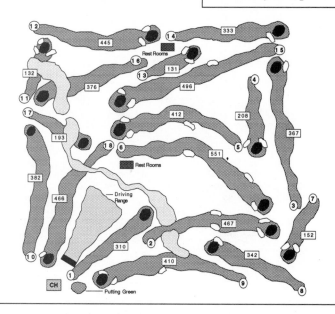

Frontier Golf Course (public, 9 hole par 3course)
2965 North Holly Street; Canby, OR 97013
Phone: (503) 266-4435. **Fax: none. Internet: none.**
Owner: Joe Sisul. Superintendent: none.
Rating/Slope: the golf course is not rated. **Course record:** 24.
Green fees: $10/$5.50 all week long; Sr. rates.
Power cart: $5. **Pull cart:** $1. **Trail fee:** personal carts not allowed.
Reservation policy: advance reservations are not required for tee-times.
Winter condition: the golf course is closed from November to March.
Terrain: flat (easy walking). **Tees:** mats. **Spikes:** metal spikes permitted.
Services: club rentals, small pro shop, snacks, beverages, putting green.
Comments: economical course. Holes range in length from a 90 yard sand
wedge to a 168 yard challenging par 3. Good track to bring the first time golfer.

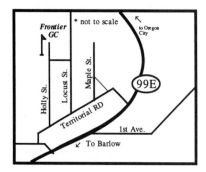

Directions: When in Canby on Highway
99E look for Ivy Street Proceed 1 block
west on Ivy Street. Proceed to Holly
Street and turn westbound. The golf
course will be located 1.8 miles ahead.
Look for signs marking your turns.

Course Yardage & Par:
M-1063 yards, par 27.
W-1063 yards, par 27.

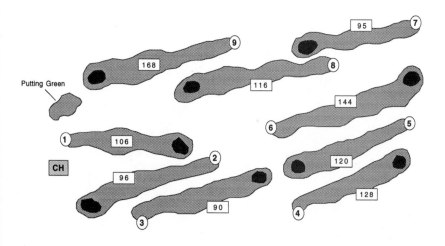

Gearhart Golf Links (public, 18 hole course)

North Marion, P.O. Box 2758; Gearhart, OR 97138
Phone: (503) 738-3538. Fax: none. Internet: none.
Pro: Jim Smith, PGA. Superintendent: Mark Kelley.
Rating/Slope: M 68.7/114; W 70.5/112. **Course record:** 63.
Green fees: $27/$14 all week long; M/C, VISA accepted.
Power cart: $25/$15. **Pull cart:** $4/$2. **Trail fee:** $25/$15.
Reservation policy: requested. Please call in advance for all tee-times.
Winter condition: course is open all year long, dry, the course drains well.
Terrain: flat, some rolling hills. **Tees:** grass. **Spikes:** metal spikes permitted.
Services: club rentals, lessons, snack bar, restaurant, lounge, beer, wine, liquor, beverages, pro shop, putting & chipping greens. **Comments:** The Gearhart Golf Links is the oldest golf course in Oregon or Washington. Established in 1892 as a 9 hole course, it was extended to 18 holes in 1913. The greens are large and well bunkered. Fairways have generous landing areas giving the golfer room off the tee. The weather on the Oregon Coast can change quickly so be prepared for anything. If the wind blows this course can play much longer than the yardage.

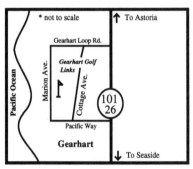

Directions: the golf course is located 1/2 of a mile west of Hwy 101 on the Oregon coast in Gearhart Oregon. **Note:** Look for the sign to the resort and the golf course from Highway 101. The path to the golf course is well marked.

Course Yardage & Par:
M-6089 yards, par 72. **W-5882 yards, par 74.**

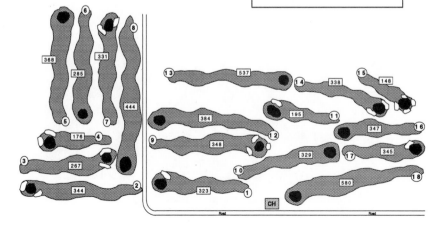

Glendoveer Golf Course (East Course) (public, 18 hole course)
14015 NE Glisan Street; Portland, OR 97230
Phone: (503) 253-7507, 292-8570, Tee-times. **Fax:** (503) 253-1772.
Director of Golf: Daran Dauble, PGA. **Head Pro:** Jim Chianello.
Rating/Slope: C 69.4/120; M 67.3/114; W 68.2/111. **Course record:** 62.
Green fees: W/D $18/$10; W/E $20/$11; Senior rates (weekdays only $7).
Power Cart: $24/$12. **Pull Cart:** $2. **Trail fee:** $7/$3.50 for personal carts.
Reservation policy: yes, call for weekends only, 6 am to 3pm for your tee times.
Winter condition: the golf course is open all year long. Dry conditions.
Terrain: undulating hills. **Tees:** all grass. **Spikes:** metal spikes permitted.
Services: club rentals, lessons, snack bar, restaurant, lounge, beer, wine, liquor, beverages, pro shop, lockers, showers, driving range, tennis, racquetball, jogging trail, putting & chipping greens, practice area. **Comments:** golf course is kept in excellent condition and can be very busy during the peak season. The course plays fairly tight in spots with trees in play off the tee. Fair public track.

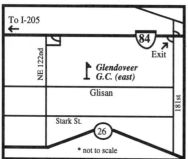

Directions: from I-84 east exit at 181st NE. Proceed southbound for 1.2 miles to Glisan Street. Turn westbound for .8 mile to the golf course. Look for signs marking your way to the golf course.

Course Yardage & Par:

M-6148 yards, par 73.
W-6148 yards, par 77.

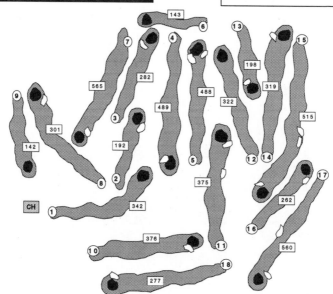

Glendoveer Golf Course (West Course) (public, 18 hole course)
14015 NE Glisan Street; Portland, OR 97230
Phone: (503) 253-7507, 292-8570, Tee-times. Fax: (503) 253-1772.
Director of Golf: Daran Dauble, PGA. Head Pro: Jim Chianello.
Rating/Slope: C 67.4/110; M 65.8/105; W 67.9/103. Course record: 62.
Green fees: W/D $18/$10; W/E $20/$11; Senior rates (weekdays only $7).
Power cart: $24/$12. Pull Cart: $2. Trail fee: $7/$3.50 for personal carts.
Reservation policy: yes, call for weekends only, 6 am to 3pm for your tee times.
Winter condition: the golf course is open all year long. Dry conditions.
Terrain: flat, some hills. Tees: all grass. Spikes: metal spikes permitted.
Services: club rentals, lessons, snack bar, restaurant, lounge, beer, wine, liquor, beverages, pro shop, lockers, showers, driving range, tennis, putting & chipping greens, racquetball, jogging trail. Comments: the golf course is in excellent condition all year long. Fairways are tree-lined and tight. Great driving range at the course location for those wanting to hit a bucket of balls. Fair public track.

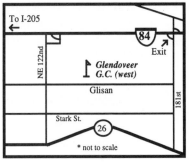

Directions: from I-84 east exit at 181st NE. Proceed southbound for 1.2 miles to Glisan Street. Turn westbound for .8 mile to the golf course. Look for signs.

Course Yardage & Par:
M-5803 yards, par 71.
W-5803 yards, par 75.

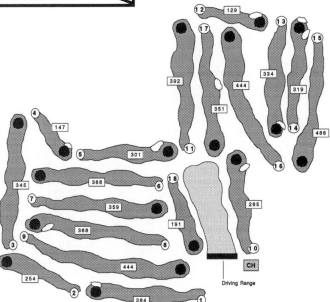

Golf City (public, 9 hole course)
2115 Highway 20; Corvallis, OR 97330
Phone: (541) 753-6213. Fax: (541) 753-6213. Internet: none.
Pro: Dick Mason, PGA. Superintendent: none.
Rating/Slope: the golf course is not rated. **Course record:** 21.
Green fees: $6 all week long; no special rates.
Power cart: power carts are not available. **Pull cart:** $1. **Trail fee:** none.
Reservation policy: advance reservations are not required for starting times..
Winter condition: the golf course is open all year long, weather permitting.
Terrain: flat, some hills. **Tees:** grass/mats. **Spikes:** no metal spikes permitted.
Services: club rentals, lessons, snack bar, coffee shop, beer, wine, pro shop, putting green, miniature golf. **Comments:** this short par 3 course is home of the shortest par 4 on record. Greens are on the small size on can be hard to hold. If you are looking for a place to take the first time golfer to try "Golf City".

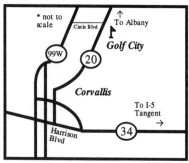

Directions: when entering Corvallis on Hwy 34. Proceed to Highway 20 and go eastbound (north to Albany). The course is located 2.1 miles ahead. Look for signs marking your turns to the golf course.

Course Yardage & Par:
M-801 yards, par 28.
W-801 yards, par 28.

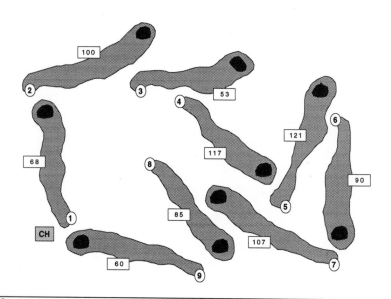

The Golf Club of Oregon (public, 18 hole course)
905 NW Spring Hill Drive; Albany, OR 97321
Phone: (541) 928-8338. Fax: (541) 928-6519. Internet: none.
Manager: Aaron O'Malley. Pro: Bill Hamilton.
Rating/Slope: C 67.8/111; M 66.5/108; W 68.9/117. **Course record: 61.**
Green fees: $22/$13; Jr. and Sr. rates (weekdays only); no credit cards.
Power cart: $20/$10. **Pull cart:** $3/$2. **Trail fee:** $10/$5 for personal carts.
Reservation policy: yes, call for weekend tee-times only, 7 days in advance.
Winter condition: the golf course is open all year long. Course drains fair.
Terrain: flat (easy walking). **Tees:** all grass. **Spikes:** no metal spikes permitted.
Services: club rentals, lessons, snack bar, beer, wine, pro shop, lockers, putting
green, driving range, irons only. **Comments:** The course is easy to walk and has
a friendly atmosphere and staff. The course has good drainage and provides
excellent play during the winter months. Fair test of golf for all level of golfers.

Directions: from I-5 N&S take exit #233
(Satiam Hwy 20) and go westbound to
Main St. and turn right. Proceed to 1st
Avenue and turn left (one way). Proceed
to Lyons and turn right. Go over the bridge
and take your first right on Spring Hill
Drive. Proceed to the golf course on your
right. Look for signs marking your way.

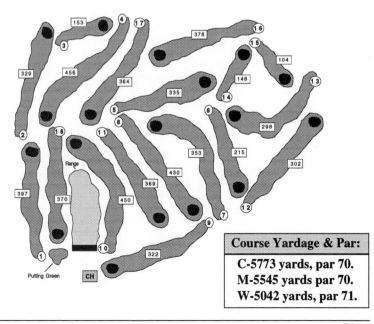

Course Yardage & Par:
C-5773 yards, par 70.
M-5545 yards par 70.
W-5042 yards, par 71.

Grants Pass Golf Club (semi-private, 18 hole course)
230 Espey Road; Grants Pass, OR 97527
Phone: (541) 476-0849. Fax: (541) 476-2807. Internet: none.
Pro: Ed Fisher, PGA. Superintendent: Scott Shillington.
Rating/Slope: C 71.1/130; M 69.8/128; W 73.5/126. **Course record:** 63.
Green fees: $30/$18 all week long; M/C, VISA are honored.
Power cart: $20/$12. **Pull cart:** $2. **Trail fee:** personal carts are not allowed.
Reservation policy: yes, please call 2 days in advance for your tee-times.
Winter condition: the golf course is open all year long, weather permitting.
Terrain: relatively hilly. **Tees:** all grass. **Spikes:** no metal spikes permitted.
Services: club rentals, lessons, snack bar, restaurant, lounge, beverages, beer, wine, liquor, pop, pro shop, lockers, showers, putting green, driving range.
Comments: Beautiful layout that winds through trees and landscaped terrain. The greens are well bunkered and fairly large. Public play is available after members play on a daily basis, so call first to find out the availability of T-times.

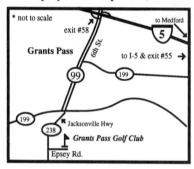

Directions: from I-5 N&S take the Grants Pass exit #55 which will put you on 6th St. Follow accross the river onto Hwy 238. Go south for 3 miles to Espey Road. Turn left to the golf course. The golf course is located approximately 6 miles from the freeway. Look for signs marking your way. The way to the golf course is well indicated.

Course Yardage & Par:
C-6409 yards, par 72.
M-6101 yards, par 72.
W-5687 yards, par 73.

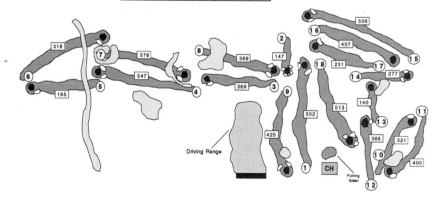

Greenlea Golf Course (public, 9 hole course)

26736 SE Kelso Road; Boring, OR 97009
Phone: (503) 663-3934. Fax: none. Internet: none.
Owner: Muriel Markham. Superintendent: none.
Rating/Slope: the golf course is not rated. **Course record:** 26.
Green fees: W/D $7; W/E & Holidays $8; no credit cards.
Power cart: power carts are not available. **Pull cart:** $2. **Trail fee:** no charge.
Reservation policy: Tee-times are on a first come first served basis.
Winter condition: the course is closed from December 1st to February 28th.
Terrain: flat, some hills. **Tees:** all grass. **Spikes:** no metal spikes permitted.
Services: club rentals, pro shop, vending machines, putting & chipping green.
Comments: two sets of tees are available for a full 18 hole round of golf. The golf course is easy to walk and has few hazards. Greens are small in size with few hazards fronting them. Great course for a shorter game of golf.

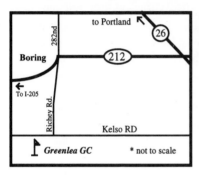

Directions: from Highway 212 trun right on Richey Road which will become SE Kelso Road. The golf course is located approximately 1.3 miles ahead on your left hand side. The golf course is located 1.5 miles south of Boring, Oregon. Look for signs marking your turn to the course.

Course Yardage & Par:
M-1510 yards, par 30.
W-1510 yards, par 30.

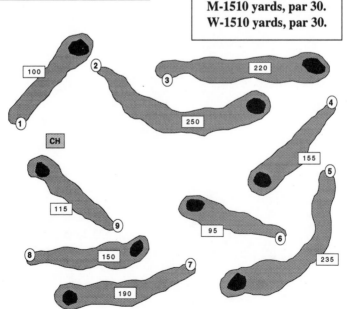

The Greens at Redmond (public)
2575 S.W. Greens Boulevard; Redmond, OR 97138
Phone: (541) 923-0694. Fax: (541) 923-1072. Internet: none.
Pro: Dick Mason, PGA. Superintendent: none.
Rating/Slope: C 58.3/97; M 57.6/95; W 57.2/93. **Course record: 25.**
Green fees: $19/$11 all week long; winter rates; M/C, VISA.
Power cart: $15/$8.50. **Pull cart:** $2. **Trail fee:** not allowed
Reservation policy: please call up to 1 week in advance for tee-times.
Winter condition: the golf course is open all year long, weather permitting.
Terrain: flat, some hills. **Tees:** all grass. **Spikes:** no metal spikes permitted.
Services: club rentals, small pro shop, snack bar, lessons, beverages.
Comments: This challenging 9 hole executive course was designed by Robert Muir Graves and opened in spring of 1996. The course features a wide variety of holes that have water or native growth area's bordering the fairways. Holes range from 108 yards to over 300 in length. Great change of pace golf course.

Directions: the golf course is located in Redmond Oregon just off of Highway 97 near the Wal-Mart store. The course is on the west side of Highway 97. You will turn on Yew Avenue. Signs are posted.

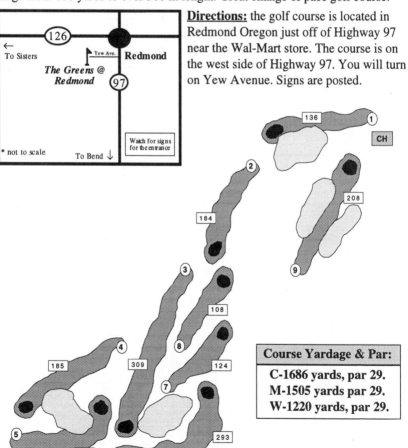

Course Yardage & Par:

C-1686 yards, par 29.
M-1505 yards par 29.
W-1220 yards, par 29.

Gresham Golf Course (semi-private, 18 hole course)
2155 NE Division; Gresham, OR 97030
Phone: (503) 665-3352. Fax: none. Internet: none.
Pro: Stuart Smart, PGA. Superintendent: Chuck Wolsborn.
Rating/Slope: C 68.1/109; M 67.2/107; W 69.0/107. **Course record:** 62.
Green fees: W/D $19/$10; W/E $22/$13; Jr. rates (Mon.-Fri.) $7; M/C, VISA.
Power cart: $24/$14. **Pull cart:** $2. **Trail fee:** personal carts are not allowed.
Reservation policy: yes, call for weekend tee-times only (advised all year long).
Winter condition: the golf course is open all year long, weather permitting.
Terrain: flat, some hills. **Tees:** all grass. **Spikes:** no metal spikes permitted.
Services: club rentals, lessons, restaurant, lounge, beer, wine, liquor, pro shop,
driving range, putting & chipping greens. **Comments:** The course is in excellent
condition all year round. Fairways have wide landing area's with few hazards to
contend with. The staff is friendly and helpful. Great walking course for seniors.

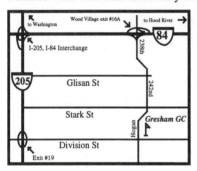

Directions: from I-205 take the Division
Street exit. Proceed eastbound for 8 miles
to the golf course. From I-84 take Wood
Village exit and go southbound. Proceed
to Division Street and turn left to the golf
course. The golf course is located 1 block
ahead on your left hand side.

Course Yardage & Par:
C-6012 yards, par 72.
M-5814 yards, par 72.
W-5284 yards, par 72.

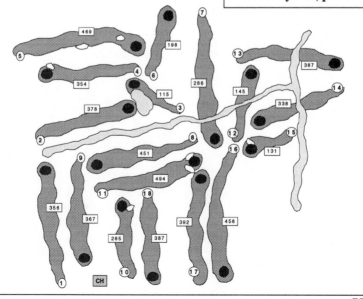

Harbor Links Golf Course (public, 18 hole course)
601 Harbor Isles Boulevard; Klamath Falls, OR 97601
Phone: (541) 882-0609. Fax: (541) 885-6833. Internet: harborlccosnet.net.
Pro: Rocky Warner, PGA. Superintendent: Paul Ludington.
Rating/Slope: C 69.3/112; M 68.5/110; W 71.4/126. **Course record:** 63.
Green fees: W/D $25/$13; W/E & Holidays $28/$16; winter rates; M/C, VISA.
Power cart: $20/$12. **Pull cart:** $3/$2. **Trail fee:** not allowed.
Reservation policy: yes, call 1 day ahead for all your tee-time reservations.
Winter condition: the course is open all year long, weather permitting, wet.
Terrain: flat (easy walking). **Tees:** all grass. **Spikes:** metal spikes permitted.
Services: club rentals, lessons, snack bar, restaurant, lounge, beer, wine, liquor,
pro shop, putting & chipping greens, driving range. **Comments:** Located on
Klamath Lake. A links type course with many water hazards. Good golf course
that can play very tough during the peak golfing season. Fair public track.

Directions: from Hwy 97 exit at Nevada
Avenue and head westbound. Turn right
at Montelus Street. Continue ahead to
Lakeport Blvd. and turn left. Proceed to
Harbor Isles Blvd. and the golf course.
The course is located on Klamath Lake.

Course Yardage & Par:
C-6272 yards, par 72.
M-6090 yards, par 72.
W-5709 yards, par 72.

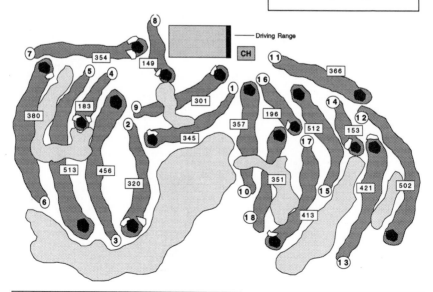

Hawk Creek Golf Course (public, 9 hole course)
48405 Hawk Street; P. O. Box 497; Neskowin, OR 97149
Phone: (503) 392-4120. **Fax:** (503) 392-4620. **Internet:** none.
Owners: Darin & Judy Galle. **Superintendent:** none.
Rating/Slope: M 63.8/103; W 64.9/104. **Course record:** 29.
Green fees: $20/$12 all week long; no special rates; M/C, VISA.
Power cart: $20/$10. **Pull cart:** $2. **Trail fee:** $5 for personal carts.
Reservation policy: yes, reservations are taken for tee times in the summer.
Winter condition: the golf course is open all year, weather permitting.
Terrain: flat, some hills. **Tees:** all grass. **Spikes:** metal spikes permitted.
Services: club rentals, snack bar, very small pro shop, beer, wine, putting green.
Comments: the golf course is beautifully situated in a valley minutes from the scenic Oregon Coast. This track is short in length and can be rustic in certain area's of the course. Greens are small and have few hazards. Great golf course if you want to play a quick nine holes or if you want a low stress round of golf.

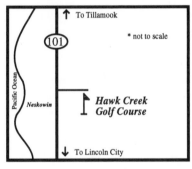

Directions: the golf course is located on the east side of Hwy 101 at Neskowin. Look for a black & white sign from Hwy 101 marking the entrance to the golf course. Your turn is well marked.

Course Yardage & Par:
M-2343 yards, par 34.
W-2343 yards, par 36.

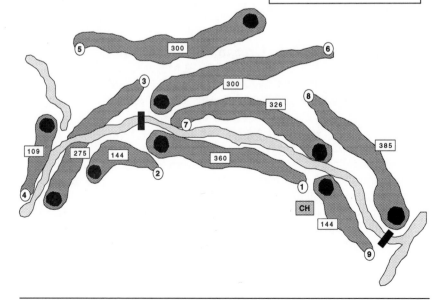

Heron Lakes Golf Club; Great Blue Course (public, 18 holes)

3500 North Victory Boulevard; Portland, OR 97217
Phone: (503) 289-1818, (503) 292-8570 Tee-times. Fax: (503) 240-1925.
Pro: Byron Wood, PGA. Superintendent: Jeese Goodling.
Rating/Slope: T 73.6/132; C 71.3/128; M 69.4/122; W 69.8/120. **Record:** 67.
Green fees: $31/$16 all week long; VISA, M/C, DISCOVER.
Power cart: $25/$12.50. **Pull cart:** $3/$2. **Trail fee:** $4/$2.
Reservation policy: 6 days by phone. 7 days when booking in person. A must.
Winter condition: the golf course is open all year long, weather permitting.
Terrain: flat (easy walking). **Tees:** all grass. **Spikes:** metal spikes permitted.
Services: club rentals, lessons, snack bar, beer, well stocked pro shop, putting &
chipping greens, driving range. **Comments:** Great Blue is one of the toughest
public courses in the northwest. It is still a great buy at less than $35 for 18 holes
of golf. The track has several bunkers fronting the large, undulating greens.
Lakes come into play on almost every hole and are a major factor off the tee.

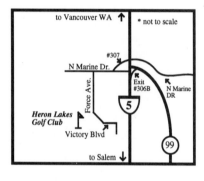

Directions: from I-5 take exit #306B
(West Delta Park/Portland International
Raceway). From the north swing sharply
to the right off exit ramp to the intersection with N. Victory Blvd. Proceed
straight to N. Broadacres Rd. Turn left
on N. Broadacres (which becomes N.
Broadacre St). Turn right at intersection
of N. Force Ave. and follow this to the
course entrance. From the south, turn left
onto N. Victory Blvd. off the freeway
exit, then right at "T" to N. Broadacres
Rd. Follow same as above from here.

Heron Lakes Golf Club; Greenback Course (public, 18 holes)

3500 North Victory Boulevard; Portland, OR 97217
Phone: (503) 289-1818, (503) 292-8570 Tee-times. Fax: (503) 240-1925.
Pro: Byron Wood, PGA. Superintendent: Jeese Goodling.
Rating/Slope: C 71.4/124; M 68.4/115; W 69.4/113. **Course record:** 66.
Green fees: W/D $19/$10; W/E $21/$11; Jr. & Sr. rates; VISA, M/C, DIS.
Power cart: $25/$12.50. **Pull cart:** $3/$2. **Trail fee:** $4/$2.
Reservation policy: 6 days by phone. 7 days when booking in person. A must.
Winter condition: the golf course is open all year long, weather permitting.
Terrain: flat (easy walking). **Tees:** all grass. **Spikes:** metal spikes permitted.
Services: club rentals, lessons, snack bar, beer, large pro shop, driving range.
Comments: Course has some of the nicest greens in Oregon. You will find the
course in excellent condition throughout the entire year. Fairways are large with
wide landing area's. Greens are large with bunkers fronting them. The course has
a driving range for those who want to practice before or after their round.

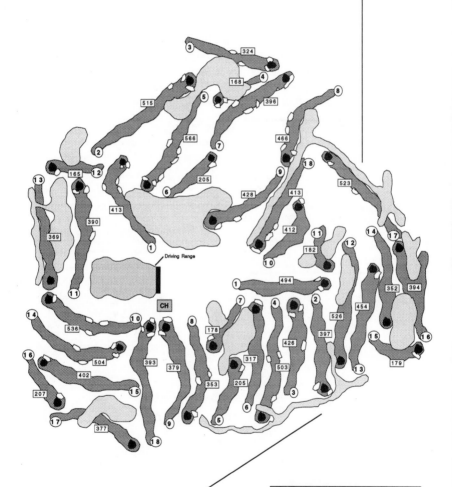

Course Yardage & Par:

(Great Blue Course)
T-6916 yards, par 72.
C-6504 yards, par 72.
M-6056 yards, par 72.
W-5285 yards, par 72.

Great Blue Course

Greenback Course

Course Yardage & Par:

(Greenback Course)
C-6595 yards, par 72.
M-5938 yards, par 72.
W-5224 yards, par 72.

Hidden Valley Golf Course (public, 9 hole course)

775 North River Road; Cottage Grove, OR 97424
Phone: (541) 942-3046. Fax: none. Internet: none.
Owners: Joel & Karen Boede. Superintendent: none.
Rating/Slope: M 66.6/108; W 68.4/114. **Course record:** 57 (18 holes).
Green fees: W/D $14/$8; W/E $16/$9; Sr. & Jr. rates (Mon.-Fri. $10/$6.50).
Power cart: $16/$11. **Pull cart:** $2. **Trail fee:** $5/$3 for personal carts.
Reservation policy: yes, call 1 week in advance for weekend tee-times.
Winter condition: the golf course is open all year, wet, with good drainage.
Terrain: flat, some hills. **Tees:** all grass. **Spikes:** metal spikes permitted.
Services: club rentals, lessons, restaurant, lounge, beer, wine, liquor, pro shop,
putting green, lockers. **Comments:** Large trees, narrow fairways and very
small greens make shot placement extremely important on this course. Great
golf course for a quick 9 holes. This track also has dual tees for 18 hole play.

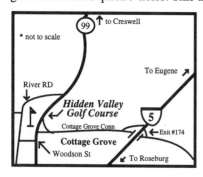

Directions: from I-5 southbound take the first Cottage Grove exit (second exit if going northbound, #174) and proceed west for 1/2 mile. Veer left at Pacific Highway. Turn right on Woodson. Turn right to the golf course. Look for signs.

Course Yardage & Par:
M-2766 yards, par 35.
W-2340 yards, par 35.
Dual tees for 18 holes:
M-5412 yards, par 70.
W-4802 yards, par 70.

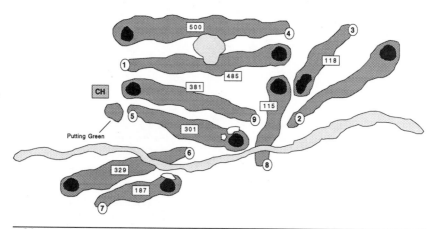

The Highlands at Gearhart (public, 9 hole course)
#1 Highlands Road; Gearhart, OR 97138
Phone: (503) 738-5248. **Fax:** none. **Internet:** none.
Pro: Dan Strite, PGA. **Superintendent:** none.
Rating/Slope: M 59.0/94; W 59.0/94. **Course record:** 25.
Green fees: $18/$10 all week long; M/C, VISA.
Power cart: not available. **Pull cart:** $2. **Trail fee:** not allowed
Reservation policy: in summer only, call up to 7 days in advance for times.
Winter condition: the golf course is open all year long, weather permitting.
Terrain: flat, some hills. **Tees:** all grass. **Spikes:** metal spikes permitted.
Services: club rentals, pro shop with large inventory, snack bar, lessons.
Comments: This challenging 9 hole course is set in a beautiful ocean view
setting. Hole #5 is the signature hole where a cliff comes into play. If you are
looking for a change of pace try "Highlands" it is a great golf course.

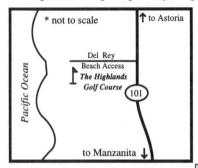

Directions: golf course is located 1 mile
north of Gearhart, Oregon off of Highway
101. Take Del Rey Beach access off of
Highway 101. Travel westbound for 1/4
mile to the golf course. Look for signs
that are posted on the highway.

Course Yardage & Par:	
Yellow Nine:	M-1776 yards, par 31.
	W-1776 yards, par 34.
Blue Nine:	M-1761 yards, par 31.
	W-1761 yards, par 33.
White Nine:	M-1618 yards, par 31.
	W-1618 yards, par 34.

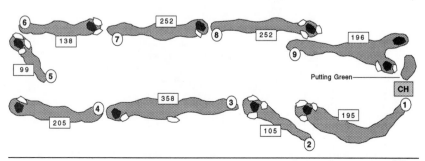

Hillebrand's Paradise Ranch Resort (resort, 3 hole course)
7000 D Monument Drive; Grants Pass, OR 97526
Phone: (541) 479-4333. Fax: none. Internet: none.
Pro: none. Superintendent: none.
Rating/Slope: the golf course is not rated. **Course record:** N/A.
Green fees: green fees are for guests staying at the ranch.; M/C, VISA.
Power cart: none. **Pull cart:** none. **Trail fee:** not allowed.
Reservation policy: tee times are for guests staying at the ranch.
Winter condition: the golf course is closed in the winter months.
Terrain: flat. **Tees:** all grass. **Spikes:** metal spikes permitted.
Services: limited golf related services.
Comments: this 3 hole course is part of the Hillebrand's Paradise Ranch Resort.
It is used by the guests staying at this dude style ranch. The three holes are
surrounded by a lake that is well stocked with catch and release trout and other
various species of fish. The course is well treed with small greens.

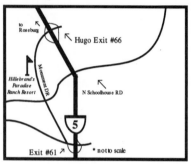

Directions: from I-5 N&S take exit #61.
Turn left at the stop sign off the ramp. Go
under freeway, right at the light, which is
monument Drive. Proceed for 2 miles to
the Ranch and the golf course.

Course Yardage & Par:
M-1310 yards, par 28.
W-1310 yards, par 28.
(3 Circuits)

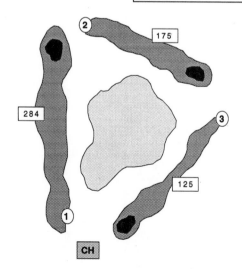

Hood River Golf & Country Club (public, 9 hole course)
1850 Country Club Road; Hood River, OR 97031
Phone: (541) 386-3009. **Fax:** (541) 386-1732. **Internet:** none.
Pro: Dave Waller, PGA. **Superintendent:** Dave Waller.
Rating/Slope: M 67.6/111; W 68.4/104. **Course record:** 64.
Green fees: W/D $17/$10; W/E $18/$10; Jr. & Sr. rates available; M/C, VISA.
Power cart: $20/$12. **Pull cart:** $2. **Trail fee:** $5 for personal carts.
Reservation policy: yes, call up to 1 week in advance for tee times.
Winter condition: the golf course is closed when snow covered only.
Terrain: relatively hilly. **Tees:** all grass. **Spikes:** metal spikes permitted.
Services: club rentals, lessons, snack bar, restaurant, lounge, beer, wine, liquor,
pro shop, driving range, putting & chipping green. **Comments:** Beautiful setting
with view's of Mount Hood and Mount Adams. The course has wide fairways
with medium to large greens. Water comes into play on three holes. Bunkers
guard some greens on your approach shots. Dual tees are available for a different
look on your 2nd nine. Hood River plans to add an additional 9 holes in 1998.

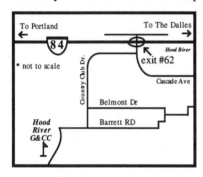

Directions: from I-84 E&W take exit #62.
Go south and take Country Club Road for
2.2 miles. At stop, where road "T,s" turn
right. The golf course is located 1.1 miles
ahead on your right hand side.

Course Yardage & Par:
M-2920 yards, par 36.
W-2695 yards, par 37.
Dual tees for 18 holes:
M-5900 yards, par 72.
W-5246 yards, par 74.

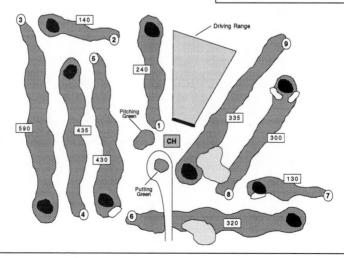

Illahe Hills Country Club (private, 18 hole course)
3376 Country Club Drive; Salem, OR 97302
Phone: (503) 581-3233. **Fax:** (503) 370-8068. **Internet:** none.
Pro: Ron Rawls, PGA. **Superintendent:** Bill Swancutt.
Rating/Slope: C 72.7/129; M 71.0/126; W 72.3/122. **Course record:** 64.
Green fees: private club, members & guests of members only; no credit cards.
Power cart: private club. **Pull cart:** complimentary. **Trail fee:** not allowed.
Reservation policy: members only & guests only, 2 days in advance for times.
Winter condition: the golf course is open all year long, damp conditions.
Terrain: flat, some hills. **Tees:** all grass. **Spikes:** metal spikes permitted.
Services: club rentals, lessons, snack bar, restaurant, lounge, beer, wine, liquor, beverages, pro shop, lockers, showers, putting & chipping greens driving range.
Comments: course has been host to several tournaments, including the 1981 U.S.G.A. Junior Girls National Championship. Great, tough golf course.

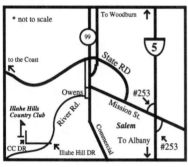

Directions: from I-5 N&S take the Mission exit and go westbound. Turn left on Commercial. At Owens, turn right. Follow Owens as it veers south and changes to River Road. Follow for 3.7 miles to the golf course. The golf course is located on the west side of the city.

Course Yardage & Par:
C-6735 yards, par 72.
M-6411 yards, par 72.
W-5621 yards, par 73.

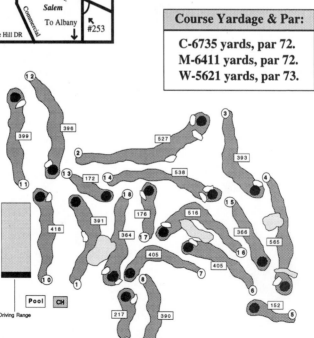

Illinois Valley Golf Club (public, 9 hole course)
Redwood Hwy 199, P.O. Box 924; Cave Junction, OR 97523
Phone: (541) 592-3151. Fax: (541) 592-3525. Internet: none.
Pro: Rex Denham, PGA. Superintendent: Matt Squire.
Rating/Slope: M 69.1/117; W 71.1/120. **Course Record:** 65.
Green fees: $16/$10 all week long; Jr & Sr rates; Thursday specials.
Power cart: $18/$9. **Pull cart:** $2/$1. **Trail fee:** not allowed.
Reservation policy: call 1 week in advance for weekends and holiday T-times.
Winter condition: course is open all year long. Dry conditions (drains well).
Terrain: flat (easy walking). **Tees:** all grass. **Spikes:** metal spikes permitted.
Services: club rentals, lessons, snack bar, beer, wine, pro shop, driving range,
putting green. **Comments:** course has two sets of tees for those who want to
play a full 18 holes. Excellent well kept golf course that plays over and through
many water hazards. Greens are medium in size and tend to be open in the front.

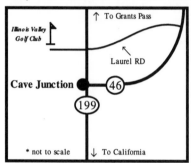

Directions: the golf course is located
1/2 mile north of the city of Cave Junction
off of Highway 199. The golf course will
be located on the west side of the Hwy.
Look for signs at your turn to the course.

Course Yardage & Par:

M-3049 yards, par 36.
W-2727 yards, par 36.
Dual tees for 18 holes:
M-6004 yards, par 72.
W-5354 yards, par 72.

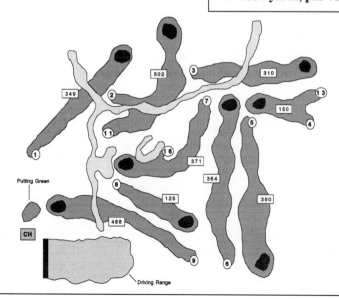

Indian Creek Golf Course (public, 18 hole course)
3605 Brookside Drive; Hood River, OR 97031
Phone: (541) 386-7770. **Fax:** (541) 386-7330. **Internet:** www.icgolf@gorge.com
Pro: Treve Gray, PGA. **Superintendent:** Marvin King.
Rating/Slope: C 70.2/124; M 67.7/112; W 67.7/116. **Course record:** 64.
Green fees: W/D $24/$13; W/E $32/$17; Sr/Jr rates $8, Sr rates M & W all day.
Power cart: $25/$13. **Pull cart:** $3. **Trail fee:** $7 for personal carts.
Reservation policy: yes, taken up to 1 week in advance, tournaments anytime.
Winter condition: the golf course is open all year long, weather permitting.
Terrain: flat, rolling terrain.**Tees:** all grass. **Spikes:** no metal spikes permitted.
Services: club rentals, lessons, pro shop, putting/chipping green, driving range.
Comments: the course provides excellent drainage for winter play. This track is
fairly easy to walk with gentle rolling hills. Great views of the countryside.

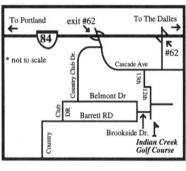

Directions: from I-84 E&W take exit #62
and turn right. Follow Cascade St. into
town. Turn right on 13th St. and proceed
approximately 1.2 miles to Brookside Dr.
Turn right to the golf course which is .8
miles ahead. Look for signs.

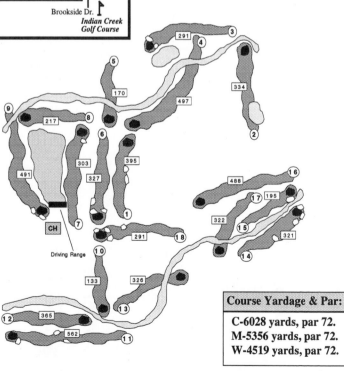

Course Yardage & Par:

C-6028 yards, par 72.
M-5356 yards, par 72.
W-4519 yards, par 72.

Jim Colbert's Hound Hollow G. C. & D. R. (public, 9 holes)

23010 West Arata Road; Wood Village, OR 97060
Phone: (503) 669-2290. Fax: (503) 667-4852. Internet: none.
Pro: Dode Forrester, PGA. Superintendent: none.
Rating/Slope: the golf course has not been rated. **Course record:** 26.
Green fees: W/D $12.50/$7.50; W/E $17/$8.50; Jr. & Sr. rates; M/C, VISA.
Power cart: $20/$11. **Pull cart:** $2. **Trail fee:** personal carts\are not allowed.
Reservation policy: call up to 1 week in advance for tee-times (recommended).
Winter condition: the golf course is open all year long, weather permitting.
Terrain: flat (easy walking). **Tees:** grass. **Spikes:** metal spikes permitted.
Services: pro shop, snack bar, driving range, 18 hole putting course, lessons,
club rentals, beer, wine. **Comments:** course is owned by Senior PGA pro Jim
Colbert. A unique feature is a miniature 18 hole all-grass putting green that is
fully lit for nighttime use. The 9 hole golf course has a very challenging layout.

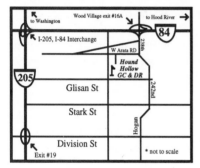

Directions: from I-84 head eastbound
and exit at Wood Village. From your exit
proceed southbound on NE 238th Drive
until you reach W. Arata Road. Turn right
on W. Arata Road and proceed to the golf
course. **Note:** Watch for signs from the
Highway marking your way to the golf
course. The golf course is adjacent to
Multnomah Greyhound Park.

Course Yardage & Par:
M-1511 yards, par 30.
W-1511 yards, par 30.

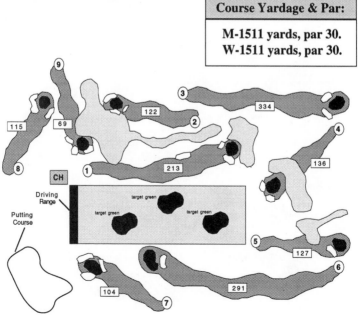

John Day Golf Club (semi-private, 9 hole course)
West Highway 26, P.O. Box 176; John Day, OR 97845
Phone: (541) 575-0170. **Fax:** none. **Internet:** none.
Manager: Bev Pierson. **Superintendent:** Tom Moore.
Rating/Slope: M 67.2/104; W 71.2/115. **Course record:** 62.
Green fees: $18/$12 all week long; VISA; the clubhouse is private.
Power cart: $18/$10. **Pull cart:** $1. **Trail fee:** $7 for personal carts.
Reservation policy: no advance reservations are needed. First come first served.
Winter condition: the golf course is closed on Mondays in winter months.
Terrain: flat, some hills. **Tees:** all grass. **Spikes:** metal spikes permitted.
Services: snack bar, beer, wine, liquor (in the clubhouse), beverages, pro shop,
lockers, driving range, putting & chipping greens. **Comments:** course has two
sets of tees to allow you to play a full 18 holes. Trees and water and narrow
fairways are a major factor when playing this golf course. Fair golf course.

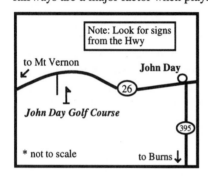

Note: Look for signs from the Hwy

to Mt Vernon
John Day
26
John Day Golf Course
395
* not to scale
to Burns ↓

Directions: the golf course is located
3.1 miles west of the city of John Day
Oregon on Highway 26. Make sure you
look for a sign posted on the Highway
to the golf course location.

Course Yardage & Par:
M-2955 yards, par 36.
W-2896 yards, par 38.
Dual tees for 18 holes:
M-5942 yards, par 71.
W-5618 yards, par 75.

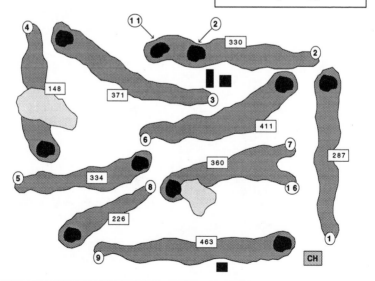

Juniper Golf Club (semi-private, 9 hole course)
139 SE Sisters Avenue; Redmond, OR 97756
Phone: (541) 548-3121. Fax: (541) 548-0808. Internet: none.
Pro: Bruce Wattenburger, PGA. Superintendent: Scott Petersen.
Rating/Slope: C 70.8/127; M 69.4/124; W 70.9/119. **Course record:** 64.
Green fees: $28/$18 all week long; Jr. and winter rates; M/C, VISA.
Power cart: $22/$14. **Pull cart:** $2/$1. **Trail fee:** $7.50 daily rate.
Reservation policy: call up to 1 month in advance for starting times.
Winter condition: the golf course is open all year long, weather permitting.
Terrain: flat, some hills. **Tees:** all grass. **Spikes:** no metal spikes permitted.
Services: club rentals, lessons, snack bar, restaurant, beer, wine, beverages,
liquor, pro shop, lockers, showers, putting & chipping greens, driving range.
Comments: This beautiful golf course wanders through Juniper trees and lava
rock. Great golf course in the great spot of Central Oregon. Worth a trip.

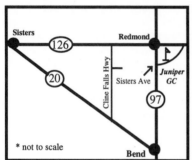

Directions: golf course located 1/4 mile
off of Highway 97 at the south end of
Redmond Oregon. Proceed east on Sisters
Avenue for 1/4 mile to the golf course.
Course located next to the City Airport.
Look for signs that are posted along the
route to the golf course.

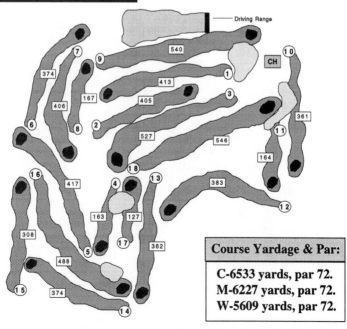

Course Yardage & Par:

C-6533 yards, par 72.
M-6227 yards, par 72.
W-5609 yards, par 72.

KAH-NEE-TA Resort (public, 18 hole course)
P.O. Box K; 100 Main Street; Warm Springs, OR 97761
Phone: (541) 553-1112 or toll free 1-800-831-0100. Fax: (541) 553-1071.
Pro: Joe C. Rauschenburg, PGA. Superintendent: Bob Wilkinson.
Rating/Slope: C 73.1/123; M 69.7/118; W 70.0/116. **Course record: 59.**
Green fees: $35/$20; Jr./Sr.; winter rates; M/C, VISA, DINERS, AMEX, DIS.
Power cart: $26/$15. **Pull cart:** $4/$2. **Trail fee:** $10 for personal carts.
Reservation policy: yes, call up to 2 weeks in advance for tee-time reservations.
Winter condition: the golf course is open all year long. Dry course conditions.
Terrain: flat (easy walking). **Tees:** all grass. **Spikes:** metal spikes permitted.
Services: club rentals, lessons, snack bar, restaurant, lounge, beer, wine, liquor,
beverages, pro shop, driving range, puuting & chipping greens, practice bunker.
Comments: The pro states "this is where the birdies fly and eagles soar in over
300 days of sunshine a year". Excellent resort facility that features full service
accomodations. Great vacation spot for the entire family. Worth a special trip.

Directions: course is located 120 miles southeast of Portland on Hwy 26. Follow the signs to the resort. Golf course is located 11 miles north of Warm Springs Oregon. Follow the signs to the resort the way is well marked along the route.

Note: Look for signs for the resort
To Portland
KAH-NEE-TA Resort
26
Warm Springs   To Madras
* not to scale

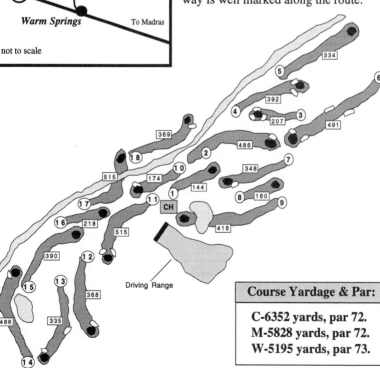

Driving Range

Course Yardage & Par:

C-6352 yards, par 72.
M-5828 yards, par 72.
W-5195 yards, par 73.

Kentuck Golf Course (public, 18 hole course)

680 Golf Course Lane; North Bend, OR 97459
Phone: (541) 756-4464. Fax: (541) 756-5722. Internet: none.
Pro: none. Manager: none. Superintendent: Wally Colt.
Rating/Slope: M 65.5/105; W 69.8/107. **Course record:** 62.
Green fees: W/D $14/$8; W/E $16/$9; Jr. rates; M/C, VISA, DISCOVER.
Power cart: $20/$10. **Pull cart:** $2. **Trail fee:** $5 for personal carts.
Reservation policy: yes, please call in advance for a tee time.
Winter condition: the golf course is open all year long. Wet conditions.
Terrain: flat (easy walking). **Tees:** all grass. **Spikes:** metal spikes permitted.
Services: club rentals, lessons, snack bar, pro shop, beer, wine, putting green.
Comments: the golf course is set in a beautiful area of Oregon and is challenging for any level of golfer. Creeks, ponds come into play on nearly every hole.

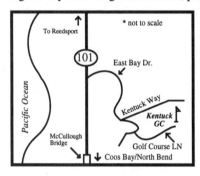

Directions: golf course located northeast of North Bend Oregon. Go eastbound on the East Bay Drive at the north end of the McCullough Bridge (where Highway 101 crosses the Coos Bay and Kentuck inlet). Follow the road to the southeast. Proceed for 3 miles to the golf course. Look for signs marking your way to the course.

Course Yardage & Par:
M-5394 yards, par 70.
W-4469 yards, par 70.

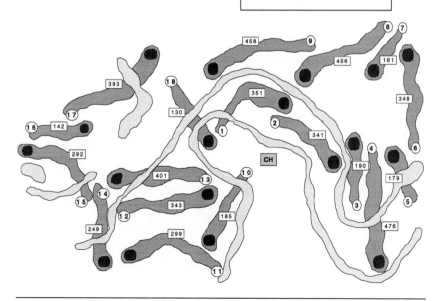

91

Killarney West Golf Club (public, 9 hole course)
1275 NW 334th; Hillsboro, OR 97124
Phone: (503) 648-7634. **Fax: none. Internet: none.**
Owner: J. E. O'Meara. Superintendent: Dave Horesky.
Rating/Slope: M 64.4/108; W 64.4/108. **Course record:** 32.
Green fees: W/D $14/$7; W/E $18/$9; no credit cards.
Power cart: $16/$8. **Pull cart:** $1. **Trail fee:** $8/$4 for personal carts.
Reservation policy: yes, taken for weekends and holidays. Call ahead 7 days.
Winter condition: the golf course is open all year. Dry conditions, drains well.
Terrain: flat, some hills. **Tees:** all grass. **Spikes:** metal spikes permitted.
Services: club rentals, snack bar, beer, wine, small pro shop, putting green.
Comments: Course is very scenic with trees lining the fairways. Greens are medium in size and fairly flat. Water is a major factor on several holes throughout the course. The course plays much tougher than the yardage would indicate.

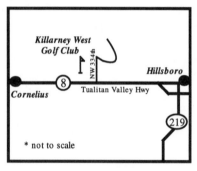

Directions: the golf course is located between Cornelius and Hillsboro Oregon off of Hwy 8. Proceed northbound on NW 334th for 1/2 mile to the golf course.

Course Yardage & Par:
M-2544 yards, par 36.
W-2544 yards, par 37.

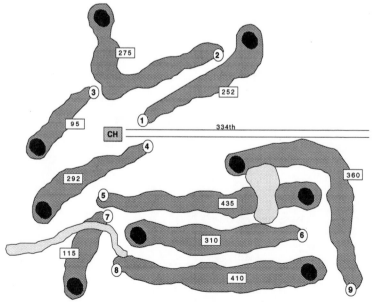

King City Golf Course (semi-private, 9 hole course)
15355 SW Royalty Parkway; King City, OR 97224
Phone: (503) 639-7986. Fax: none. Internet: none.
Pro: Bob Gasper, PGA. Superintendent: Steve Fletchell.
Rating/Slope: M 61.9/90; W 64.6/96. **Course record:** 59.
Green fees: Mon.-Th. $22/$11; Friday-Sun. & Hol. $24/$12; no credit cards.
Power cart: $20/$10. **Pull cart:** $2. **Trail fee:** personal carts are not allowed.
Reservation policy: yes, call for reservations during the summer, 7 days.
Winter condition: the golf course is open all year long with wet conditions.
Terrain: flat (easy walking). **Tees:** all grass. **Spikes:** metal spikes permitted.
Services: club rentals, pro shop, lockers, showers, putting & chipping greens.
Comments: the golf course is an excellent par 33 tract. The course is very easy to walk with very few hazards to contend with. Worth a trip if you are in the mood for something a little different than the 6400+ back-breaker golf course.

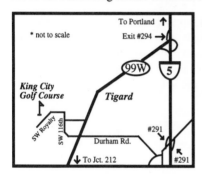

Directions: from I-5 N&S take exit for Hwy 99W #294 (West Pacific Highway). Travel south to King City. When in King City turn right on Durham Road. Proceed to SW 116th and go north then take the first left to SW Royalty and proceed ahead to the golf course. Look for signs that are posted along the way. The route is well marked.

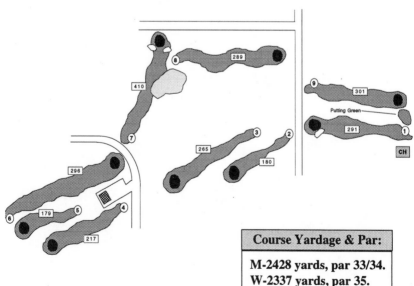

Course Yardage & Par:
M-2428 yards, par 33/34.
W-2337 yards, par 35.

Kinzua Hills Golf Club (semi-private, 6 hole course)
Off of Highway 19; Fossil, OR 97830;
Phone: none. Fax: none. Internet: none.
Manager: none. Pro: none.
Rating/Slope: M 58.3/92; W 61.3/97. **Course record:** 20.
Green fees: $8 all day rate; no credit cards.
Power cart: none available. **Pull cart:** none. **Trail fee:** not allowed.
Reservation policy: advance reservations are not taken. First come first served.
Winter condition: the golf course is open all year, weather permitting.
Terrain: flat, some hills. **Tees:** all grass. **Spikes:** metal spikes permitted.
Services: the golf course has very limited services, putting green.
Comments: The only 6 hole golf course in Oregon. Each hole has 3 sets of tees for 18 hole play. The greens and course are on the rough side but if you need a quick 9 holes give Kinzua Hills a try. Course is often on the honor system.

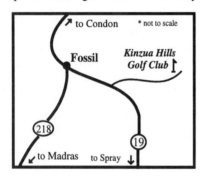

Directions: the golf course is located off Highway 19 in Fossil, Oregon. From Highway 19 go east toward Kinzua. While in Kinzua on Highway 19 travel northbound to the golf course. Look for signs.

Course Yardage & Par:
M-1463 yards, par 22.
W-1388 yards, par 24.
(the par for 9 holes is 32).

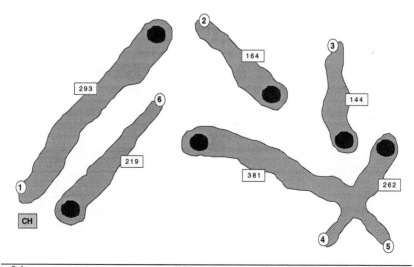

La Grande Country Club (private, 9 hole course)

10605 South McAlister Road, P.O. Box 836; Island City, OR 97850
Phone: (541) 963-4241. Fax: (541) 963-3891. Intenet: none.
Pro: Bill Rosholt, PGA. Superintendent: none.
Rating/Slope: M 70.6/123; W 70.9/120. **Course record:** 63.
Green fees: private club members & guests of members only; reciprocates.
Power cart: private club, members only. **Pull cart:** private club. **Trail fee:** $7.
Reservation policy: private club members & guests of members only.
Winter condition: the golf course is open all year long, weather permitting.
Terrain: flat, some hills. **Tees:** all grass. **Spikes:** metal spikes permitted.
Services: club rentals, lessons, lounge, beer, wine, pro shop, driving range.
Comments: Long narrow course built amidst an apple orchard. Trees are in
play off the tee as well as on your approach shots. Well bunkered postage
stamp greens make this lush golf course a challenge for any level of golfer.

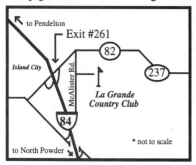

Directions: from I-84 E&W take the exit
for Highway 82 exit in Island City, Ore.
Proceed east for 2 miles then turn right on
McAllister to the golf course which is 2
blocks ahead on your left hand side. Look
for a sign marking your turn to the course.

Course Yardage & Par:
M-3267 yards, par 36.
W-2849 yards, par 38.
<u>Dual tees for 18 holes:</u>
M-6514 yards, par 72.
W-5653 yards, par 75.

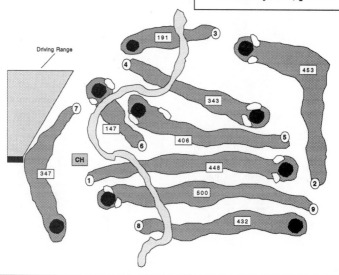

Lake Oswego Golf Course (public, 18 hole executive course)
17525 SW Stafford Road; Lake Oswego, OR 97034
Phone: (503) 636-8228. Fax: (503) 699-7465. Internet: none.
Pro: John Welsh. Manager: Cindy Lincoln.
Rating/Slope: the golf course is not rated. **Course Record:** 51.
Green fees: W/D $12/$6.50; W/E $13/$7.50; Jr. & Sr. rates $9/$5 (M-F).
Power cart: $6 handicapped only. **Pull cart:** $2. **Trail fee:** not allowed.
Reservation policy: Monday through Thursday first come first served basis.
Friday through Sunday make reservations by calling 7 days in advance for times.
Winter condition: the golf course is open all year long, damp conditions.
Terrain: flat, some hills. **Tees:** all grass. **Spikes:** metal spikes permitted.
Services: club rentals, lessons, snack bar, covered & lighted driving range.
Comments: golf course is great for seniors and those who want to practice their
short game. Driving range is partially covered for use during inclement weather.

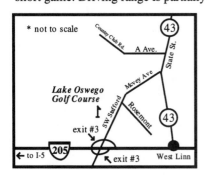

Directions: from I-205 exit (#3) at SW
Stafford. Proceed for 2.5 miles northbound on SW Stafford. The golf course
will be located on your left hand side.
You can also reach the golf course by
taking Highway 43. Look for signs.

Course Yardage & Par:
M-2695 yards, par 54.
W-2695 yards, par 54.

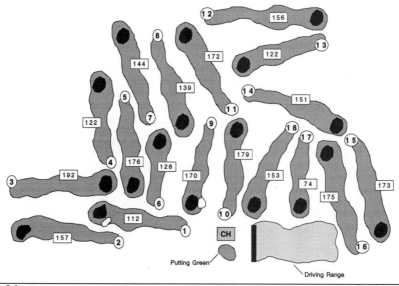

Lakeridge Golf & Country Club (semi-private, 9 holes)
Highway 140 West; HC 60, Box 199; Lakeview, OR 97630
Phone: (541) 947-3855. Fax: none. Internet: none.
Owners: Ed & Diane Almojuela. Superintendent: none.
Rating/Slope: M 70.0/119; W 71.6/121. **Course record**: 65.
Green fees: $18/$10 all week long; Jr. rates; M/C, VISA.
Power cart: $15/$7.50. **Pull cart**: $3/$2. **Trail fee**: $8/$4 for personal carts.
Reservation policy: none taken. T-times are on a first come first served basis.
Winter condition: the course is closed from November 15th to February 15th.
Terrain: flat (easy walking). **Tees**: all grass. **Spikes**: metal spikes permitted.
Services: club rentals, lessons, snack bar, restaurant, beer, wine, beverages, pro shop, lockers, grass teed driving range, putting & chipping greens.
Comments: This picturesque golf course is surrounded by the Warner Mountains and the Fremont National Forest. The golf course is in excellent condition during the summer months providing the golfer with lush fairways and firm greens. Worth a trip to the golf course if you are in the area.

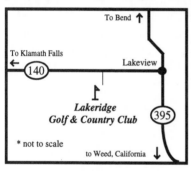

Directions: the golf course is located 3 miles west of Lakeview off Highway 140. From Klamath Falls travel 90 miles east on Highway 140 to the golf course. Look for signs marking your way to the course.

Course Yardage & Par:
M-3323 yards, par 36.
W-2965 yards, par 37.
Dual tees for 18 holes:
M-6647 yards, par 72.
W-5863 yards, par 74.

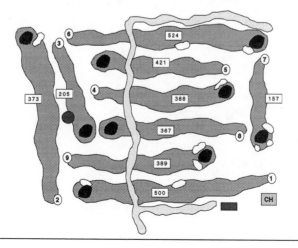

Lakeside Golf & Racquet Club (public, 18 hole course)
3245 Club House Drive; Lincoln City, OR 97367
Phone: (541) 994-8442. Fax: (541) 994-2066. Internet: lakeside@wcn.net.
PGA Director of Golf: Todd Young. Superintendent: Jody Piconni.
Rating/Slope: C 62.0/102; M 61.1/99; W 66.2/113. **Course record:** 60.
Green fees: $32/$18 all week long; Jr. & Sr. rates; M/C, VISA.
Power cart: $25/$15. **Pull cart:** $3/$2. **Trail fee:** no personal carts allowed.
Reservation policy: yes, please call ahead for tee times (a must in the summer).
Winter condition: the golf course is open all year long, weather permitting.
Terrain: relatively hilly, walkable. **Tees:** grass. **Spikes:** metal spikes permitted.
Services: club rentals, lessons, snack bar, beer, wine, pop, pro shop, lockers, driving range (irons only), racquet ball, tennis, health & fitness center, daycare.
Comments: good test golf with conditions improving yearly. Greens are medium in size well bunkered and tricky. Fairways are rolling and narrow in spots.

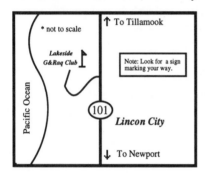

Directions: the golf course is located on the west side of Highway 101 at the north end of Lincoln City. Turn off Highway 101 at the last light at the north end of Lincoln City. Follow Clubhouse Drive to the golf course complex. Look for a sign marking the entrance to the course.

Course Yardage & Par:
C-5116 yards, par 66.
M-4769 yards, par 66.
W-4318 yards, par 71.

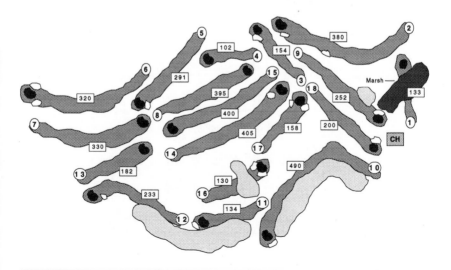

Langdon Farms Golf Club (public, 18 hole course)
24377 NE Airport Road; Aurora, OR 97002
Phone: (503) 678-GOLF (4653). **Fax:** (503) 678-3263. **Internet: none.**
Pro: Bryan Tunstill, PGA. **Superintendent:** N/A.
Rating/Slope: P 73.3/125; C 71.2/121; R 68.9/116; PL 64.8/108. **Record:** 67.
Green fees: fluctuates, please call (cart included); M/C, VISA, DISCOVER.
Power cart: included. **Pull cart:** N/A. **Trail fee:** personal carts not allowed.
Reservation policy: yes, please call up to 30 days in advance for tee times.
Winter condition: the golf course is open year round, weather permitting, dry.
Terrain: links style, depressed fairways. **Tees:** grass. **Spikes:** no metal spikes.
Services: club rentals, lessons, snack bar, lounge, restaurant, pro shop, practice range, putting greens, putting course (bentgrass), learning center, showers.
Comments: Designed by award winning architects John Fought & Robert Cupp. Depressed fairways give Langdon Farms a very unique look, one not found in the State of Oregon. Large Bentgrass greens highlighted with ground contours create chipping zones which truely makes Langdon Farms "one of a kind". A "state of the art" practice area boasts the largest grass teeing surface in the NW. Langdon Farms is truely one of the finest golf venues in the Northwest.

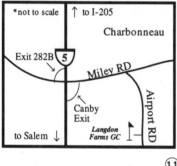

Directions: from I-5S take exit #282B. Travel eastbound then turn right on NE Airport Road. Travel 1 mile to the main entrance. From I-5N take the Canby exit turn right and then turn right on NE Airport Road. Follow to main entrance.

Course Yardage & Par:		
Professional: 6911 yards, par 71.		
Champion: 6577 yards, par 71.		
Resort: 6088 yards, par 71.		
Player: 5283 yards, par 71.		

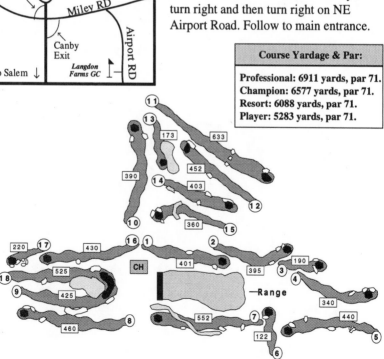

Laurel Hill Golf Course (public, 9 hole course)

9450 Old Stage Road; P.O. Box 167; Gold Hill, OR 97525
Phone: (541) 855-7965. Fax: none. Internet: none.
Managers: Jan & Peter Fish. Superintendent: none.
Rating/Slope: M 62.0/102; W 62.3/103. **Course record:** 27.
Green fees: W/D $12/$7; W/E $13/$7.50; Jr. & Sr. rates; M/C, VISA.
Power cart: not available. **Pull cart:** $1. **Trail fee:** no charge for your cart.
Reservation policy: yes, call ahead of time, (recommended on the weekends).
Winter condition: the golf course is open all year long, damp to dry course.
Terrain: flat, some hills. **Tees:** grass & mats. **Spikes:** metal spikes permitted.
Services: club rentals, lessons, snack bar, beer, wine, beverages, pro shop, driving range, putting & chipping greens, GHIN 18 hole handicapping service.
Comments: A challenging irons course of great scenic beauty, but not intimidating for beginners. Greens are on the small size and can be difficult to hold. Great golf course to bring the entire family to.

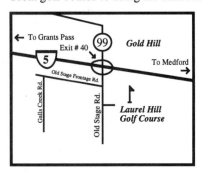

Directions: from I-5 N&S take exit #40 (Gold Hill/Jacksonville). Travel east for .25 miles on Old Stage Road to the golf course. The golf course will be located on your left hand side. Look for signs marking your turn to the parking lot.

Course Yardage & Par:
M-1915 yards, par 31.
W-1915 yards, par 31.

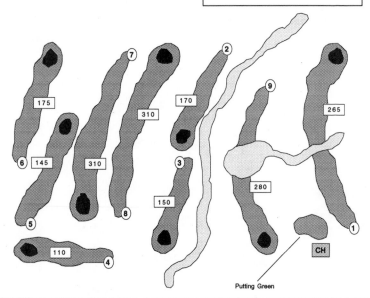

Putting Green

Laurelwood Golf Course (public, 9 hole course)
2700 Columbia Avenue; Eugene, OR 97403
(541) 687-5321, Tee-times 484-4653. Fax: (541) 343-3012.
Pro: Christopher Wibur. Superintendent: none.
Rating/Slope: C 69.5/129; M 68.1/125; W 70.4/124. **Course record:** 59.
Greens fee: W/D \$14/\$8; W/E \$16/\$9; Jr. & Sr. rates; M/C, VISA.
Power cart: \$17/\$9. **Pull cart:** \$3/\$2. **Trail fee:** \$4 (9 holes).
Reservation policy: yes, please call ahead, especially in the summer months.
Winter condition: the course is open all year long, weather permitting, damp.
Terrain: relatively hilly. **Tees:** all grass. **Spikes:** metal spikes permitted.
Services: club rentals, lessons, sandwiches, beer, juices, pro shop, covered driving range, putting & chipping greens, full club repair, wedding receptions.
Comments: The course is in excellent condition after significant changes last year. Lots of hills for interesting shot making and exercise. Good public course.

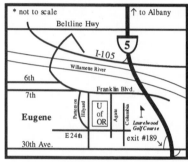

Directions: I-5 northbound take 30th Ave. exit to Hilyard. Turn right on Hilyard to E 24th turn right on E 24th. Proceed to Columbia and take a right. Proceed to the top of the hill. The pro shop is on the lower level. From I-5 southbound take the Eugene/University exit. Follow signs to the University of Oregon (Franklin Blvd to Agate St). Turn right on Agate St. to E 24th. Turn left on E 24th for 1 block. Turn right on Columbia St. to the course.

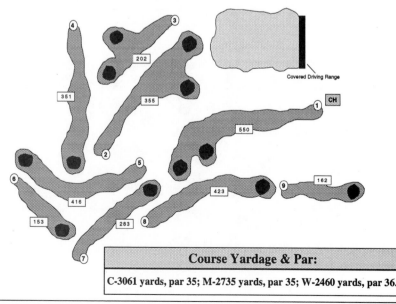

Course Yardage & Par:
C-3061 yards, par 35; M-2735 yards, par 35; W-2460 yards, par 36.

Lone Pine Village Golf (public, 9 hole course)
355 Lone Pine Drive; The Dalles, OR 97058
Phone: (541) 298-2800. Fax: none. Internet: none.
Manager: Bill Blackburn. Pro: Steve Welker.
Rating/Slope: to be determined. **Course record:** to be determined.
Green fees: to be determined upon opening of the golf course.
Power cart: to be determined. **Pull cart:** to be determined. **Trail fee:** N/A.
Reservation policy: to be determined upon opening of the golf course.
Winter condition: the course will be open all year long, weather permitting.
Terrain: flat (easy walking). **Tees:** all grass. **Spikes:** metal spikes permitted.
Services: club rentals, snack bar, lessons, lounge, restaurant, beer, wine, liquor, beverages, pro shop, driving range, putting & chipping greens, motel, RV park.
Comments: golf course is now in the early construction stages and should be open sometime in 1999. The full service driving range is now open to serve you.

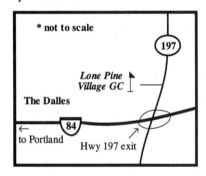

Directions: from I-84 East & West exit at the junction for Highway 197. Turn northoff the exit. The golf course and the driving range will be immediately on your left hand side. Look for a sign posting your turn into the complex.

Course Yardage & Par:
(Yardage & Par are tenative)
M-2500 yards, par 32.
W-2500 yards, par 32.

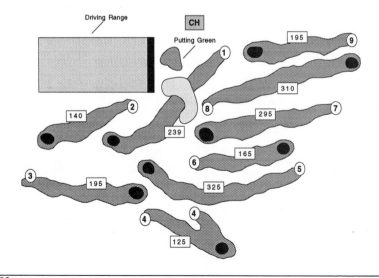

Lost Tracks Golf Club (public, 18 hole course)

60205 Sunset View Drive; Bend, OR 97702
Phone: (541) 385-1818.. Fax: (541) 317-9589. Internet: none.
Director of Golf: Steve Bruening. Superintendent: N/A.
Rating/slope: C 72.4/129; M 69.6/122; W 70.2/111. **Course record:** 68.
Green fees: $45/$25 all week long; Jr. & Sr., resident and twilight rates;
hotel packages available for those who want lodging; M/C, VISA.
Power cart: $26/$15. **Pull cart:** $3/$1.50. **Trail fee:** not allowed.
Reservation policy: call up to 30 days in advance with a credit card guarantee.
Winter condition: dry, the golf course is closed during inclement weather.
Terrain: rolling terrain. **Tees:** all grass. **Spikes:** metal spikes permitted.
Services: rentals, lessons, lounge, restaurant, snack bar, beer, pro shop, range.
Comments: the golf course is bordered by national forest land and carved out of
a stand of Ponderosa and high desert pines. Lava rock outcroppings, sparkling
lakes, and seaside sand filled bunkers are everywhere. Worth a special trip.

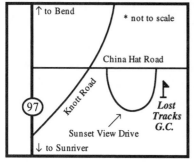

Directions: from Hwy 97 South turn
east on China Hat Road. Proceed straight
ahead, crossing Knott Road. Turn right
on Sunset View Drive to the golf course.

Course Yardage & Par:		
C-7003 yards, par 72.		
M-6245 yards, par 72.		
W-5287 yards, par 72.		

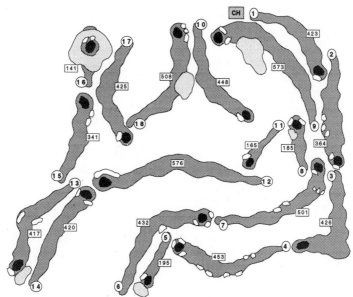

Manzanita Golf Course (public, 9 hole course)

P.O. Box 21; Lakeview Drive; Manzanita, OR 97130
Phone: (503) 368-5744. Fax: none. Internet: none.
Owners: Steve and Penny Erickson.
Rating/Slope: M 61.8/97; W 63.2/102. **Course record:** 29.
Green fees: $24/$13 all week long; M/C, VISA.
Power cart: none. **Pull cart:** $1 (per 9 holes). **Trail fee:** not allowed.
Reservation policy: yes, taken 7 days in advance and recommended in summer.
Winter condition: the golf course is open all year long, damp turf conditions.
Terrain: flat, some hills. **Tees:** all grass. **Spikes:** metal spikes permitted.
Services: club rentals, snack bar, pro shop, driving range, putting green.
Comments: Picturesque course located on the beautiful Oregon coast. Greens are on medium in size and well bunkered. Fairways are narrow giving the golfer tight landing area's. This golf course which is not a back-breaker is worth the trip if you are driving the Oregon coast and want to play a quick 9 holes.

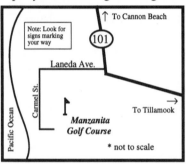

Directions: from Hwy 101 N&S take Manzanita Junction exit toward the beach. You will be on Laneda Avenue. Follow Laneda for .6 miles to S Carmel Avenue (there is a sign to the golf course) turn left. Go through residential area for .8 miles to the golf course on your left. The golf course is located at the intersection of Lakeview Drive and NeCarney Blvd.

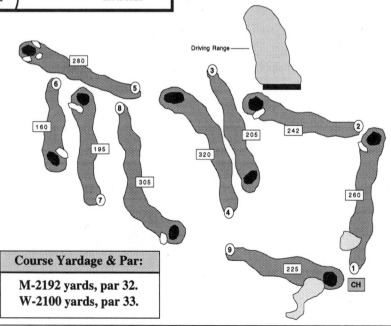

Course Yardage & Par:

M-2192 yards, par 32.
W-2100 yards, par 33.

Marysville Golf Course (public, 9 hole course)

2020 SW Allen Lane: P.O. Box 1203; Corvallis, OR 97339
Phone: (541) 753-3421. **Fax:** none. **Internet:** none.
Owner: R. M. Hoselton & Sons. **Superintendent:** none.
Rating/Slope: M 69.0/114; W 71.8/109. **Course record:** 31.
Green fees: W/D $16/$10; W/E $17/$11; annual memberships; no credit cards.
Power cart: none available. **Pull cart:** $3. **Trail fee:** no charge for your cart.
Reservation policy: call in advance to the golf course for the tee time policy.
Winter condition: the course is open all year long, weather permitting, dry.
Terrain: flat, walkable course. **Tees:** all grass. **Spikes:** metal spikes permitted.
Services: club rentals, beer, small pro shop, practice area, putting green.
Comments: Family owned course that is well kept and offers a great family golfing atmosphere. The golf course is fairly wide open with only a few hazards coming into play off the tee. The course plays much longer than the yardage.

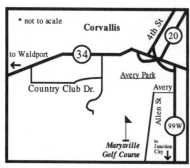

Directions: from Highway 20, take Avery Park exit. When entering the park, take left hand fork. Go to four way stop. Continue straight on S.W. Allen Lane to the golf course. From Hwy 99W south of Corvallis go to Avery Lane & turn west. Go to four way stop. Turn left on S.W. Allen Lane. Go straight on S.W. Allen Lane to the golf course.

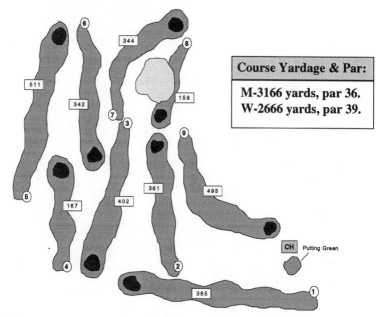

Course Yardage & Par:

M-3166 yards, par 36.
W-2666 yards, par 39.

McKay Creek Golf Course (public, 9 hole course)

1416 N.W. Jackson Street; Hillsboro, OR 97124;
Phone: (503) 693-7612. Fax: none. Internet: none.
Owners: John & Jane Reding. Superintendent: none.
Rating/Slope: M 64.4/101; W 64.4/101. **Course record:** 68.
Green fees: W/D $13/$7; W/E $17/$9; no special rates.
Power cart: $16/$8. **Pull cart:** $1. **Trail fee:** $ 4 for personal carts.
Reservation policy: please call ahead for tee-time reservation policies.
Winter condition: the golf course is closed during the winter months.
Terrain: flat, easy walking. **Tees:** all grass. **Spikes:** metal spikes permitted.
Services: club rentals, snack bar, beer, wine, pro shop, driving range.
Comments: this 9 hole track opened for play in 1996. The golf course features
tree-lined fairways, medium sized greens and McKay Creek running through
many holes. Work on the clubhouse and the 50 acre facility continue.

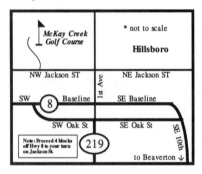

Directions: the golf course is located
off of Hwy 8 in Hillsboro Oregon. Turn
north on 1st Avenue. Follow 1st (about
3-4 blocks) until you reach Jackson
Street. Turn left on Jackson. Proceed to
the golf course which will be on your
left hand side. Look for signs.

Course Yardage & Par:
M-2727 yards, par 36.
W-2492 yards, par 36.

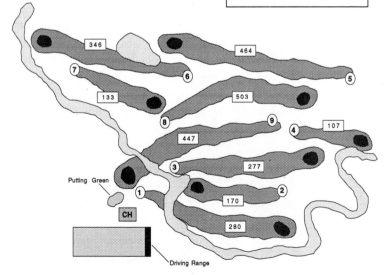

McKenzie River Golf Course (public, 9 hole course)

Mailing Address: P. O. Box 98; Walterville, OR 97489
Street Address: 41723 Madrone Street; Springfield OR 97478
Phone: (541) 896-3454. Fax: none. Internet: none.
Owners: Rod & Diane Omlid. Superintendent: none.
Rating/Slope: M 66.7/106; W 71.2/116. **Course record:** 29.
Green fees: W/D$19/$12; W/E $20/$12; Jr. rates weekdays only; credit cards.
Power cart: $11 per nine holes. **Pull cart:** $2. **Trail fee:** $7.50.
Reservation policy: yes, call 3 days in advance for your starting times.
Winter condition: the golf course is open all year long, dry (drains well).
Terrain: flat (easy walking). **Tees:** grass. **Spikes:** metal spikes permitted.
Services: club rentals, snack bar, beer, pro shop, putting & chipping green.
Comments: The golf course has a 10 hole punch card for your green fees at
$95. Pride of ownership shows on this well kept manicured facility that is
nestled in between the McKenzie River and surrounding mountains. The
owners of the course invite you to see why they are the " Jewel on the river".

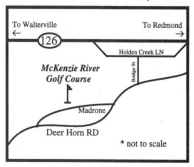

Directions: from Highway 126 exit at
Holden Creek Lane. Follow the road
past mile post 17 to Bridge Street which
crosses the river. Turn right on Deerhorn
Road then another right on Madrone
Street which leads to the clubhouse.

Course Yardage & Par:
M-2783 yards, par 35.
W-2304 yards, par 35.
Dual tees for 18 holes:
M-5629 yards, par 70.
W-4746 yards, par 70.

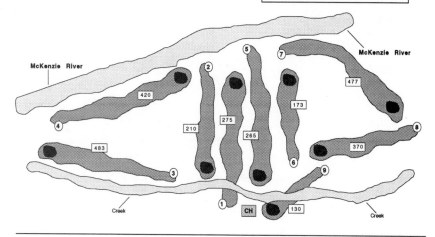

McNary Golf Club (semi-private, 18 hole course)
155 McNary Estates Drive North; Keizer, OR 97303
Phone: (503) 393-4653. Fax: none. Internet: none.
Pro: Rich Brown, PGA. Superintendent: not available.
Rating/Slope: C 69.2/121; M 67.9/119; W 71.2/116. **Course record**: 62.
Green fees: $35/$20 all week long; Sr. rates; M/C, VISA.
Power cart: $20/$11. **Pull cart:** $2. **Trail fee:** not allowed.
Reservation policy: yes, call up to 5 days in advance your for tee-times.
Winter condition: the golf course is open all year long, damp conditions.
Terrain: flat, easy walking. **Tees:** grass. **Spikes:** metal spikes permitted.
Services: club rentals, lessons, snack bar, restaurant, lounge, beer, wine, liquor,
pro shop, putting & chipping greens, lockers, showers. **Comments:** this chal-
lenging course offers wide, open fairways with large well bunkered greens. The
facility is well taken care of and offers the golfer a country club look and feel.

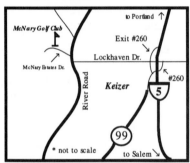

Directions: from I-5 N&S take exit #260
(Lockhaven) and go west on Lockhaven
proceed for 1.3 miles to River Road, turn
right and proceed to McNary Estates Dr.
and turn left to the golf course. Look for
signs marking your entrance to the course.

Course Yardage & Par:
C-6187 yards, par 71.
M-5899 yards, par 71.
W-5370 yards, par 71.

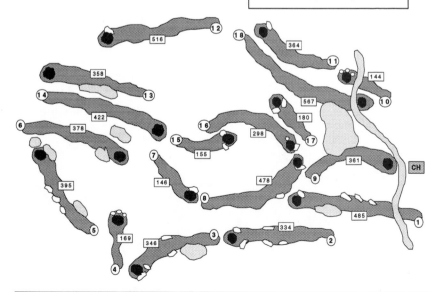

Meadow Lakes Golf Course (public, 18 hole course)
300 Meadow Lakes Drive; Prineville, OR 97754
Phone: (541) 447-7113, 1-800-577-2797. Fax: (541) 447-7831.
Pro: Jay Kinzel, PGA. Superintendent: Wayne Van Matre.
Rating/Slope: T 73.1/131; C 71.8/128; M 69.1/121 W 69.0/121. Record: 66.
Green fees: Monday-Friday $18; Saturday-Sunday $29; winter rates.
Power cart: $22/$12. Pull cart: $3/$2. Trail fee: personal carts not allowed.
Reservation policy: call 6 days ahead or 1 year in advance with a credit card.
Winter condition: the golf course is open all year long, weather permitting.
Terrain: beautifully mounded. Tees: grass. Spikes: metal spikes permitted.
Services: fully stocked pro shop, club rentals, lessons, lounge, restaurant, snack
bar, liquor, putting green, driving range. Comments: A beautiful newer course.
Ten ponds, 16 surface acres of water, 2000 trees, and 66 bunkers will challenge
you at every turn. *Golf Digest* "Environmental Leader in Golf" award winner. If
you get the chance be sure to include Meadow Lakes on any golf trip to Oregon.

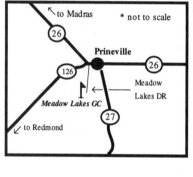

Directions: from Portland take Hwy 26
through Madras to Prineville. In Prineville
the highway becomes 3rd street. Meadow
Lakes Dr. will be on your right. There will
be signs to mark your way to the course.

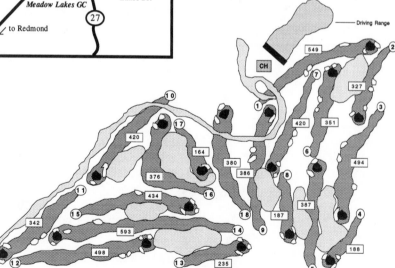

Course Yardage & Par:	
T-6731 yards, par 72.	M-5849 yards, par 72.
C-6398 yards, par 72	W-5155 yards, par 72.

109

Meadowlawn Golf Club (public, 9 hole course)
3898 Meadowlawn Loop SE; Salem, OR 97303
Phone: (503) 363-7391. Fax: none. Internet: none.
Pro: Greg Ganson, PGA. Superintendent: Jeff Halfman.
Rating/Slope: M 58.5/92; W 60.5/98. **Course record:** 26.
Green fees: $22/$11 all week long; no special rates; M/C, VISA.
Power cart: $20/$10. **Pull cart:** $2. **Trail fee:** $10/$5 for personal carts.
Reservation policy: yes, call 1 day in advance for your starting times.
Winter condition: the golf course is open all year long. Wet during the winter.
Terrain: very flat. **Tees:** all grass. **Spikes:** metal spikes permitted.
Services: club rentals, lessons, beverages, snack bar, pro shop, putting green.
Comments: The course has rolling hills and is very easy to walk. The golf
course plays very tight in places, putting an emphasis on shot placement. This
Salem golf course is a senior and first time golfer favorite.

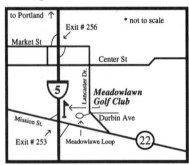

Directions: from I-5 exit #256 (Market St-Silverton). Eastbound on Market St. for .6 mi to Lancaster Dr. Turn right on Lancaster Dr. Proceed for 1.9 mi to Durbin St. then take a right, then immediate right on Meadowlawn Loop SE which curves around to the course on your left. Or take exit #253 and go east on Mission to the first exit you come to and go north on Lancaster Dr. Proceed to Durbin St. and turn left to Meadowlawn Loop Rd. and to the course. Look for signs.

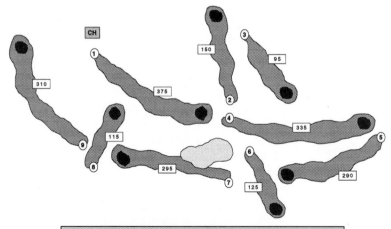

Course Yardage & Par:
M-2090 yards, par 32; W-2090 yards, par 34.

Meriwether National Golf Club (public, 27 hole course)
5200 SW Roodbridge Road; Hillsboro, OR 97123
Phone: (503) 648-4143. Fax: (541) 640-9757. Internet: none.
Pro: Jim Petersen, PGA. Superintendent: Bob Short.
Rating/Slope: North/West C 71.3/121; M 69.5/118; W 72.3/113. **Record: 64.**
Greens fee: W/D $16/$9; W/E $18/$10; Jr./monthly Sr. rates; no credit cards
Power cart: $20/$11. **Pull cart:** $2. **Trail fee:** no personal carts allowed.
Reservation policy: yes for weekends and holidays. A must in the summer.
Winter condition: the golf course is open all year long. Damp conditions.
Terrain: flat (easy walking). **Tees:** all grass. **Spikes:** metal spikes permitted.
Services: clubhouse with banquet facilities, club rentals, lessons, snack bar, pro
shop, driving range. **Comments:** course is very challenging, and includes one of
the toughest par 4's in the state. In additon to the existing 27 holes, Meriwether
has plans for another 9 holes, an 18 hole putting green and a covered driving
range. All should be in place by spring of 1998. Great public golf course.

Directions: the course is located at the
west edge of Hillsboro, OR. From Hwy 8,
proceed east to River Rd. Turn south on
River Rd. Turn right on Rood-bridge Rd
and follow this to the course.

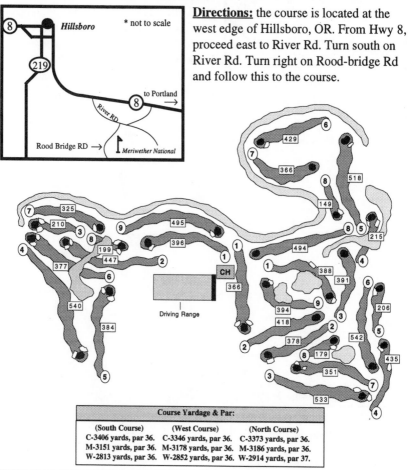

Course Yardage & Par:		
(South Course)	(West Course)	(North Course)
C-3406 yards, par 36.	C-3346 yards, par 36.	C-3373 yards, par 36.
M-3151 yards, par 36.	M-3178 yards, par 36.	M-3186 yards, par 36.
W-2813 yards, par 36.	W-2852 yards, par 36.	W-2914 yards, par 37.

Michelbook Country Club (private, 18 hole course)
1301 Michelbook Lane; McMinnville, OR 97128
Phone: (503) 472-8079. **Fax:** (503) 435-1334. **Internet:** none.
Pro: Mel Chaufty, PGA. **Superintendent:** John Lof.
Rating/Slope: C 71.4/126; M 69.9/124; W 72.2/122. **Course record:** 63.
Green fees: private club, members & guests only, reciprocates .
Power cart: private club. **Pull cart:** private club. **Trail fee:** private club.
Reservation policy: private club members & guests of members only.
Winter condition: the golf course is open all year long. Dry conditions.
Terrain: flat (easy walking). **Tees:** grass. **Spikes:** metal spikes permitted.
Services: club rentals, lessons, snack bar, restaurant, beer, lounge, pro shop,
driving range, putting & chipping greens. **Comments:** The golf course can be
very tight in places. Lakes, bunkers and tree lined fairways put and emphasis on
shot making. Greens are fast and can be hard to hold in summer. Great course.

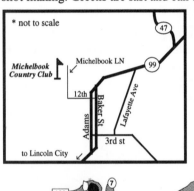

Directions: from Hwy 99 (Pacific Hwy
W). Follow Hwy 99 into town and make
a right turn onto 12th Avenue. Proceed to
Michelbook Lane and the golf course.
From Hwy 18 (River Hwy) come into
town and go north on Baker St. and then
take a left on 12th Ave. to the golf course.

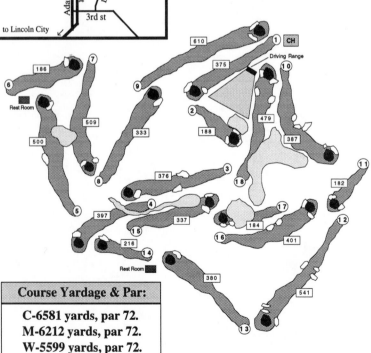

Course Yardage & Par:
C-6581 yards, par 72.
M-6212 yards, par 72.
W-5599 yards, par 72.

Middlefield Village G. C. & D. R. (public, 18 hole course)
91 Village Drive; Cottage Grove, OR 97424
Phone: (541) 942-8730. **Fax:** (541) 942-7745. **Internet:** none.
Manager: Jeff Bridges. **Superintendent:** none.
Rating/Slope: M 63.7/104; W 63.4/102. **Course record:** 64.
Green fees: W/D $20/$14; W/E $24/$16; Jr. & Sr., college rates W/D $16/$10.
Power cart: $20/$14. **Pull cart:** $3/$2. **Trail fee:** $8/$4 for personal carts.
Reservation policy: please call 1 week in advance for tee times.
Winter condition: the golf course is open all year long. Drains well in winter.
Terrain: flat (easy walking). **Tees:** all grass. **Spikes:** metal spikes permitted.
Services: full service facility, club rentals, lessons, snack bar, beer, wine, pro shop, covered driving range, changing room. **Comments:** excellent easy to play course that is well kept. Great learning center and practice facility for those wanting to take lessons. The gentle rolling fairways and the scenic setting along the Row River add to this Bunny Mason designed track. Worth a special trip.

Directions: from I-5 north and south in Cottage Grove take exit # 174. Proceed to Middlefield Village and the golf facility. Look for signs marking your turns to the golfing facility. The course is located 20 minutes south of Eugene, Oregon.

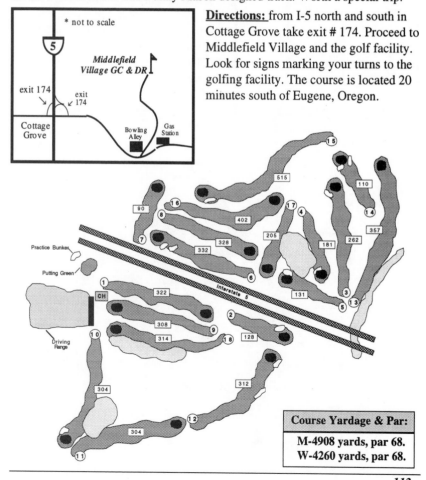

Course Yardage & Par:
M-4908 yards, par 68.
W-4260 yards, par 68.

Milton-Freewater Golf Course (public, 18 hole course)
W 301 Catherine Street; Milton-Freewater, OR 97862
Phone: (541) 938-7284. Fax: (541) 938-6411
Pro/Manager: G.R. Gillette. 18 hole executive course.
Rating/Slope: M 55.4/80; W 58.1/83. **Course record:** 54.
Green fees: $14/$9; Jr. rates $10/$6, Sr. rates $12/$8; no credit cards.
Power cart: $20/$14. **Pull cart:** $1. **Trail fee:** $5 for personal carts.
Reservation policy: yes, call 3 days in advance for weekends, holiday T-times.
Winter condition: the golf course is open all year long. Dry (drains well).
Terrain: flat, back 9 is hilly. **Tees:** grass. **Spikes:** metal spikes permitted.
Services: club rentals, lessons, restaurant, lounge, pro shop, putting green.
Comments: the golf course is tight in places and is perfect to help you improve your iron play. Water comes into play on several holes. Fair public course.

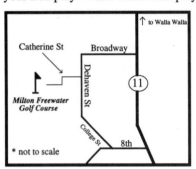

Directions: golf course located in Milton-Freewater behind high school, west on Hwy 11. Look for sign on highway for the turn to the golf course. When in Milton-Freewater turn westbound on 2nd NW for .2 miles. Turn right on Dehaven Street. Proceed to Catherine Street and turn left.

Course Yardage & Par:
M-3346 yards, par 60.
W-3314 yards, par 61.

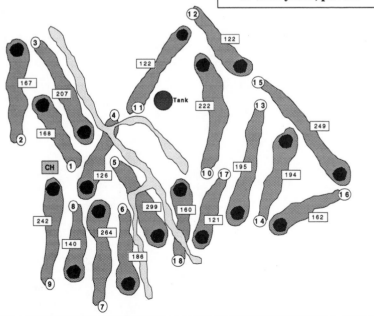

Mountain High Golf Course (public, 18 hole course)
60650 China Hat Road; Bend, OR 97702
Phone: (541) 382-1111. Fax: (541) 382-0364. Internet: none.
Manager: Ed Cecil. Superintendent: Ron Loucks.
Rating/Slope: C 72.0/131; M 69.2/122; F 67.3/115; W 69.2/120. **Record:** 69.
Green fees: $40/$24, includes cart; spring rates; M/C, VISA.
Power cart: includued in fee. **Pull cart:** none. **Trail fee:** not allowed.
Reservation policy: yes, call 7 days in advance for all tee-times.
Winter condition: the golf course is closed from November 1st to mid-March.
Terrain: flat, rolling hills. **Tees:** all grass. **Spikes:** metal spikes permitted.
Services: club rentals, pro shop, snack bar, beer, wine, lessons, driving range.
Comments: Fantastic island green on hole #5. Water will come into play on
over half the course. O.B. is everywhere and puts a real emphasis on accuracy.
Fairways are lined with large Pondersa Pines and are spectacular. Great course.

Directions: from Bend go south on Hwy 97. Take left on China Hat Road. Proceed approximately .25 miles to the entrance of the golf course. Look for signs from Hwy 97.

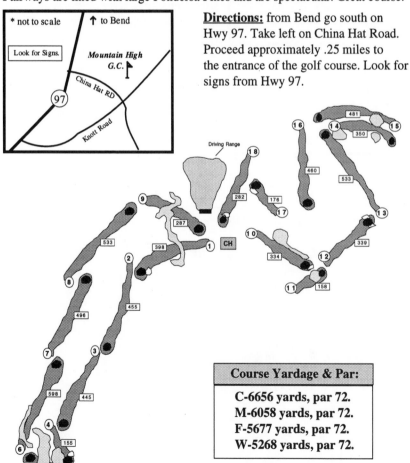

Course Yardage & Par:

C-6656 yards, par 72.
M-6058 yards, par 72.
F-5677 yards, par 72.
W-5268 yards, par 72.

Mountain View Golf Course (public, 18 hole course)
27195 SE Kelso Road; Boring, OR 97009
Phone: (503) 663-4869. Fax: (503) 663-4515. Internet: none.
Pro: Toby Tommaso. Superintendent: not availble.
Rating/Slope: C 68.0/118; M 66.0/113; W 69.2/111. **Course record:** 61.
Green fees: W/D $18.50$10; W/E $21.50/$12.50; Jr. & Sr. rates; M/C, VISA.
Power cart: W/D $20/$12; W/E $24/$14. **Pull cart:** $3. **Trail fee:** $11/$6.
Reservation policy: yes, call 1 week in advance for your starting time.
Winter condition: the golf course open, weather permitting. Dry winter course.
Terrain: flat, some hills. **Tees:** all grass. **Spikes:** metal spikes permitted.
Services: club rentals, lessons, snack bar, restaurant, lounge, beer, wine, liquor,
pro shop, putting & chipping greens, driving range. **Comments:** this golf course
offers beautiful mountain views and some of the driest winter play in the area.

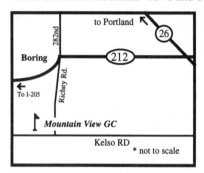

Directions: from Hwy 26 turn west at flashing yellow light in Boring, proceed 3 miles to the course on your right. You can also exit at Boring Rd (212) and go west to Richey Road. Turn left and proceed to Kelso Road and turn right to the course.

Course Yardage & Par:
C-6041 yards, par 71.
M-5572 yards, par 71.
W-5348 yards, par 73.

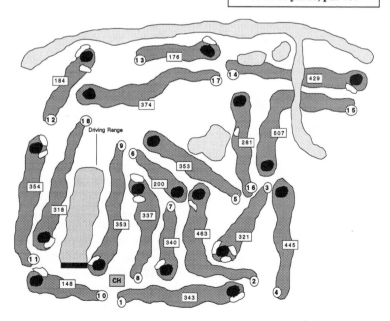

Myrtle Creek Golf Course (public, 18 hole course)
P.O. Box 6007; Fairway Drive; Myrtle Creek, OR 97457
Phone: 888-T-MYRTLE, (541) 863-GOLF. Fax: (541) 863-4768.
Pro: Keith Johnson, PGA. Superintendent: N/A.
Rating/Slope: C 72.3/135; M 67.5/124; W 69.4/124. **Course record:** 67.
Green fees: W/D $20; W/E $25; winter rates; Jr. & Sr. rates.
Power cart: $20/$12. **Pull cart:** $4/$2.50. **Trail fee:** $7 for personal carts.
Reservation policy: please call up to 30 dyas in advance for tee times.
Winter condition: the golf course is open, weather permitting. Dry course.
Terrain: flat, some hills. **Tees:** all grass. **Spikes:** metal spikes permitted.
Services: club rentals, lessons, snack bar, restaurant, pro shop, driving range.
Comments: this golf course offers beautiful views of the surrounding country-
side. Opened in early summer of 1997 this Graham Cooke designed layout
features large, well bunkered greens. Great new golf course that is worth a trip.

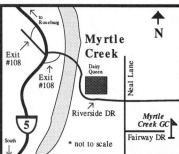

Directions: from I-5 N&S take the
Myrtle Creek exit #108. Proceed
eastbound and head through the downtown Myrtle Creek. Proceed through the
traffic light, cross the bridge and make a
hard left onto Riverside Drive. Take a
right off Riverside at Neal Lane, then
turn left at Fairway Drive to the course.

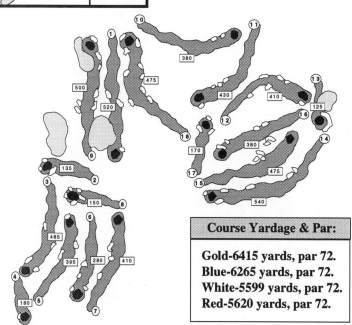

Course Yardage & Par:
Gold-6415 yards, par 72.
Blue-6265 yards, par 72.
White-5599 yards, par 72.
Red-5620 yards, par 72.

Neskowin Beach Golf Course (public, 9 hole course)
Hawk Avenue; P.O. Box 855; Neskowin, OR 97149
Phone: (503) 392-3377. Fax: none. Internet: none.
Pro: Tom Clark, PGA. Superintendent: none.
Rating/Slope: M 65.3/103; W 67.7/110. **Course record:** 28.
Green fees: $20/$12 all week long; M/C, VISA.
Power cart: $20/$10. **Pull cart:** $2. **Trail fee:** $20 for personal carts.
Reservation policy: yes, recommended but not required (a must in summer).
Winter condition: the course is closed from November 1st to March 15th.
Terrain: flat (easy walking). **Tees:** grass/mats. **Spikes:** metal spikes permitted.
Services: club rentals, lessons, snack bar, bevrages, pro shop, putting green.
Comments: this course has fabulous, well kept turf which is seems to always
be green no matter the weather conditions or the time of year. Small flat greens
and creeks that wander through the track make this golf course a real challenge.
The track is tucked away from the wind even though the course is located on
the scenic Oregon Coast. Tee-times are a must during the peak summer season.

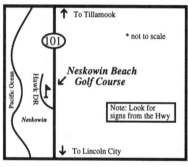

Directions: from Highway 101, turn
north on Hawk Avenue. The golf course
is located 1/4 mile ahead on your right
hand side. Look for a sign on Highway
101 marking your turn to the golf course.

Course Yardage & Par:
M-2616 yards, par 35.
W-2516 yards, par 35.

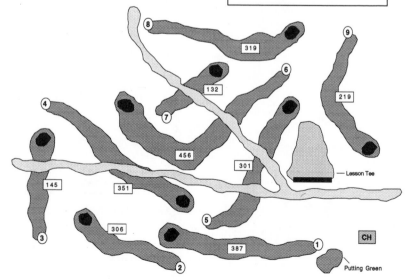

Nine Peaks Golf Course (public, 18 hole course)

1152 NW Golf Course Road; Madras, OR 97741
Phone: (541) 475-3511. Fax: none. Internet: none.
Owners: Kevin & Deirdre O'Meara. Superintendent: none.
Rating/Slope: M 67.8/103; W 70.0/107. **Course record:** 61.
Green fees: $18/$9 all week long; M/C, VISA, DISCOVER, NOVUS.
Power cart: $18/$10. **Pull cart:** $1. **Trail fee:** $6/$3 for personal carts.
Reservation policy: please call ahead for tee-times policies.
Winter condition: open all year, however closed periodically due to snow.
Terrain: flat (easy walking). **Tees:** grass. **Spikes:** metal spikes permitted.
Services: club rentals, lessons, snack bar, beer, wine, pro shop, putting green.
Comments: The course very flat and is easy to walk. The new nine has several
challenging greens guarded by bunkers and water. Great views of the Cascade
Mountain Range. This golf course is worth a special trip if in Central Oregon.

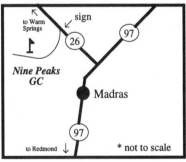

Directions: the golf course is located
off of Highway 26, 1.25 miles west of
Madras, Oregon. Look for the signs on
Highway 26 marking your turn to the
golf course. The location of your turn
to the golf course is well marked.

Course Yardage & Par:
C-6582 yards, par 72.
M-6280 yards, par 72.
W-5745 yards, par 72.

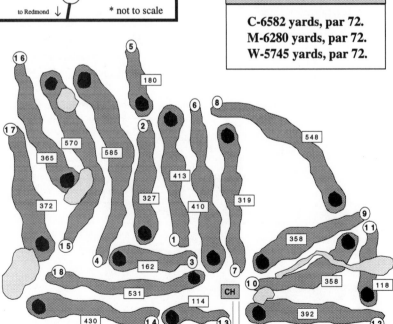

Oak Knoll Public Golf Course (public, 9 hole course)
3070 Highway 66; Ashland, OR 97520
Phone: (541) 482-4311. Fax: none. Internet: none.
Pro: Bob Haney. Superintendent: none.
Rating/Slope: M 69.1/119; W 70.5/116. **Course record:** 62.
Green fees: October-April $14/$9; May-September $18/$12; M/C, VISA.
Monday thru Friday Green fee cart combo (summer) $23/$16, lower in winter.
Power cart: $18/$12. **Pull cart:** $3/$2. **Trail fee:** $7 for personal carts.
Reservation policy: yes, please call ahead for tee-times. 7 days maximum.
Winter condition: the golf course is open all year long. Very dry winter course.
Terrain: flat, some hills. **Tees:** all grass. **Spikes:** metal spikes permitted.
Services: club rentals, lessons, restaurant, lounge, beer, wine, liquor, pro shop.
Comments: course has 2 sets of tees for those people wanting to play a full 18
holes. Fairways are narrow in spots putting emphasis on driving accuracy.
Creeks are factors on other holes. Your company tournaments are welcome.

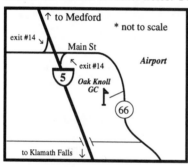

Directions: from I-5 take exit #14
(Southern Oregon State College). Head
east on Hwy 66. The golf course will
be located .75 miles on your right hand
side. **Note:** The golf course is located
across from the Ashland City Airport.
Look for signs marking your way.

Course Yardage & Par:
M-3020 yards, par 36.
W-2656 yards, par 38.
Dual tees for 18 holes:
M-6035 yards, par 71.
W-5229 yards, par 74.

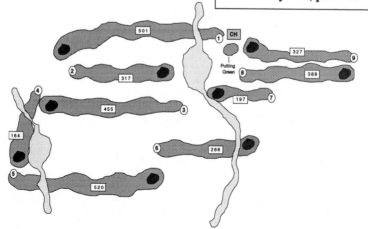

Oak Knoll Golf Course (public, 18 hole course)

6335 Highway 22; Independence, OR 97351
Phone: (503) 378-0344. Fax: (503) 585-7944. Internet: none.
Pro: John McComish, PGA. Superintendent: Kirk Anderson.
Rating/Slope: C 68.6/113; M 67.1/111, W 69.2/113. **Course record:** 63.
Green fees: $25/$15 all week long; Senior rates $22/$12; VISA, M/C.
Power cart: $20/$10. **Pull cart:** $2. **Trail fee:** $10/$5.
Reservation policy: yes, please call in advance for your tee-times (a must).
Winter condition: the golf course is open all year long, damp conditions.
Terrain: flat (easy walking). **Tees:** grass. **Spikes:** metal spikes permitted.
Services: club rentals, lessons, snack bar, restaurant, lounge, beer, wine, liquor,
pro shop, lockers, putting green, driving range. **Comments:** one of the area's
most popular courses. You will always find the greens and golf course in great
condition. Excellent public course that can get very busy during the summer.

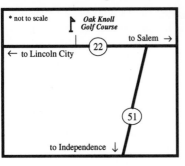

Directions: the golf course is located
7 miles west of Salem on the north side
of Highway 22. Take exit #253 off of
I-5 to Highway 22 in Salem, Oregon.
Look for signs to Dallas, Ocean Beaches
this will help direct you to the course
which is right off Hwy 22.

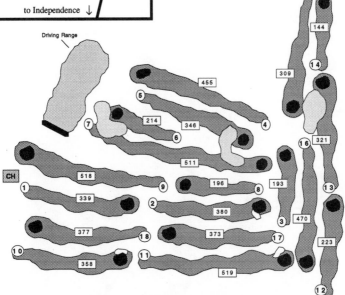

Course Yardage & Par:
C-6266 yards, par 72. M-5909 yards, par 72. W-5069yards, par 72.

Oakway Golf Course (public, 9 hole course)
2000 Cal Young Road; Eugene, OR 97401
Phone: (541) 484-1927. Fax: (541) 485-5899. Internet: none.
Manager: Tom DeCuman. Superintendent: Loren Erickson.
Rating/Slope: M 58.6/91; W 59.0/92. **Course record:** 54.
Green fees: W/D $20/$12; W/E $22/$14; Sr. rates $16/$10 (M-F); M/C, VISA.
Power cart: $18/$10. **Pull cart:** $2. **Trail fee:** personal carts are not allowed.
Reservation policy: none needed. Course is run on a 1st come 1st served basis.
Winter condition: the golf course is open all year long. Wet conditions.
Terrain: flat, some hills. **Tees:** all grass. **Spikes:** metal spikes permitted.
Services: club rentals, restaurant, beer, wine, pro shop, putting/chipping greens.
Comments: One of the nicest short courses in the state of Oregon. The course is easy to walk. Excellent course for seniors who want to play a highly competive course but do not want the length. Fairways can play very tight on certain holes.

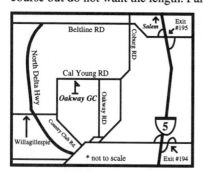

Directions: from I-5 take exit #195. Head west on Beltline Road. Take the Coburg Road exit and go south. At Cal Young Road turn right. The golf course will be 1/4 mile ahead on your left hand side.

Course Yardage & Par:
M-3609 yards, par 61.
W-3117 yards, par 61.

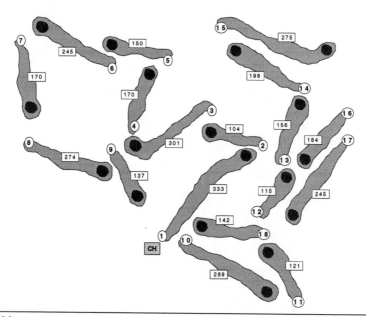

Ocean Dunes Golf Links (public, 18 hole course)

3345 Munsel Lake Road; Florence, OR 97439
Phone: (541) 997-3232; 800-468-4833. Fax: (541) 997-3232.
Pro: Vern Smith, PGA. Superintendent: Mark Shepherd.
Rating/Slope: C 70.0/124; M 68.0/119; W 70.6/121. **Course record:** 68.
Green fees: $28/$15 all week long; Sr. rates; M/C, VISA.
Power cart: $24. **Pull cart:** $3/$2. **Trail fee:** $10 for personal carts.
Reservation policy: yes, please call ahead for weekend reservations (a must).
Winter condition: the golf course is open all year long. Very dry conditions.
Terrain: flat, rolling some hills. **Tees:** grass. **Spikes:** metal spikes permitted.
Services: club rentals, lessons, snack bar, beer, wine, pro shop, driving range,
putting/chipping greens. **Comments:** This course is built on sand dunes which
keeps it dry during the winter. The course plays like a real links course that you
would find in Scotland. Greens are large and rolling and can be a good test for
the best putter. Fairways give the golfer a wide variety of lies. Worth a trip.

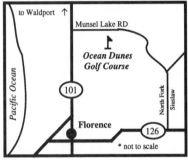

Directions: from Highway 101 turn
eastbound on Munsel Lake Road and
proceed to the golf course. From Hwy
126 (Florence Hwy) go north on North
Fork Siuslaw. When you reach Munsel
Lake Road turn left to the golf course.
The golf course will be located on your
left hand side. Look for signs marking
your turn to the golf course.

Course Yardage & Par:
C-6018 yards, par 71.
M-5601 yards, par 71.
W-5044 yards, par 72.

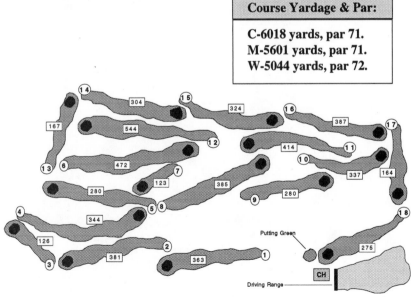

Olalla Valley Golf Course (public, 9 hole course)
1022 Olalla Road; Toledo, OR 97391
Phone: (541) 336-2121. **Fax:** (541) 336-4024. **Internet: none.**
Owner: Gary L. Lau. Superintendent: Rosco Baptiste.
Rating/Slope: M 69.2/127; W 72.7/124. **Course record:** 63.
Green fees: $20/$12 all week long; M/C, VISA.
Power cart: $20/$10. **Pull cart:** $2. **Trail fee:** $3.
Reservation policy: yes, required for weekend tee times. Call 7 days ahead.
Winter condition: the golf course is open all year long, course drains very well.
Terrain: course is very hilly. **Tees:** all grass. **Spikes:** metal spikes permitted.
Services: club rentals, restaurant, beer, wine, beverages, pro shop, putting green.
Comments: Excellent winter course. Nine hole golf course that has 2 sets of tees for 18 hole play. Water comes into play on nearly every hole. The course can be very demanding in spots so concentration is a must for a good score.

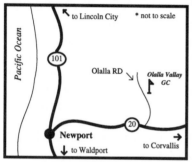

Directions: on Highway 101 the golf course is located 6 miles east of Newport. From Highway 20 (from Corvallis) go west 45 minutes to the golf course. Exit on to Olalla Road from Highway 20. There are signs from each direction you can follow to the golf course.

Course Yardage & Par:
M-2949 yards, par 36.
W-2587 yards, par 37.
Dual tees for 18 holes:
M-6027 yards, par 72.
W-5507 yards, par 74.

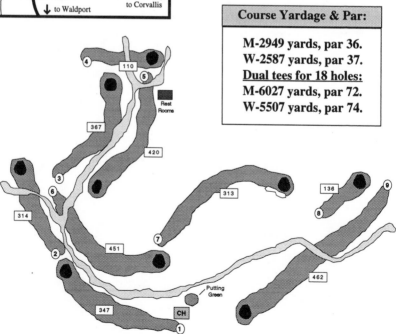

Oregon City Golf Club (public, 18 hole course)
20124 South Beaver Creek Road; Oregon City, OR 97045
Phone: (503) 656-2846. Fax: (503) 656-0290. Internet: none.
Pro: Bill Hagedon. Owner: John Herberger.
Rating/Slope: M 67.9/116; M 66.2/111; W 69.4/113. **Course record: 62.**
Green fees: W/D $20/$10; W/E $25/$12.50; Jr. & Sr. rates (M-F); M/C, VISA.
Power cart: $25/$15. **Pull cart:** $3. **Trail fee:** $5 for personal carts.
Reservation policy: yes, a must, call 2 weeks in advance for your tee-times.
Winter condition: the golf course is open all year long, dry (drains well).
Terrain: gentle, rolling hills. **Tees:** grass. **Spikes:** metal spikes permitted.
Services: club rentals, lessons, snack bar, beer, pop, pro shop, putting green,
banquet room (seats up to 160 persons). **Comments:** This is the 3rd oldest golf
courses in the state of Oregon still in full operation. Excellent drainage and a
good maintenance schedule provide a very dry course conditions even in winter.
Very friendly public course that has been a joy to play every time I have visited.

Directions: from I-205 N&S take exit # 10 (Park Place). Head southbound on Highway 213. At the 3rd light go left (eastbound) on Beaver Creek Road. The golf course is located 1.5 miles ahead on your left. Look for signs along the way.

Course Yardage & Par:

C-5872 yards, par 71.
M-5516 yards, par 71.
W-5198 yards, par 75.

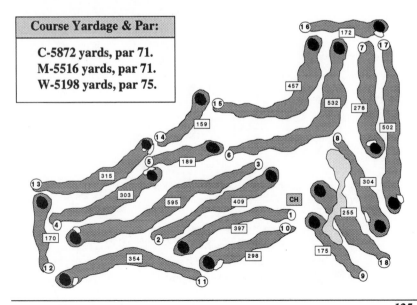

The O.G.A. Members Course @ Tukwila (public, 18 holes)

2990 Boones Ferry Road; Woodburn, OR 97071
Phone: (503) 981-6105. **Fax:** none. **Internet:** none.
Pro: Chuck Siver, PGA. **Superintendent:** none.
Rating/Slope: T 71.6/126; C 70.4/123; 71.9/123; W 71.9/127. **Record:** 65.
Green fees: W/D $38/$23; W/E $43/$25; special rates for OGA members.
Power cart: $22/$12. **Pull cart:** $2. **Trail fee:** personal carts are not allowed.
Reservation policy: call up to 5 days in advance for all your tee-times.
Winter condition: the course is open, weather permitting. Drains very well.
Terrain: rolling hills. **Tees:** all grass. **Spikes:** metal spikes permitted.
Services: club rentals, lessons, snack bar, beer, wine, pro shop, driving range.
Comments: This course has a unique double green on holes 9 and 18. Water comes into play on several holes, some holes offer a peek-a-boo view of Mount Hood. This course is worth a trip anytime. Lower rates for all OGA members.

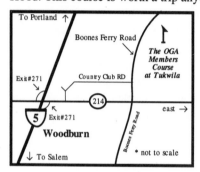

Directions: From I-5 N&S take exit #271, Woodburn. Head eastbound for approximately 1.5 miles to Boones Ferry Road and turn left. The golf course is ahead on the right hand side of the road. Look for signs marking your way to the golf course.

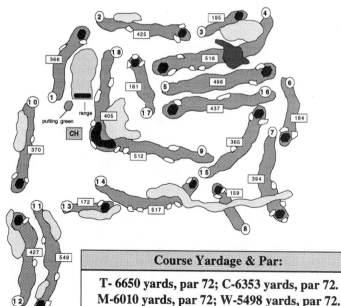

Course Yardage & Par:
T- 6650 yards, par 72; C-6353 yards, par 72.
M-6010 yards, par 72; W-5498 yards, par 72.

The Oregon Golf Club (private, 18 hole course)

25700-A SW Pete's Mountain Road; West Linn, OR 97068
Phone: (503) 650-7805. **Fax:** (503) 650-7580. **Internet:** none.
Pro: Gary Dowen, PGA. **Superintendent:** John Andersen
Rating/Slope: J 74.4/135; C 72.1/132; M 69.8/123; W 71.1/125. **Record:** 63.
Green fees: private club, members & guests only; limited reciprocation.
Power cart: private club. **Pull cart:** yes. **Trail fee:** personal carts not allowed.
Reservation policy: private club, members & guests only. No public play.
Winter condition: the golf course is open all year long. Dry conditions.
Terrain: very hilly. **Tees:** all grass. **Spikes:** no metal spikes in summer.
Services: full service private facility, driving range, putting & chipping greens.
Comments: the golf course was co-designed by PGA Tour player Peter
Jacobsen. Layout is of championship caliber with sand on nearly every hole.
Host of the annual Fred Meyer Challenge. This private track is spectacular.

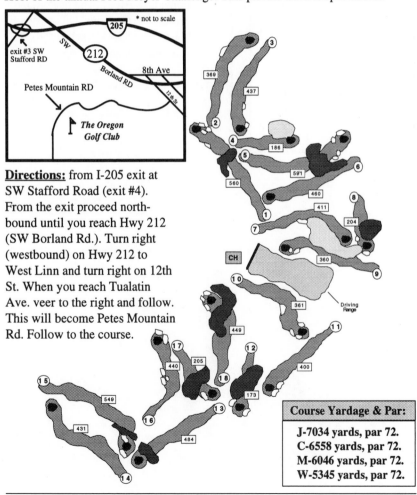

Directions: from I-205 exit at
SW Stafford Road (exit #4).
From the exit proceed north-
bound until you reach Hwy 212
(SW Borland Rd.). Turn right
(westbound) on Hwy 212 to
West Linn and turn right on 12th
St. When you reach Tualatin
Ave. veer to the right and follow.
This will become Petes Mountain
Rd. Follow to the course.

Course Yardage & Par:

J-7034 yards, par 72.
C-6558 yards, par 72.
M-6046 yards, par 72.
W-5345 yards, par 72.

Orenco Woods Golf Club (public, 9 hole course)
22200 NW Birch; P.O. Box 25; Hillsboro, OR 97123
Phone: (503) 648-1836. **Fax:** none. **Internet:** none.
Pro: Rich Haaland, PGA. **Superintendent:** Tim Hamel.
Rating/Slope: M 65.9/109; W 67.3/109. **Course record:** 63.
Green fees: $17/$9 all week long; Jr. & Sr. rates; M/C, VISA.
Power cart: $20/$10. **Pull cart:** $2. **Trail fee:** $9/$5 for personal carts.
Reservation policy: yes, call 7 days in advance for times (a must for weekends).
Winter condition: the golf course is open all year long, damp conditions.
Terrain: very hilly. **Tees:** all grass. **Spikes:** metal spikes permitted.
Services: club rentals, lessons, snack bar, beer, wine, pro shop, driving range.
Comments: course is hilly and presents a good challenge. The greens are small
which puts a premium on shot making. A creek is in play on nearly every hole.

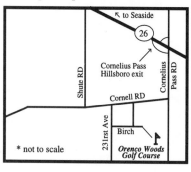

Directions: take Hwy 26 out of Portland
going west. Take Cornelius Pass/Hillsboro
exit. Proceed south on Cornelius Pass Rd.
to NW Cornell Rd. and turn right. Proceed
to NW 231st Ave. and turn left to NW
Birch. Proceed and turn left to the course.

Course Yardage & Par:
M-2626 yards, par 35.
W-2454 yards, par 36.
Dual tees for 18 holes:
W-5080 yards, par 72.
M-5376 yards, par 71.

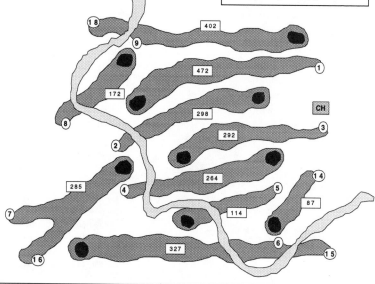

Orion Greens Golf Course (public, 9 hole course)
61525 Fargo Lane; Bend, OR 97702
Phone: (541) 388-3999. **Fax:** (541) 318-8538. **Internet:** none.
Manager: Bud Lamarche. **Superintendent:** Rich Colantino.
Rating/Slope: M 58.3/96; W 62.0/95. **Course record:** 26.
Green fees: $21/$13 all week long; M/C, VISA.
Power cart: $19/$10. **Pull cart:** $3/$2. **Trail fee:** $10/$5.
Reservation policy: call the pro shop for advance reservation policies.
Winter condition: the golf course is open all year long, weather permitting.
Terrain: flat (easy walking). **Tees:** grass. **Spikes:** metal spikes permitted.
Services: club rentals, lessons, snack bar, restaurant, lounge, beer, wine, liquor,
putting green. **Comments:** This facility is well kept. Greens are medium in
size and are well bunkered. Great views of the surrounding countryside abound
from nearly every tee. If you are looking for a change of pace Orion Greens
G.C. is sure to please. The golf course is in excellent condition most of the year.
Good walking golf course that is great for the first time or senior golfer.

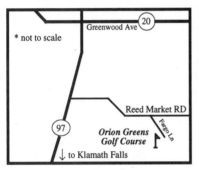

Directions: take Highway 97. Go east on
Reed Market Road. Proceed 1.5 miles to
Fargo Lane. Turn right on Fargo Lane and
follow this to the golf course which will
be on your right hand side. Look for signs
from Highway 97 in Bend, Oregon to the
golf course. The way is well marked.

Course Yardage & Par:
White tees: 2075 yards, par 31.
Gold tees: 1939 yards, par 31.
Red tees: 1738 yards, par 31.

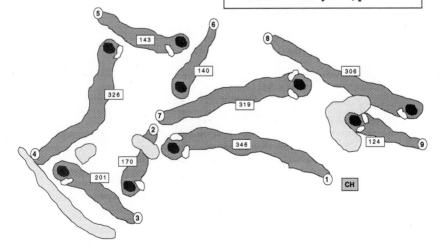

Oswego Lake Country Club (private, 18 hole course)

20 Iron Mountain Boulevard: P.O. Box 508; Lake Oswego, OR 97034
Phone: (503) 635-3659. Fax: (503) 636-4362. Internet: none.
Pro: Brent Murray, PGA. Superintendent: Dick Fluter
Rating/Slope: T 71.9/132; C 70.6/127; M 68.7/123; W 73.4/124. **Record: 65.**
Green fees: private club members & guests only; reciprocates; no credit cards.
Power cart: private club. **Pull cart:** private club. **Trail fee:** not allowed.
Reservation policy: for members and guests only. Call 2 days in advance.
Winter condition: the golf course is open all year long, damp conditions.
Terrain: very hilly. **Tees:** all grass. **Spikes:** metal spikes permitted.
Services: lessons, snack bar, restaurant, lounge, beer, wine, liquor, pro shop,
lockers, showers, driving range, putting & chipping greens, club memberships.
Comments: The golf course is noted for the many picturesque golf holes it has.
Course can play very tough at times with large well bunkered greens.

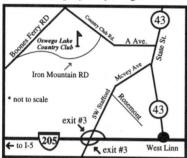

Directions: from I-5 take Hwy 217 exit into Lake Oswego. Take left onto Boones Ferry then a right onto Country Club. Take a right onto Iron Mountain Blvd. the course will be on your right side. From I-205 exit to go north at either Pacific Hwy 43 Willamette Drive or at SW Stafford and proceed north to State and turn left onto "A" Ave. to Country Club Road.

Course Yardage & Par:
T-6557 yards, par 71.
C-6286 yards, par 71.
M-5910 yards, par 71.
W-5382 yards, par 73.

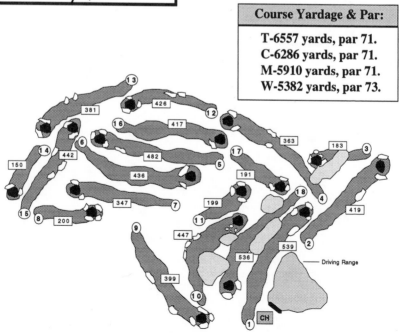

Pendleton Country Club (private)

69772 Hwy 395 S; Route 2, Box 94; Pendleton, OR 97801
Phone: (541) 443-4653. Fax: none. Internet: none.
Pro: Doug Newman, PGA. Superintendent: Ross Noble.
Rating/Slope: C 69.8/116; M 68.6/113; W 70.3/117. **Course record:** 63.
Green fees: private club members & guests only; reciprocates; M/C, VISA.
Power cart: private club. **Pull cart:** private club. **Trail fee:** private club.
Reservation policy: private club members & guests of members only.
Winter condition: the golf course is open all year long, weather permitting.
Terrain: flat (easy walking). **Tees:** grass. **Spikes:** metal spikes permitted.
Services: club rentals, lessons, snack bar, restaurant, lounge, beer, wine, liquor, pro shop, showers, driving range, putting green. **Comments:** The course is well conditioned during the golf season. Lush fairways with medium to fast greens.

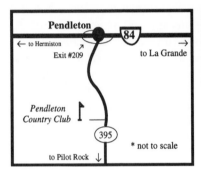

Directions: the golf course is located 8 miles south of Pendleton. From I-84 E&W take exit #209 to Highway 395. Follow Highway 395 for 7.7 miles to the golf course on your right hand side.

Course Yardage & Par:

C-6317 yards, par 72.
M-6060 yards, par 72.
W-5483 yards, par 74.

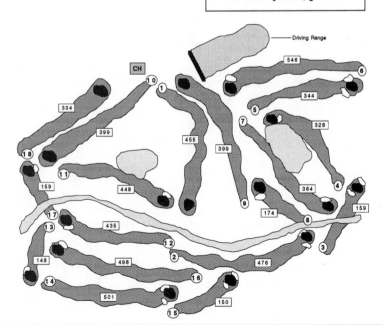

Persimmon Country Club (semi-private)
500 SE Butler Road; Gresham, OR 97080
Phone: (503) 661-1800. Fax: (503) 667-3885. Internet: none.
Pro: Larry Skreen, PGA. Superintendent: N/A.
Rating/Slope: C 71.2/125; M 69.5/122; W 70.3/122; W 66.1/112. Record: 63.
Green fees: Weekdays $70; Weekends $85 (fees include a cart).
Power cart: included in fees. Pull cart: $4/$2. Trail fee: not allowed.
Reservation policy: members 7 days ahead; non members 3 days in ahead.
Winter condition: the golf course open all year long, weather permitting.
Terrain: gently sloping. Tees: all grass. Spikes: metal spikes permitted.
Services: club rentals, lessons, swing analysis, outdoor practice cages, pro shop,
club repair, driving range, grill room with beer & wine, lockers, putting green.
Comments: golf course designed by Bunny Mason with incredible views of the
Cascade Mtns. Great newer golf course that will challenge you at every turn.

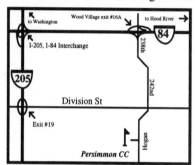

Directions: from I-84 take the Wood Village 16A exit and go south on 238th. 238th will become 242nd, then becomes Hogan Road. Proceed to the golf course which will be located on your right. The course is approximately 4.5 miles from your I-84 exit. Look for signs marking your way to the golf course.

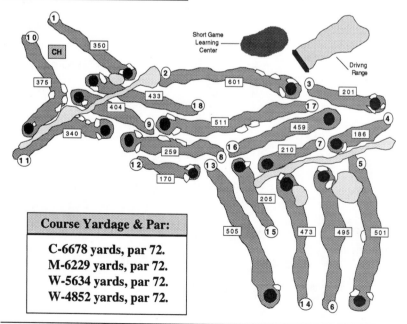

Course Yardage & Par:
C-6678 yards, par 72.
M-6229 yards, par 72.
W-5634 yards, par 72.
W-4852 yards, par 72.

Pine Hollow Golf Course (public, 9 hole course)
8-A South County Road; Tygh Valley, OR 97063
Phone: (541) 544-2035. Fax: (541) 544-2350.
Owner: Irl Davis. Superintendent: none.
Rating/Slope: M 61.6/95 W 60.9/101. **Course record:** 30.
Green fees: $14/$7 all week long; M/C, VISA.
Power cart: $15/$7.50. **Pull cart:** $2.50. **Trail fee:** not allowed.
Reservation policy: reservations can be made up to 1 month in advance.
Winter condition: the golf course is open from April until October.
Terrain: flat, some hills. **Tees:** all grass. **Spikes:** metal spikes permitted.
Services: club rentals, lounge, beer, wine, limited pro shop, driving net, putting green, tournament planning, club memberships. **Comments:** this golf course was designed in by Irl Davis and plays to a par of 34. The fairways are narrow in spots leaving the golfer little room off the tee. Dual tees are available for those wanting to play a full 18 hole round. Call ahead as some open play is restricted.

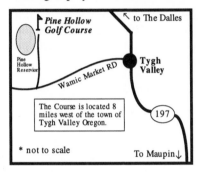

Directions: from Highway 197 turn westbound on Wamic Market Road when in the town of Tygh Valley. Proceed on Wamic Market Road to the Pine Hollow Reservoir. The course is located at the Pine Hollow Reservoir. Look for signs that are posted.

Course Yardage & Par:
M-2234 yards, par 34.
W-1954 yards, par 34.

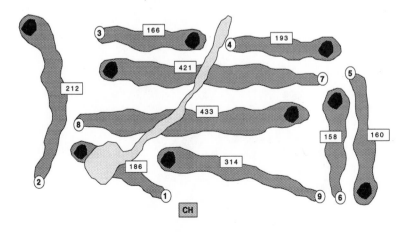

133

Pineway Golf Course (public, 9 hole course)

30949 Pineway Road; Lebanon, OR 97355
Phone: (541) 258-8815. Fax: none. Internet: none.
Pros: Jim Glasser, Mickie Price. Superintendent: none.
Rating/Slope: M 68.1/108; W 73.8/ 122. **Course record:** 64.
Green fees: W/D $20/$10; W/E $20/$10; Jr. & Sr. rates $17 (M-F); M/C, VISA.
Power cart: $20/$10. **Pull cart:** $2. **Trail fee:** $10/$5 for personal carts.
Reservation policy: yes, call 1 week in advance for your tee-times.
Winter condition: the golf course is open all year long, dry (drains very well).
Terrain: relatively hilly. **Tees:** all grass. **Spikes:** metal spikes permitted.
Services: club rentals, lessons, restaurant, lounge, beer, pro shop, snack bar, lockers, driving range, practice green. **Comments:** course is in great condition all year round. The terrain is up and down giving the golfer a wide variety of lies from the fairway. Dual tees will give you a different look if you are playing a full 18 holes. New 9 is in the planning stages and should be ready in the future.

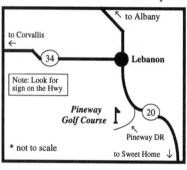

Directions: the golf course is located just off of Highway 20 4.3 miles southeast of Lebanon, Oregon. A sign will indicate the location of the golf course.

Course Yardage & Par:
M-2967 yards, par 36.
W-2960 yards, par 37.
Dual tees for 18 holes:
M-5927 yards, par 72.
W-5919 yards, par 74.

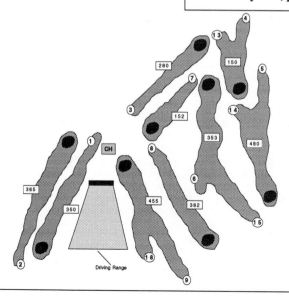

Pleasant Valley Golf Club (private, 18 hole course)
12300 SE 162nd Avenue; Clackamas, OR 97105
Phone: (503) 658-3101. Fax: (503) 658-7702.
Pro: Derek Peterson, PGA. Superintendent: John McDonald.
Rating/Slope: C 72.4/132; M 70.1/128; W 71.9/119. **Course record:** 66.
Green fees: private club, members & guests of members only; reciprocates.
Power cart: private club. **Pull cart:** private club. **Trail fee:** not allowed.
Reservation policy: private club, members & guests of members only.
Winter condition: the golf course is open all year long, dry conditions.
Terrain: flat, some hills. **Tees:** all grass. **Spikes:** no metal spikes in summer.
Services: club rentals, lessons, snack bar, restaurant, beer, liquor, pro shop,
lockers, putting green. **Comments:** private club, members and guests only.
The course is well conditioned and offers challenging golf. Great golf course.

Directions: from Highway 205 exit eastbound on SE Sunnyside which. Follow for 3.4 mi to 162nd and turn left for .5 mi to the golf course on your right. **Note:** sign indicating your turn.

Course Yardage & Par:
C-6593 yards, par 72.
M-6164 yards, par 72.
W-5410 yards, par 73.

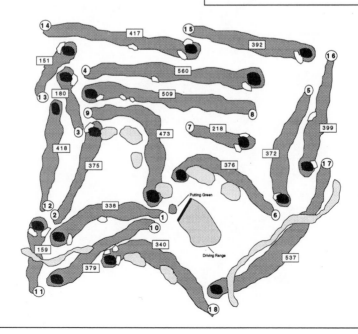

Portland Golf Club (private, 18 hole course)
5900 SW Scholls Ferry Road; Portland, OR 97225
Phone: (503) 292-2778. **Fax:** unavaiable. **Internet:** none.
Pro: Larry Lamberger Jr., PGA. **Superintendent:** Forest Goodling.
Rating/Slope: C 72.4/131; M 70.8/127; W 74.0/127. **Course record:** 64.
Green fees: private. Must be a guest of a member and be with the member.
Power cart: private club members only. **Pull cart:** private club members only.
Reservation policy: private club members and guests for members only.
Winter condition: the golf course is open all year long, damp conditions.
Terrain: relatively hilly. **Tees:** all grass. **Spikes:** metal spikes permitted.
Services: club rentals, lessons, snack bar, restaurant, lounge, beer, wine, liquor, beverages, pro shop, lockers, showers, driving range, putting & chipping greens.
Comments: Beautiful, old, historical golf course. Home to numerous past major tournaments, P.G.A. Championship, Ryder Cup, Western Open and the United State Senior Open. The golf course is rated #3 in the state of Oregon and is nothing short of spectacular. Excellent track that is rich in golf tradition.

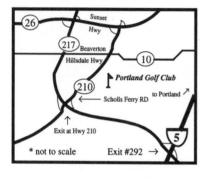

Directions: from I-5 take exit # 217. Follow SW Scholls Ferry Road and proceed 3 miles north to the golf course.

Course Yardage & Par:
C-6683 yards, par 72.
M-6323 yards, par 72.
W-5868 yards, par 73.

Portland Meadows Golf Course (public, 9 hole course)
901 North Schmeer Road; Portland, OR 97217
Phone: (503) 289-3405. Fax: none. Internet: none.
Pro: teaching pro during the summer. Superintendent: none.
Rating/Slope: the golf course is not rated. **Course record:** 57.
Green fees: Monday's $5; Tuesday thru Friday $7; Sat., Sun. & holidays $8.
Power cart: none available. **Pull cart:** $2. **Trail fee:** not allowed.
Reservation policy: advance tee-time reservations are not needed or required.
The course opens at 7am Saturday, Sunday & holidays. 8:30am Tuesday-Friday.
Winter condition: the golf course is open from May 1st to September 30th. The
course is closed Monday through Friday during the months of October to April.
Terrain: flat (easy walking). **Tees:** grass. **Spikes:** metal spikes permitted.
Services: club rentals, snack bar, beer, driving range, lessons, limited pro shop.
Comments: Unusual setting. Greens are small, postage stamp type style. Very
few hazards come into play off the tee or on your approach shots. The golf
course is situated in the center of the Portland Meadows horse racing track.

Directions: from I-5 N&S take exit # 306B (Delta Park). Turn left at the stop sign on North Victory Boulevard. Get in the right hand lane. Curve to the right for 1/2 mile to North Schmeer Road. The golf course will be located .2 miles ahead to your left at the race track. **Note:** Look for the Portland Meadows race track and you will find the course.

Course Yardage & Par:
M-1983 yards, par 31.
W-1983 yards, par 35.

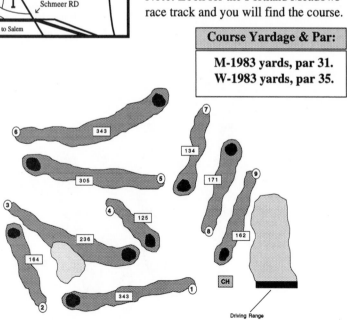

Prineville Golf & Country Club (private)

232204 E Highway 26; Prineville, OR 97754;
Phone: (541) 447-7225. Fax: (541) 447-6714. Internet: none.
Pro: Tom Brown, PGA. Superintendent: Dan Severance.
Rating/Slope: M 64.1/112; W 65.9/107. **Course record: 59.**
Green fees: private club members only, reciprocates; M/C, VISA.
Power cart: private club. **Pull cart:** private club. **Trail fee:** private club.
Reservation policy: private club members only, reciprocates call in advance.
Winter condition: the golf course is open all year long, dry (drains very well).
Terrain: flat, some slight hills. **Tees:** all grass. **Spikes:** metal spikes permitted.
Services: rentals, lessons, snack bar, restaurant, lounge, beer, wine, liquor, pro
shop, showers, driving range, putting & chipping greens, club memberships.
Comments: in excellent condition April through September. The golf course
is very beautiful, tricky but fair. Separate tees for 18 hole play. Good course.

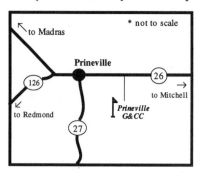

Directions: the golf course is located 3
mile east of Prineville, Oregon off of
Highway 26. Look for a sign marking
your entrance to the Country Club.

Course Yardage & Par:
M-2525 yards, par 33.
W-2268 yards, par 34.
Dual tees for 18 holes:
M-4959 yards, par 65.
W-4662 yards, par 68.

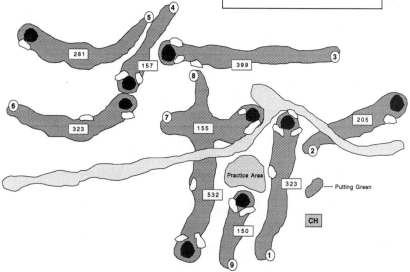

Progress Downs Municipal Golf Course (public, 18 holes)

8200 Scholls Ferry Road; Beaverton, OR 97008
Phone: (503) 646-5166. **Fax:** none. **Internet:** none.
Pro: Mark Bolton, PGA. **Superintendent:** John Standard.
Rating/Slope: C 69.8/112; M 68.4/110; W 71.7/115. **Course record:** 64.
Green fees: W/D $19/$10; W/E $21/$11; Jr. & Sr. rates are available.
Power cart: $22/$11; **Pull cart:** $3/$2. **Trail Fee:** $4 for personal carts.
Reservation policy: yes, please call up to 7 days in advance for your tee-time.
Winter condition: the golf course is open all year long. Dry conditions.
Terrain: flat, some hills. **Tees:** all grass. **Spikes:** metal spikes permitted.
Services: club rentals, lessons, restaurant, lounge, pro shop, driving range,
putting & chipping greens. **Comments:** well kept public facility. Driving range
is double decked, covered and lighted. Great public golf center that includes a
fantastic on course pro shop that will meet all your golfing needs.

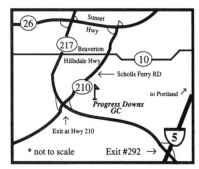

Directions: Hwy 217 exit at Progress
exit. Go left on SW Hall Boulevard.
Take first left at the light after proceed-
ing over the overpass onto Scholls
Ferry Road. Go for .3 miles to the golf
course on your right. Look for signs
directing your turns to the golf course.

Course Yardage & Par:
C-6426 yards, par 71.
M-6122 yards, par 71.
W-5626 yards, par 73.

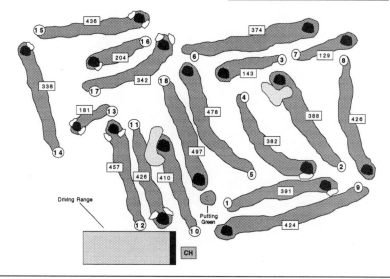

Pumpkin Ridge Golf Club (Ghost Creek) (semi-private, 18 holes)
12930 NW Old Pumpkin Ridge Road; Cornelius, OR 97113-6147
Phone: (503) 647-4747 or 647-9977. **Fax:** (503) 647-2002. **Internet: none.**
Pro: Ken Jack, PGA. **Superintendent:** Bill Webster.
Rating/Slope: T 73.6/135; C 71.4/132; M 69.0/130; W 70.4/117. **Record:** 65.
Green fees: $80 Monday-Thursday; $100 Friday-Sunday & Hol.; VISA, M/C.
Power cart: $30. **Pull cart:** $3. **Trail Fee:** personal carts are not allowed.
Reservation policy: yes, call 6 days ahead by phone. 7 days ahead in person.
Winter condition: the golf course is open all year long. Very dry conditions
Terrain: gentle rolling hills. **Tees:** grass. **Spikes:** no metal spikes in summer.
Services: club rentals, lessons, restaurant, beer, wine, pro shop, driving range.
Comments: ranked #74 in *Golf Digest's* best 100 golf courses in the U.S. Robert
Cupp Design. Pumpkin Ridge was host to the 1996 US Amateur. In 1997 the US
Womens Open Championship came to this outstanding one-of-kind golf course.

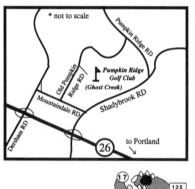

Directions: From Hwy 26 (Sunset Hwy) take Dersham exit #55. Proceed north for .3 miles, take right onto Mountaindale Rd., proceed east for 1.0 miles, take a left onto Old Pumpkin Ridge Rd. Proceed for .3 miles to the entrance on your right.

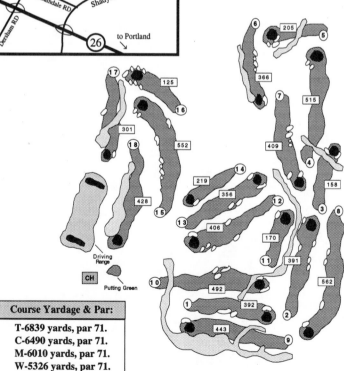

Course Yardage & Par:
T-6839 yards, par 71.
C-6490 yards, par 71.
M-6010 yards, par 71.
W-5326 yards, par 71.

Pumpkin Ridge Golf Club (Witch Hollow) (private, 18 holes)

12930 NW Old Pumpkin Ridge Road; Cornelius, OR 97113-6147
Phone: (503) 647-4747 or 647-2500. Fax: (503) 647-2002. Internet: none.
Pro: Ken Jack, PGA. Superintendent: Bill Webster.
Rating/Slope: T 74.8/141; C 72.3/138; M 70.1/133; W 70.4/121. **Record:** 64.
Green fees: private club members and guests of members only.
Power cart: private club. **Pull cart:** private club. **Trail Fee:** private club.
Reservation policy: private club members and guests of members only.
Winter condition: the golf course is open all year long. Dry conditions.
Terrain: flat, some hills. **Tees:** all grass. **Spikes:** no metal spikes in summer.
Services: club rentals, lessons, restaurant, beer, wine, pro shop, driving range.
Comments: ranked #72 in *Golf Digest's* best 100 in the U.S. Robert Cupp
design. The course sports bentgrass tees, fairways and greens. Pumpkin Ridge
was host to the 1996 U.S. Amateur and hosted the 1997 U.S. Womens Open
Championship in the summer. A true gem that is nothing short of spectacular.

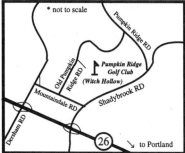

Directions: From Hwy 26 (Sunset Hwy)
take Dersham exit. Proceed north for .3
miles, take right onto Mountaindale Road,
proceed east for 1.0 miles, take a left onto
Old Pumpkin Ridge Road. Proceed for .3
miles to the entrance on your right.

Course Yardage & Par:
T-7014 yards, par 72; C-6513 yards, par 72.
M-6009 yards, par 72; W-5277 yards, par 72.

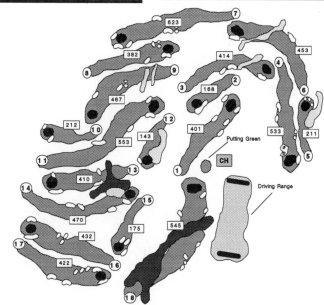

Quail Point Golf Course (semi-private, 9 hole course)
1200 Mira Mar; Medford, OR 97504
Phone: (541) 857-7000. Fax: (541) 857-7074. Internet: none.
Pro: Mike Byrd, PGA. Superintendent: Eric Breitling.
Rating/Slope: C 69.8/126; M 68.8/123; W 68.4/115. **Course record:** 30.
Green fees: $22/14 B-4 noon; $20/$12 after noon; call for any special rates.
Power cart: $20/$12. **Pull cart:** $3/$2. **Trail fee:** not allowed.
Reservation policy: please call 7 days in advance to schedule tee-times.
Winter condition: the golf course open all year long, weather permitting.
Terrain: relatively hilly. **Tees:** all grass. **Spikes:** metal spikes permitted.
Services: club rentals, lessons, snack bar, pro shop, driving range, putting green.
Comments: This challenging new nine hole course opened in August of 1993.
The golf course offers resort conditions year round. Water comes into play on
6 holes. The hilly terrain makes this course play longer than yardage indicates.

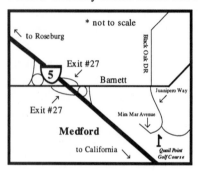

Directions: From I-5 N&S take exit #27
in Medford to Barnett Road. Travel east
to Ellendale, turn right on Ellendale and
then follow this to the golf course.

Course Yardage & Par:
C-3056 yards, par 35.
M-2949 yards, par 35.
W-2557 yards, par 35.

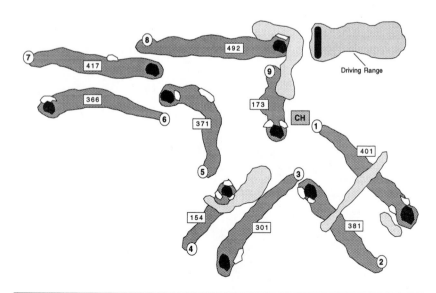

Quail Run Golf Course (public, 9 hole course)

16725 Northridge Drive; P.O. Box 4279; Sunriver, OR 97707
Phone: (541) 536-1303. Fax: (541) 536-1076. Internet: none.
Pro: Bill Martin. Superintendent: none.
Rating/Slope: C 72.2/126; M 70.9/123; M 69.6/119 W 69.6/116. **Record:** 33.
Green fees: $30/$17 all week long. Call for additional special rates.
Power cart: $20/$12. **Pull cart:** $3/$2. **Trail fee:** $5 for personal carts.
Reservation policy: yes, please call ahead 7 days for your starting times.
Winter condition: the golf course is closed December through February.
Terrain: flat, some undulations. **Tees:** grass. **Spikes:** metal spikes permitted.
Services: club rentals, lessons, coffee shop, beer, wine, pro shop, driving range, putting & chipping greens. **Comments:** USGA spec built greens. Very scenic golf course with views of Mount Bachelor and the surrounding countryside. Excellent 9 hole course to play when visting or vacationing in Central Oregon.

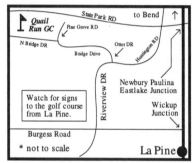

Directions: the golf course is located 8 miles south of Sunriver Oregon off of Highway 97. Turn right on the Newbury Paulina/Eastlake Junction. Go across the railroad tracks and follow signs to the golf course. Look for signs marking your way to the golf course from Hwy 97.

Course Yardage & Par:
C-3512 yards, par 36.
M-3185 yards, par 36.
M-3023 yards, par 36.
W-2707 yards, par 36.

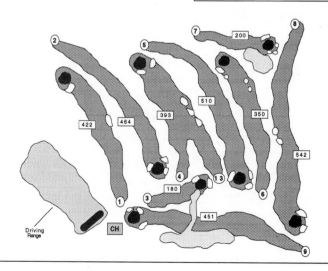

Quail Valley Golf Course (public, 18 hole course)

12565 NW Aerts Road; P.O. Box 200; Banks, OR 97106
Phone: (503) 324-4444. Fax: (503) 324-7500. Internet: none.
Pro: Doug Hixson, PGA. Superintendent: N/A.
Rating/Slope: C 71.6/122; M 68.9/114; W 71.5/117. **Course record:** 66.
Green fees: Monday-Thursday $29/$15; Friday-Sunday & holidays $32/$18.
Power cart: $22/$11. **Pull cart:** $3/$1.50. **Trail fee:** not allowed.
Reservation policy: please call the pro shop 7 days in advance for tee times.
Winter condition: the golf course open, weather permitting. Dry conditions.
Terrain: mounded. **Tees:** all grass. **Spikes:** metal spikes permitted.
Services: fully stocked pro shop, club rentals, lessons, lounge, snack bar, driving range, putting/chipping green. **Comments:** A beautiful newer course that is worth a special trip. Four lakes, 12 surface acres of water, 600 small trees, and 44 bunkers will challenge your golfing skill at every turn. Great track.

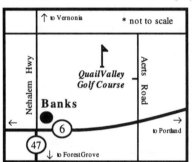

Directions: From Portland, Oregon take highway 26 westbound to Highway 6. Exit onto Highway 6 and proceed to NW Aerts Road, (just 1.5 miles from Highway 26). Turn right on NW Aerts Road and proceed to the golf course. Look for signs marking your way to the golf course.

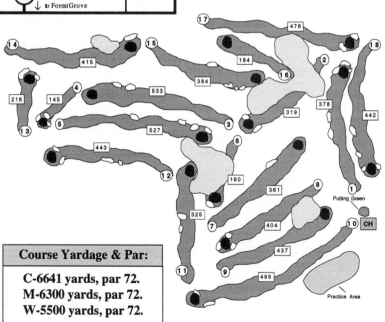

Course Yardage & Par:

C-6641 yards, par 72.
M-6300 yards, par 72.
W-5500 yards, par 72.

Ranch Hills Golf Club (public, 9 hole course)

26710 South Ranch Hills Road; Mulino, OR 97042
Phone: (503) 632-6848, (503) 829-5666. Fax: none.
Owners: Dewey & Dinene Wyatt.
Rating/Slope: M 65.0/108; W 68.8/108.   **Course record:** 28 nine/59 eighteen.
Green fees: W/D $18/$9; W/E $20/$10; Sr. rates; no credit cards.
Power cart $20/10. **Pull cart:** $1.50. **Trail fee:** $3 for personal carts.
Reservation policy: yes, please call up to 3 days in advance for tee-times.
Winter condition: the golf course is open all year long, wet conditions.
Terrain: flat (easy walking). **Tees:** all grass. **Spikes:** metal spikes permitted.
Services: club rentals, snack bar, beer, wine, pop, pro shop, putting green.
Comments: Mill Creek wanders throughout this nine hole golf course putting an emphasis on accuracy off the tee. Golf course can play very tight at times.

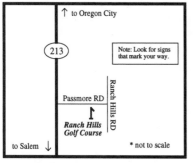

Directions: from Highway 213 S turn left on Passmore Road. Proceed straight ahead for 1.3 miles to the golf course. From Highway 213 N turn right on Passmore Road. Make sure you look for a sign marking your way to the course.

Course Yardage & Par:
C-2895 yards, par 36.
M-2838 yards, par 36.
W-2636 yards, par 37.

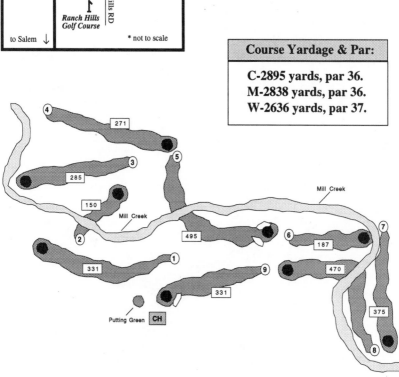

Reames Golf & Country Club (private, 18 hole course)
4201 Highway 97 South; Klamath Falls, OR 97603
Phone: (541) 884-7446. Fax: (503) 882-0391. Internet: none.
Pro: Rick Verbarendse, PGA. Superintendent: Rich Flink.
Rating/Slope: C 71.2/124; M 70.3/123; W 73.3/127. **Course record:** 65.
Green fees: private club, members & guests only; reciprocates; no credit cards.
Power cart: private club. **Pull cart:** private club. **Trail fee:** private club.
Reservation policy: yes, 1 week in advance for members and guests only.
Winter condition: the golf course is open all year, weather permitting, good.
Terrain: flat, some hills. **Tees:** all grass. **Spikes:** metal spikes permitted.
Services: club rentals, lessons, restaurant, lounge, beer, wine, beverages, pro
shop, lockers, showers, putting & chipping greens, driving range, club member-
ships. **Comments:** this is an outstanding golf facility. Large well bunkered
greens and tree-lined fairways make this course a good test of your game.
Landing area's are small in certain parts of the course putting emphasis on shot
placement. If you get a chance to play Reames G&CC be sure not to pass it up.

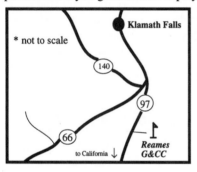

Directions: the golf course is located of Highway 97 south of Klamath Falls. You can see the golf course from the Highway. You will turn east to get to the clubhouse from Highway 97.

Course Yardage & Par:

C-6564 yards, par 72.
M-6371 yards, par 72.
W-5855 yards, par 74.

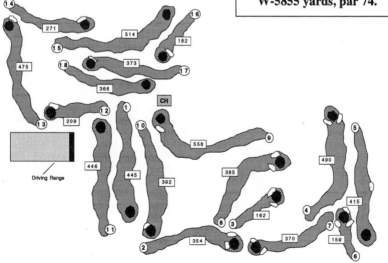

Red Mountain Golf Course (public, 9 hole course)

324 North Schoolhouse Creek Road; Grants Pass, OR 97526
Phone: (541) 479-2297. Fax: none. Internet: none.
Owner: Dave Snook. Superintendent: none.
Rating/Slope: the golf course is not rated. **Course record:** 54.
Green fees: $12/$7; Monday through Friday you can play all day for $15.
Power cart: $8 per nine holes. **Pull cart:** $1. **Trail fee:** $3 for personal carts.
Reservation policy: T-times on a 1st come 1st served basis. Walk-ons welcome.
Terrain: flat, some hills. **Tees:** all grass. **Spikes:** metal spikes permitted.
Services: club rentals, beer, beverages, snack bar, pro shop, putting green.
Comments: formerly Shoestring Golf Course this executive tract sports tree lined fairways and challenging golf. This family run course is a bright spot on the southern Oregon golf scene. Worth a trip if you have time for a quick nine.

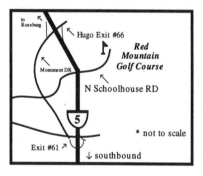

Directions: From I-5 N&S take the Merlin or Hugo exit. Proceed to Monument Drive. Follow to North Schoolhouse Road. Turn east and follow this to the golf course.

Course Yardage & Par:
Blue tees-1049 yards, par 27.
White tees-1265 yards, par 30.
<u>Dual tees for 18 holes:</u>
Blue tees-2314 yards, par 57.
White tees-2314 yards, par 57.

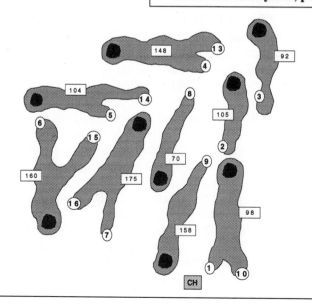

The Reserve Vineyards & G.C.; Cupp Course (semi-private)

4747 S.W. 229th Avenue; Aloha, OR 97007   **(18 hole Course)**

Phone: (503) 649-2345. Fax: 848- 3425. Internet: none.

Pro: Andy Deiro, PGA. Superintendent: none.

Rating/Slope: the golf course is not rated. **Course Record:** 68.

Green fees: weekdays $75 includes cart; weekends $85 includes cart.

Power Cart: included with green fee. **Pull cart:** yes. **Trail fee:** N/A.

Reservation policy: you may call ahead up to 30 days in advance.

Winter Condition: the course is considered dry and open all year long.

Terrain: some hills. **Tees:** all grass. **Spikes:** metal spikes permitted.

Services: club rentals, lessons, lounge, restaurant, snack bar, beer, wine, liquor, showers, lockers, pro shop, driving range, state of the art practice facility.

Comments: the course promises to be one of the premier courses in the Pacific NW. Designed for golfers who appreciate the games tradition the Cupp course is more open with many water hazards and rolling mounds. Both courses wind along the Gordon and Butternut Creeks.

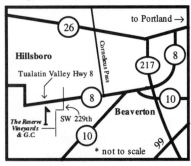

Directions: from Highway 26 West Cornelius Pass. Turn right on the Tualatin Valley Highway 8 exit at SW 229th where you will turn left. Proceed on SW 229th to the golf course. Look for signs that are posted along the way.

The Reserve Vineyards & G.C.; Fought Course (semi-private)

4747 S.W. 229th Avenue; Aloha, OR 97007   **(18 hole Course)**

Phone: (503) 649-2345. Fax: 848- 3425. Internet: none.

Pro: Tim Berg, PGA. Superintendent: none.

Rating/Slope: T 74.3/134; C 72.7/129; M 69.7/124; &0.1/121.

Green fees: weekdays $75 includes cart; weekends $85 includes cart.

Power Cart: included with green fee. **Pull cart:** yes. **Trail fee:** N/A.

Reservation policy: you may call ahead up to 30 days in advance.

Winter Condition: the course is considered dry and open all year long.

Terrain: some hills. **Tees:** all grass. **Spikes:** metal spikes permitted.

Services: club rentals, lessons, lounge, restaurant, snack bar, beer, wine, liquor, showers, lockers, pro shop, driving range, state of the art practice facility.

Comments: designed by award winning architects John Fought and Robert Cupp the golf experience at The Reserve promises to be unique. The Fought course is the more traditional of the two, there are numerous sand bunkers, dramatic terrain changes, and many older established tree stands. The vineyard/ winery theme will be woven throughout the architecture of both the courses.

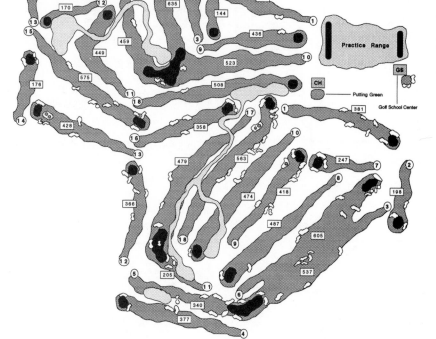

The Cupp Course

Practice Range

GS

CH

Putting Green

Golf School Center

The Fought Course

The Resort at the Mountain (public, 27 hole course)
68010 E Fairway Avenue; Welches, OR 97067
Phone: (503) 622-3151. Fax: none. Internet: none.
Pro: Darrin Nash, PGA. Superintendent: Tony Lasher. Course record: 64.
Green fees: Mon.-Thur. $32/$22; Fri.-Sun. $38/$22; M/C, VISA, AMEX, DIS.
Power cart: $26/$16. **Pull cart:** $4/$2. **Trail fee:** not allowed.
Reservation policy: yes, please call 2 weeks in advance, maximum non guests.
Winter condition: the golf course is open all year long. Fair conditions
Terrain: flat, some hills. **Tees:** all grass. **Spikes:** metal spikes permitted.
Services: club rentals, lessons, snack bar, restaurant, lounge, beer, wine, liquor,
pro shop, lockers, showers, driving range, complete resort. **Comments:** These
27 holes wander through an alpine setting. The facility has a excellent resort
tied to the golf course for those wanting to take a golfer's vacation. Good course.

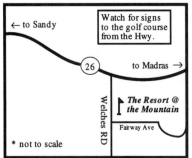

Directions: from Highway 84 proceed
east to the Woodvillage exit to Hwy 26.
Proceed east to Welches, Oregon. South
on Welches Road to the golf course.

Rating/Slope:
Thistle/Foxglove: M 70/119; W 74/123.
Foxglove/Pine Cone: M 68/116; W 70/116.
Pine Cone/Thistle: M 68/114; W 70/115.

Course Yardage & Par:
Thistle Nine:
M-3351 yards, par 36. W-2954yards, par 37.
Fox Glove Nine:
M-3092/3062 yards, par 36. W-2739 yards, par 37.
Pine Cone Nine:
M-2681/2626 yards, par 34. W-2292/2071 yards, par 34.

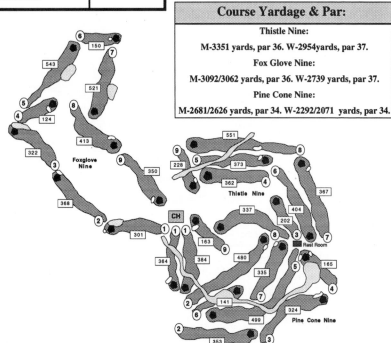

Riveridge Golf Course (public, 18 hole course)

3800 North Delta; Eugene, OR 97408
Phone: (541) 345-9160. **Fax:** (541) 345-1202. **Internet: none.**
Pros: Ric Jeffries, PGA, Al Mundle, PGA. **Superintendent:** Richard Fallon.
Rating/Slope: C 68.6/116; M 67.2/112; W 67.7/112. **Course record:** 63.
Green fees: $24/$15 all week long; $3 off per 9 holes if you wear soft spikes, the pro shop sells them. Sr. rates (Monday through Friday); M/C, VISA.
Power cart: $20/$12. **Pull cart:** $2. **Trail fee:** personal carts not allowed.
Reservation policy: yes, please call 7 days in advance for your tee-times.
Winter condition: the golf course is open all year long, weather permitting.
Terrain: flat, some hills. **Tees:** all grass. **Spikes:** metal spikes permitted.
Services: club rentals, lessons, snack bar, beer, pro shop, driving range, putting & chipping greens. **Comments:** the course has a covered and lighted driving range. The golf course is kept in excellent condition and is worth a stop if in the area. Complete practice facility with putting green, chipping green and bunkers.

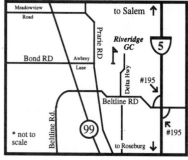

Directions: from I-5 N&S take (exit 195) go west on Beltline to Delta Highway. Go north on Delta Highway for 1.5 miles to the golf course which will be located on your left hand side of the road. Look for signs marking your way to the golf course.

Course Yardage & Par:

C-6262 yards, par 71.
M-6007 yards, par 71.
M-5560 yards, par 71.
W-5197 yards, par 71.

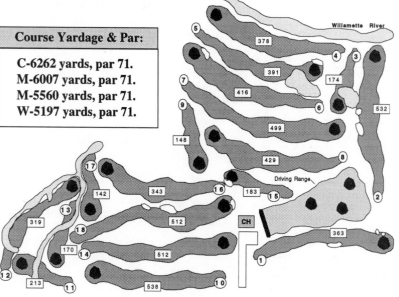

River's Edge Golf Resort (public, 18 hole course)
400 Pro Shop Drive; Bend, OR 97701
Phone: (541) 389-2828. Fax: (541) 389-0870. Internet: none.
Pro: Lyndon Blackwell, PGA. Superintendent: Clint Handsschuch.
Rating/Slope: C 72.6/137; M 71.6/135; M 70.5/129; W 71.8/135. **Record:** 68.
Green fees: $39/$24 all week long; winter and Jr. rates; M/C, VISA.
Power cart: $26/$16. **Pull cart:** $3/$2. **Trail fee:** personal carts not allowed.
Reservation policy: public 1 week ahead. Hotel guests w/ room confirmation.
Winter condition: the course is open all year long depending upon conditions.
Terrain: hillside course. **Tees:** all grass. **Spikes:** metal spikes permitted.
Services: club rentals, lessons, snack bar, beer, wine, pro shop, driving range.
Comments: 2 different nines one narrow and short. The other is longer and
more open. Very scenic with picturesque waterfalls and serene surroundings.
This course will challenge you at every turn. Good central Oregon track.

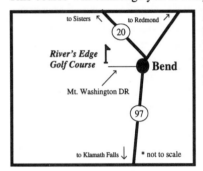

Directions: from Hwy 97, turn into the
road at the south end of the Riverhouse
Motor Inn. Course will be ahead. Course
located at the north end of Bend. Look
for signs marking your turn to the course.

Course Yardage & Par:
C-6683 yards, par 72.
M-6440 yards, par 72.
M-6128 yards, par 72.
W-5381 yards, par 73.

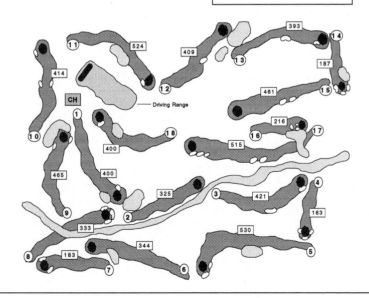

Riverside Golf & Country Club (private, 18 hole course)

8105 NE 33rd Drive; Portland, OR 97211
Phone: (503) 282-7265. Fax: (503) 282-1383. Internet: none.
Pro: Pat Sutton, PGA. Superintendent: Tom Christy.
Rating/Slope: C 72.2/129; M 71.4/128; M 70.4/125; W 70.4/130. **Record:** 65.
Green fees: private club, members & guests of members only; M/C, VISA.
Power cart: private club. **Pull cart:** private club. **Trail fee:** not allowed.
Reservation policy: private club, members & guests of members only.
Winter condition: the golf course is open all year long. Fair conditions
Terrain: flat. **Tees:** all grass. **Spikes:** no metal spikes March to September.
Services: club rentals, lessons, restaurant, lounge, beer, wine, liquor, pro shop,
lockers, showers, driving range, putting & chipping greens, club memberships.
Comments: Mature trees abound at this picturesque course. One of Portland's
best private clubs. Course plays very tough in places. Excellent golf course.

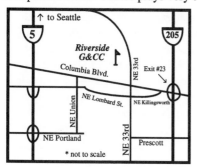

Directions: from I-5 take the Columbia
Street exit and go eastbound to NE 33rd.
Turn left to the course. From I-205 take
the Columbia St. exit and go westbound
for 2 miles to NE 33rd. Turn right.

Course Yardage & Par:
C-6624 yards, par 72.
M-6393 yards, par 72.
M-6075 yards, par 72.
W-5738 yards, par 73.

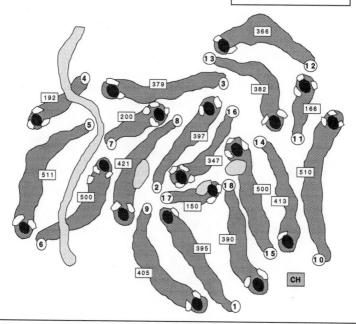

Riverwood Golf Course (public, 9 hole course)

21050 SE Riverwood Road; Dundee, OR 97115
Phone: (503) 864-2667. Fax: (503) 864-2660. Internet: none.
Pro: Gregory C. Brown, PGA. Superintendent: Earl Brown.
Rating/Slope: M 67.4/117; W 69.3/118. **Course record:** 65.
Green fees: W/D $18/$9.50; W/E $19/$11; Jr./Sr. rates, (M-F); no credit cards.
Power cart: $16/$8. **Pull cart:** $1.50. **Trail fee:** $8/$4 for personal carts.
Reservation policy: yes, please call for your tee-times 7 days in advance.
Winter condition: the golf course is open all year long, damp conditions.
Terrain: flat (easy walking). **Tees:** all grass. **Spikes:** metal spikes permitted.
Services: club rentals, lessons, snack bar, beer, wine, pro shop, driving range.
Comments: Course is flat and very easy to walk. This course was built in 1932
and displays many mature trees. Recent improvements make for a challenging 9
hole round. Greens are medium in size and have some green-side bunkers.

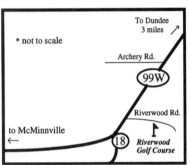

Directions: the golf course is located
1 mile off of Hwy 99W. After traveling
3 miles on Hwy 99W look for Riverwood Road. Turn right to the golf
course. Look for a sign on the east side
of the highway. The golf course located
south of Newburg Oregon.

Course Yardage & Par:
M-2861 yards, par 35.
W-2483 yards, par 35.
Dual tees for 18 holes:
M-5805 yards, par 71.
W-5205 yards, par 71.

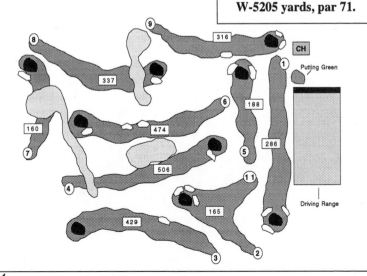

Rock Creek Country Club (private, 18 hole course)

5100 NW Neakahnie; Portland, OR 97213
Phone: (503) 645-1101. Fax: none. Internet: none.
Pro: Rob Croskrey. Superintendent: Pat Hamlin.
Rating/Slope: C 71.9/123; M 71.0/122; W 72.5/125. **Course record:** 63.
Green fees: private, members only; reciprocates; no credit cards.
Power cart: private club. **Pull cart:** private club. **Trail fee:** no charge.
Reservation policy: private club, members and guests of members only.
Winter condition: the golf course is open all year long. Dry conditions.
Terrain: flat, some rolling terrain. **Tees:** grass. **Spikes:** metal spikes permitted.
Services: club rentals, lessons, restaurant, lounge, beer, wine, liquor, pro shop, lockers, showers, driving range, putting and chipping greens, club memberships.
Comments: Beautiful private club in Portland. The course sports several ponds and greenside bunkers to catch any errant shots. Excellent private golf course.

Directions: from I-5 exit on Highway 26 (Sunset Highway West). Go 10 miles to 185th. Turn northbound on 185th and proceed approximately 1.1 miles to the West Union Road Intersection. Turn left and travel westbound for .5 miles to Neakahnie and the golf course.

Course Yardage & Par:
C-6634 yards, par 72. M-6371 yards, par 72. W-5629 yards, par 74.

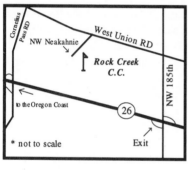

155

Rogue Valley Country Club (private, 27 hole course)
2660 Hillcrest Road; Medford, OR 97504
Phone: (541) 772-4050. Fax: (541) 776-0960
Pro: Jim Wise, PGA. Superintendent: Ken Johnson.
Rating/Slope: Course #1: C 72.1/128; M 70.3/126; W 70.1/122. **Record:** 63.
Green fees: private club, members and guests only; reciprocates ; M/C,VISA.
Power cart: private club. **Pull cart:** private club. **Trail fee:** private club.
Reservation policy: private club, members and guests only.
Winter condition: the golf course is open all year long, weather permitting
Terrain: flat, some hills. **Tees:** all grass. **Spikes:** no metal spikes in summer.
Services: club rentals, lessons, snack bar, restaurant, lounge, beer, wine, liquor,
beverages, pro shop, lockers, showers, driving range, putting & chipping greens.
Comments: Host of the Southern Oregon Golf Championship. Great private
golf course that has large, well bunkered greens and fairly wide fairways.

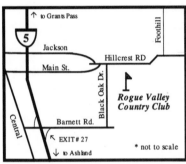

Directions: from I-5 take the Barnett exit.
Travel east on Barnett to Black Oak Rd,
turn left. Proceed straight to Hillcrest Rd.
Turn right on Hillcrest Road to the course.

Course Yardage & Par:
Course #1
T-6666 yards, par 72.
C-6353 yards, par 72.
M-5980 yards, par 72.
W-5283 yards, par 72.

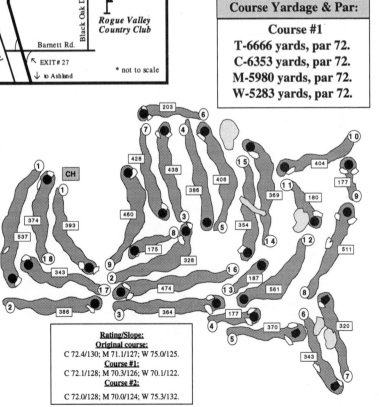

Rating/Slope:
Original course:
C 72.4/130; M 71.1/127; W 75.0/125.
Course #1:
C 72.1/128; M 70.3/126; W 70.1/122.
Course #2:
C 72.0/128; M 70.0/124; W 75.3/132.

Rose City Golf Course (public, 18 hole course)

2200 NE 71st Avenue; Portland, OR 97213
Phone: (503) 253-4744, 292-8570 for Tee-times. **Fax:** (503) 255-8189.
Pro: Hank Childs, PGA. **Superintendent:** Jim Heck.
Rating/Slope: C 70.9/118; M 69.2/115; W 74.4/122; W 71.6/111. **Record:** 61.
Green fees: W/D $19/$10; W/E $21/$11; Jr. & Sr. rates.
Power cart: $24/$12. **Pull cart:** $3/$2. **Trail fee:** $4/$2 for personal carts.
Reservation policy: yes, call six days in advance or visit a week in advance.
Winter condition: the golf course is open all year long. Dry (drains well).
Terrain: flat, some hills. **Tees:** all grass. **Spikes:** metal spikes permitted.
Services: club rentals, lessons, snack bar, restaurant, beer, wine, pop, pro shop, putting green, club memberships. **Comments:** Beautiful old clubhouse surrounded by mature trees. Fairways are tree-lined and can be a factor off of the tee. Greens can generally be found in kept in excellent condition throughout the year. Good public track that can get very busy during the summer months.

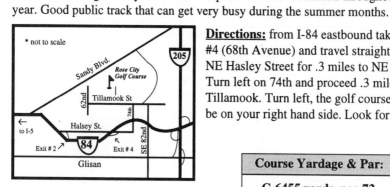

Directions: from I-84 eastbound take exit #4 (68th Avenue) and travel straight on NE Hasley Street for .3 miles to NE 74th. Turn left on 74th and proceed .3 miles to Tillamook. Turn left, the golf course will be on your right hand side. Look for signs.

Course Yardage & Par:
C-6455 yards, par 72.
M-6166 yards, par 72.
W-5619 yards, par 74.

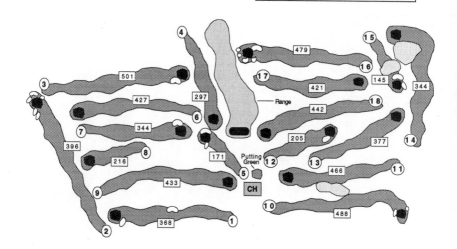

Roseburg Country Club (private, 18 hole course)
5051 NW Garden Valley Road; Roseburg, OR 97470
Phone: (541) 672-4041. Fax: none. Internet: none.
Pro: Pat Huffer, PGA. Superintendent: Gary Whittacker.
Rating/Slope: C 70.5/125; M 68.6/121; W 70.8/116. **Course record:** 62.
Green fees: private club, members & guests of members only; reciprocates.
Power cart: private club. **Pull cart:** private club. **Trail fee:** private club.
Reservation policy: private club, members can call up to 8 days in advance.
Winter condition: the course is open all year long weather permitting, damp.
Terrain: some hills, flat areas. **Tees:** grass. **Spikes:** metal spikes permitted.
Services: club rentals, lessons, snack bar, restaurant, lounge, beer, wine, liquor,
pop, pro shop, lockers, showers, driving range, putting & chipping greens, pool.
Comments: Relatively short course with well bunkered, undulating greens. The
fairways are tree-lined with narrow landing area's. The pro states that "no one
ever tears this course up". Excellent country club with a relaxed look and feel.

Directions: from I-5 take exit #125 at
Roseburg (Garden Valley). Travel west
for 4.5 miles on NW Garden Valley Road
to the golf course which will be on your
right hand side. Look for a sign at the turn.

Course Yardage & Par:
C-6316 yards, par 71.
M-5965 yards, par 71.
W-5529 yards, par 72.

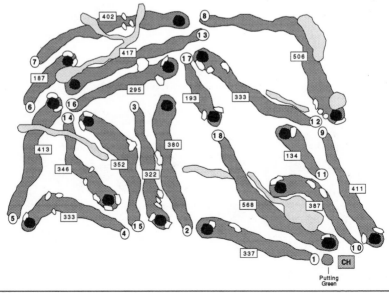

Round Lake Resort (public, 9 hole course)
4000 Round Lake Road; Klamath Falls, OR 97601
Phone: (541) 884-2520. **Fax: none. Internet: none.**
Manager: Walt Zelinski. Pro: Chuck Michielsen.
Rating/Slope: the golf course is not rated. **Course record:** 25.
Green fees: $11/$7 all week long; student & Sr. rates; no credit cards.
Power cart: none available. **Pull cart:** $1. **Trail fee:** not allowed.
Reservation policy: not needed. Tee-times are on a first come first served basis.
Winter condition: course is closed March or April depending on the weather.
Terrain: flat (easy walking). **Tees:** all grass. **Spikes:** metal spikes permitted.
Services: club rentals, snack bar, lessons, beverages, pro shop, RV parking.
Comments: the golf course offers discount greens fee rates for people who are staying at the RV park. This short has some trees lining the fairways but is fairly wide open. Greens are on the small side leaving you a real test at scoring from the fairway. The course sports one lake and a stream that runs through 2 holes.

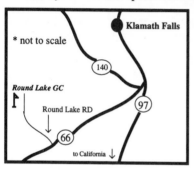

Directions: from Hwy 97 take Hwy 66 (Ashland Highway) to Round Lake Road. The golf course is located approximately 3.5 miles up Round Lake Road. The golf course will be located on your right hand side. Look for signs marking your way to the golf course.

Course Yardage & Par:
M-1512 yards, par 29.
W-1512 yards, par 29.

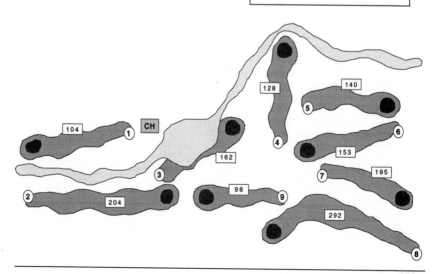

Running Y Ranch Resort (resort, 18 hole course)
5790 Coopers Hawk Road; Running Y, OR 97601
Phone: (541) 880-5580. Fax: (541) 850-5581. Internet: none.
Manager: Michael Justin. Superintendent: Larry Raschko.
Rating/Slope: T 73.0/125; C 70.4/121; M 67.6/116; W 66.3/120. **Record:** 67.
Green fees: $42/$24 all week long; M/C, VISA.
Power cart: $26/$18. **Pull cart:** $4/$2. **Trail fee:** not allowed.
Reservation policy: you may call up to 2 weeks in advance for tee-times.
Golf packages may call well in advance. No time limit.
Winter condition: the golf course is open all year depnding on the weather.
Terrain: flat, some hills. **Tees:** all grass. **Spikes:** metal spikes permitted.
Services: club rentals, snack bar, beer, wine, pro shop, driving range, putting
& chipping greens, practice bunker. **Comments:** this Arnold Palmer designed
championship course is nothing short of spectacular. Be sure to make a reserva-
tion to play as this is a must come and play golf course. Worth a special trip.

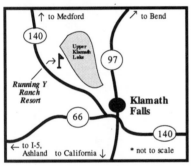

Directions: the golf course is located
off of Hwy 140, 7.5 miles west of
Klamath Falls, Oregon. Look for signs.

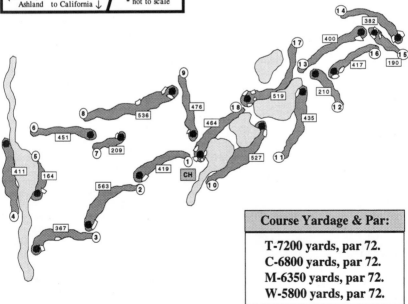

Course Yardage & Par:

T-7200 yards, par 72.
C-6800 yards, par 72.
M-6350 yards, par 72.
W-5800 yards, par 72.

Sah-Hah-Lee Golf Course & Driving Range (public, 18 holes)
17104 SE 130th Ave; Clackamas, OR 97015
Phone: (503) 655-9249, 655-3215 (range). **Fax:** (503) 655-0970.
Pro: Don Otto, PGA. **Superintendent:** not available.
Rating/Slope: the golf course is not rated. **Course record:** 47.
Green fees: W/D $12/$7; W/E $13/$8; Jr. & Sr. rates weekdays only, $10/$6.
Power cart: none. **Pull cart:** $2/$1. **Trail fee:** personal carts not allowed.
Reservation policy: call 1 week in advance, 7 days a week for tee-times.
Winter condition: the golf course is open all year long. Excellent drainage.
Terrain: flat (easy walking). **Tees:** all grass. **Spikes:** metal spikes permitted.
Services: club rentals, lessons, snack bar, beer, pop, pro shop, driving range.
Comments: great par 3 layout, you will use every iron in your bag. Excellent driving range and practice facility for those wanting to practice their games.

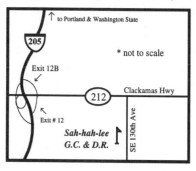

Directions: from I-205 northbound & southbound exit at Highway 212 going eastbound. Proceed to SE 130th Avenue and head southbound to the golf course. Look for signs to the golf course.

Course Yardage & Par:
M-2477 yards, par 54.
W-2294 yards, par 54.

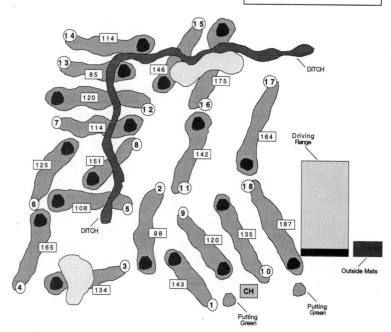

Saint Helens Golf Course (public, 9 hole course)

57246 Hazen Road; Warren, OR 97053
Phone: (503) 397-0358. Fax: (503) 397-1408. Internet: none.
Pro: Jeff Stirling, PGA. Superintendent: Jeff Stirling.
Rating/Slope: M 68.0/116; W 70.3/108. **Course record:** 65.
Green fees: W/D $17/$9; W/E $22/$12; Sr. rates $15/$8; M/C, VISA.
Power cart: $24/$12. **Pull cart:** $2. **Trail fee:** $10/$5 for personal carts.
Reservation policy: yes, please call 7 days in advance for your tee-times.
Winter condition: the golf course is open all year long, weather permitting.
Terrain: flat, some hills. **Tees:** all grass. **Spikes:** metal spikes permitted.
Services: club rentals, snack bar, beer, wine, pro shop, practice range.
Comments: Course has challenging greens and lush fairways. The varied terrain gives the golfer a wide variety of lies from the fairway. The course can usually be found in fair shape in the summer months. Not a bad walking golf course.

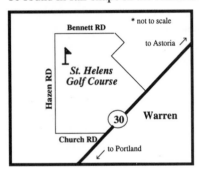

Directions: from Highway 30 go west on Church Road for 1.5 miles. At Hazen Road turn right. The golf course is located .5 miles ahead on your right hand side. **Note:** Look for signs marking the way to the course from the highway.

Course Yardage & Par:
M-2934 yards, par 36.
W-2663 yards, par 36.
Dual tees for 18 holes:
M-6003 yards, par 71.
W-5503 yards, par 73.

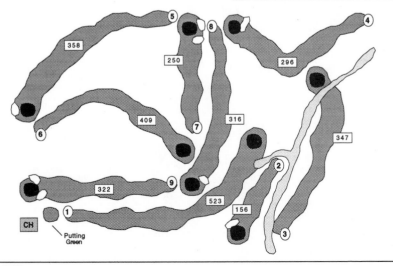

Salem Golf Club (semi-private, 18 hole course)
2025 Golf Course Road South; Salem, OR 97302
Phone: (503) 363-6652. Fax: none. Internet: none.
Pro: Danny Moore, PGA. Superintendent: Mike O'Neill.
Rating/Slope: C 69.6/118; M 68.0/114; W 72.9/119. **Course record:** 64.
Green fees: $35/$18 all week long; call for special rates; M/C, VISA.
Power cart: $20/$10. **Pull cart:** $1. **Trail fee:** $20/$10 for personal carts.
Reservation policy: call ahead for play after men's and women's clubs daily.
Winter condition: the golf course open all year long. Fair conditions.
Terrain: flat, some hills. **Tees:** all grass. **Spikes:** metal spikes permitted.
Services: club rentals, lessons, custom club fitting, snack bar, restaurant,
beer, wine, pro shop. **Comments:** club was established in 1928. Beautiful old
colonial style clubhouse in a picturesque setting. Visitors are welcome with re-
stricted tee-times so be sure to call ahead. Excellent course that is worth a trip.

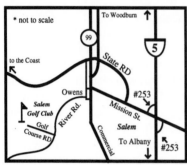

Directions: from I-5 N take the Parkway
exit #248 and proceed north on Commercial to Owens. Turn left on Owens which
turns into River Road. Course located 1.9
miles ahead. From I-5 S take the North
Santiam exit #253 (Mission St.). Proceed
west on Mission to Commercial turn left.
Proceed to Owens and turn right, Owens
turns into River Road. Course located 1.9
miles ahead on the right hand side.

Course Yardage & Par:
C-6200 yards, par 72; M-5939 yards, par 72; W-5163 yards, par 72.

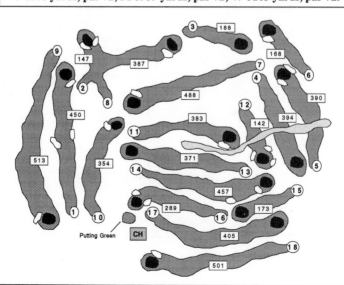

Salemtowne Golf Club (private, 9 hole course)
2900 Oakcrest Drive NW; Salem, OR 97304
Phone: (503) 362-2215. Fax: none. Internet: none.
Manager/Superintendent: Gary Schafer.
Rating/Slope: C 55.9/82; M 55/79; W 58.5/86. **Course record:** 25.
Green fees: private club, members and guests of members only.
Power cart: none. **Pull cart:** none. **Trail fee:** personal carts are not allowed.
Reservation policy: private club, members and guests of members only.
Winter condition: the golf course is open all year long weather permitting, dry.
Terrain: flat, some hills. **Tees:** all grass. **Spikes:** metal spikes permitted.
Services: full service private golf club, beverages, putting & chipping greens.
Comments: The golf course is well manicured with excellent greens. The golf course sports many greenside bunkers that will challenge any level of golfer. The course is fairly flat and easy to walk giving the golfer a relaxed round.

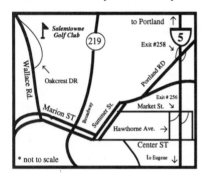

Directions: from I-5 take exit #256 (Market Street Silverton). West on Market Street for 1.6 miles to Summer Street. Turn left on Summer Street and proceed .5 miles to Marion Street. Turn right on Marion St. As you approach the bridge stay right and follow signs for Edgewater Street, Dayton (Highway 221). Proceed for 3.4 miles to Oakcrest Drive. Turn right. The pro shop will be on your left hand side.

Course Yardage & Par:
M-1690 yards, par 30.
W-1657 yards, par 32.

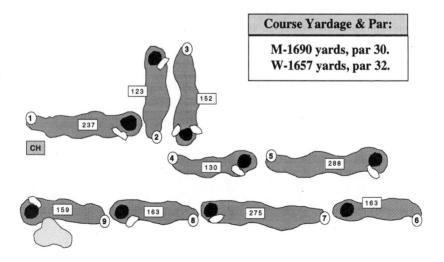

Salishan Golf Links (resort course, 18 hole course)

Highway 101; P.O. Box 118; Gleneden Beach, OR 97388
Phone: (541) 764-3632, 1-800-890-0387. **Fax: none. Internet: none.**
Pro: Grant Rogers, PGA. **Superintendent:** Mark Snider.
Rating/Slope: C 72.3/132; M 70.4/130; W 72.3/128. **Course record:** 66.
Green fees: $60/$35; lower rates lodge guests; seasonal rates; M/C, VISA, DIS.
Power cart: $26/$15. **Pull cart:** $5/$3. **Trail fee:** personal carts not allowed.
Reservation policy: yes, please call up to 2 weeks in advance for tee times.
Winter condition: the golf course is open all year long. Damp conditions.
Terrain: flat, some hills. **Tees:** all grass. **Spikes:** metal spikes permitted.
Services: club rentals, lessons, restaurant, beer, wine, pro shop, driving range,
full service accommodations, putting & chipping greens, 18 hole putting course.
Comments: Course was selected as one of the top resort courses in America by
Golf Digest in 1992. The course has gone through some reconstruction phases
in the past year that should enhance the tracks playability. Excellent facility.

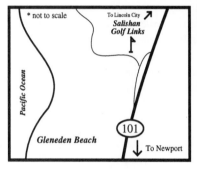

Directions: from I-5 take Ocean Beaches
Highway to Highway 101. The golf course
is located just south of Lincoln City in the
town of Gleneden Beach on the west side
of Highway 101. Look for signs marking
your turn to the golf course.

Course Yardage & Par:
C-6453 yards, par 72.
M-6203 yards, par 72.
W-5389 yards, par 72.

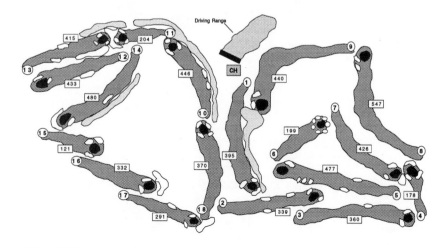

Sandelie Golf (public, 27 hole course)

28333 SW Mountain Road; West Linn, OR 97068
Phone: (503) 682-2022. Fax: none. Internet: none.
Owners: Bill & Jan Kaiser. Superintendent: Bill Kaiser.
Rating/Slope: M 66.6/99; W 72.0/109. **Course record:** 66.
Green fees: W/D $18/$9; W/E $20/$10; Sr. rates on W/D's; no credit cards.
Power cart: power carts are not available. **Pull cart:** $2. **Trail fee:** N/A.
Reservation policy: please call in 7 days in advance for tee-times.
Winter condition: the golf course is open all year long weather permitting.
Terrain: flat, some hills. **Tees:** all grass. **Spikes:** metal spikes permitted.
Services: club rentals, snacks, beverages, small pro shop club memberships.
Comments: fair conditioned golf course set back in the country among rolling
hills and tree lined fairways. Greens are large with few hazards fronting them.
The course does have some water that the golfer will have to contend with.

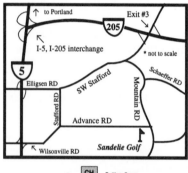

Directions: from I-205 N&S take exit #3
(Stafford Road). Travel west on Stafford
Road for .8 miles to SW Mountain Road.
Turn left. The golf course is located 3.3
miles ahead on your right. Look for signs
that are posted along your route to the
golf course. The way is well marked.

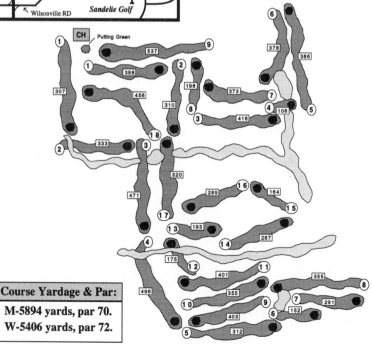

Course Yardage & Par:
M-5894 yards, par 70.
W-5406 yards, par 72.

Sandpines Golf Links (public, 18 hole course)

1201 35th Street; Florence, OR 97439
Phone: (541) 997-1940 or call 1-800-917-4653. Fax: none.
Pro: Jim Skaugstad, PGA. Superintendent: Darrell Fields.
Rating/Slope: T 74.0/129; C 71.7/125; M 69.5/120; W 71.1/123. **Record:** 67.
Green fees: $45/$35 summer rates; $25 winter rates; M/C, VISA, AMEX.
Power cart: $26/$18. **Pull cart:** $4/$2. **Trail fee:** not allowed.
Reservation policy: you may call up to 14 days in advance for tee-times.
Winter condition: the golf course open all year long. Very dry conditions.
Terrain: flat, some small hills. **Tees:** grass. **Spikes:** metal spikes permitted.
Services: club rentals, lessons, snack bar, beer, pro shop, driving range.
Comments: a newer Rees Jones design, this golf course is built on the Oregon sand dunes. The course is a links style course where water comes into play on three holes. The course was voted best new public course in the United States for 1993 by *Golf Digest*. Be sure to include Sandpines G.L. in any vacation.

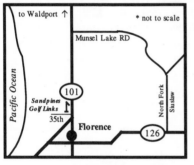

<u>Directions:</u> From Highway 101 turn west on 35th street to the golf course. The course is located in the north city limits. Look for signs marking your way to the golf course the way is well marked.

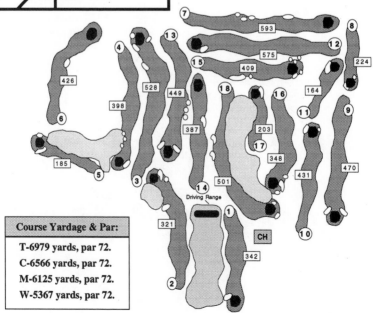

Course Yardage & Par:
T-6979 yards, par 72.
C-6566 yards, par 72.
M-6125 yards, par 72.
W-5367 yards, par 72.

Santiam Golf Club (public, 18 hole course)

off of Highway 22; P.O. Box 447; Stayton, OR 97383
Phone: (503) 769-3485. Fax: none. Internet: none.
Pro: Jack Coppedge, PGA. Superintendent:
Rating/Slope: C 69.9/1123; M 68.8/119; W 72.2/122. **Course record:** 63.
Green fees: $25/$15 all week long; M/C, VISA; senior rates on Friday, $20/$15.
Power cart: $20/$11. **Pull cart:** $2. **Trail fee:** $10 for personal carts.
Reservation policy: yes, please call 7 days in advance for weekends, holidays.
Winter condition: the golf course is open all year long. Dry, drains very well.
Terrain: flat (easy walking). **Tees:** grass. **Spikes:** metal spikes permitted.
Services: club rentals, lessons, snack bar, restaurant, lounge, beer, wine, liquor, driving range, putting & chipping greens. **Comments:** Course is a good test of golf with lots of trees, water and creeks to challenge any golfer. Good walking course that is popular with the locals. This course can get very busy in summer.

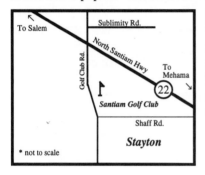

Directions: from I-5 take the Stayton exit. Travel approximately 12 miles eastbound on Highway 22 to the course. The golf course is located on the south side of the Highway 22. **Note:** be sure to look for the sign to the golf course from the Highway marking your turn to the clubhouse.

Course Yardage & Par:
C-6387 yards, par 72.
M-6157 yards, par 72.
W-5697 yards, par 75.

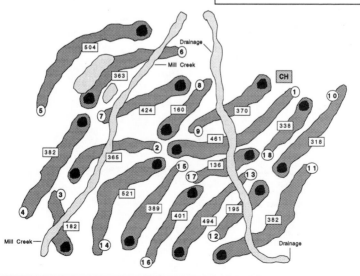

Seaside Golf Course (public, 9 hole course)
451 Avenue U; Seaside, OR 97138
Phone: (503) 738-5261. Fax: none. Internet: none.
Manager/Pro: Wayne Fulmer. Superintendent: Wayne Fulmer.
Rating/Slope: M 64.9/104; W 69.6/106. **Course record:** 28.
Green fees: Mon.-Thur. $16/$8; Fri.-Sunday $18/$9; M/C, VISA, DISCOVER.
Power cart: $20/$10. **Pull cart:** $1.50. **Trail fee:** $5 for personal carts.
Reservation policy: not required, course is run on a first come first served basis.
Winter condition: the golf course is open all year long, wet conditions.
Terrain: flat (easy walking). **Tees:** grass. **Spikes:** metal spikes permitted.
Services: club rentals, snack bar, restaurant, lounge, beer, wine, liquor, pro shop.
Comments: easy to walk and friendly track. Course located on the fantastic Oregon coast. The Necamicum River runs through the whole golf course and is a major factor. Fair public course that is great for quick 9 hole golf fix.

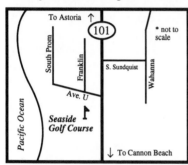

Directions: from Highway 101 turn west on Avenue U. The golf course will be located on your left hand side. (The golf course is located at the south end of the town of Seaside Oregon). The golf course can be seen from Highway 101.

Course Yardage & Par:
M-2593 yards, par 35.
W-2593 yards, par 35.

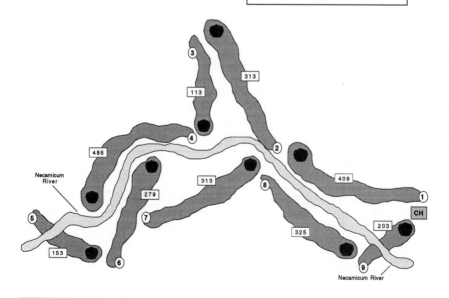

Senior Estates Golf & Country Club (private, 18 hole course)
1776 Country Club Drive; Woodburn, OR 97071
Phone: (503) 981-0189. Fax: none. Internet: none.
Pro: Jim White, PGA. Superintendent: Curt Smith.
Rating/Slope: M 65.5/100; W 67.7/109. **Course record:** 63.
Green fees: private club members & guests only; reciprocates; M/C, VISA.
Power cart: private club. **Pull cart:** private club. **Trail fee:** not allowed.
Reservation policy: no, private club, members & guests of members only.
Winter condition: the golf course is open all year long. Wet conditions.
Terrain: very flat. **Tees:** all grass. **Spikes:** metal spikes permitted.
Services: club rentals, lessons, restaurant, beer, wine, pro shop, putting green.
Comments: Easy walking golf course. The course is well taken care of. Very
popular senior course with many retirement homes around the layout.

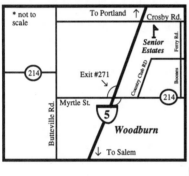

Directions: From I-5 take the Woodburn
exit. Travel east on Newberg Hwy for .5
miles to Country Club Dr. Turn left.
Follow for .3 miles to the course entrance
on your right.

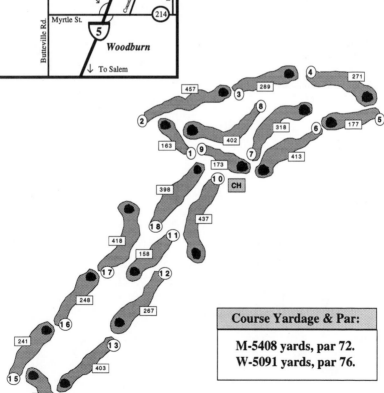

Course Yardage & Par:

M-5408 yards, par 72.
W-5091 yards, par 76.

Shadow Butte Municipal Golf Course (public, 18 holes)

Butler Boulevard; Box 684; Ontario, OR 97914
Phone: (541) 889-9022. Fax: none. Internet: none.
Pro: John Wallace, PGA. Superintendent: none.
Rating/Slope: C 70.4/112; M 69.3/110; W 73.3/120. **Course record:** 64.
Green fees: $11.50/$9.50; M/C, VISA. Special rates on Mondays $10 all day.
Power cart: $15/$7.50. **Pull cart:** $3/$2. **Trail fee:** $5 for personal carts.
Reservation policy: not needed. Tee-times are on a first come first served basis.
Winter condition: the course is closed from November 15th to February 15th.
Terrain: flat, some hills. **Tees:** all grass. **Spikes:** metal spikes permitted.
Services: club rentals, lessons, snack bar, lounge, beer, wine, liquor, pro
shop, lockers, putting & chipping greens, driving range, club memberships.
Comments: The greens are large and have bunkers fronting them on nearly
every hole. Easy walking course that is challengeing to every level of golfer.

Directions: from I-84 take exit #376 and
proceed westbound on Idaho. Turn left
on 9th and proceed to 4th Avenue. At 4th
Avenue turn right to Cairo Boulevard.
Turn left on Cairo Boulevard. Proceed
to Butler Blvd. and turn right on Butler
Blvd. Follow to Golf Course Road and
turn right to the golf course. The golf
course is located next to the airport on
the southwest edge of the city.

Course Yardage & Par:
C-6847 yards, par 72.
M-6542 yards, par 72.
W-5727 yards, par 74.

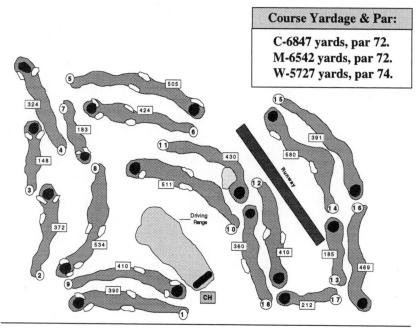

Shadow Hills Country Club (private, 18 hole course)

92512 River Road; Junction City, OR 97448
Phone: (541) 998-8441. Fax: (541) 998-6779. Internet: none.
Pro: Mark Keating, PGA. Superintendent: Randy Marshall.
Rating/Slope: C 73.4/132; M 71.6/130; M 71.0/128; W 70.4/118. **Record:** 61.
Green fees: private, members & guests only, reciprocates; M/C, VISA.
Power cart: private club. **Pull cart:** private club. **Trail fee:** not allowed.
Reservation policy: reciprocates please call 2 days in advance for tee-times.
Winter condition: the golf course is open all year long weather permitting.
Terrain: flat (easy walking). **Tees:** all grass. **Spikes:** no metal spikes.
Services: lessons, restaurant, lounge, beer, wine, liquor, beverages, pop, shop,
showers, lockers, driving range, putting & chipping greens, club memberships.
Comments: Course is noted for the lush fairways and some of the best greens
in Oregon. The course sports a great deal of water and many greenside bunkers.

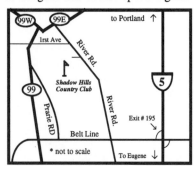

Directions: from I-5 N&S take exit #195
and travel west on Beltline to River Road.
Travel northbound on River Road. The
golf course is about 10 minutes from here.
From Highway 99 travel eastbound on
River Road to the golf course.

Course Yardage & Par:
C-7007 yards, par 72.
M-6726 yards, par 72.
M-6447 yards, par 72.
W-5830 yards, par 72.

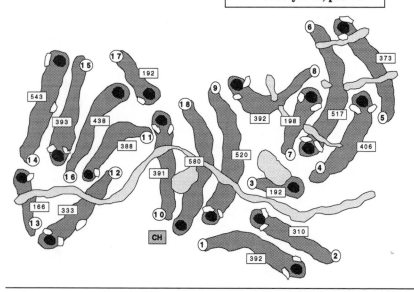

Shield Crest Golf Course (public, 18 hole course)

3151 Shield Crest Drive; Klamath Falls, OR 97603
Phone: (541) 884-1493. Fax: (541) 884-8946. Internet: none.
Pro: John Humphrey, PGA. Superintendent: Ward Walters
Rating/Slope: C 72.1/122; M 70.6/120; M 68.6/109; W 73.4/118. **Record: 65.**
Green fees: W/D $22/$14; W/E $25/$18; (Sr. rates Mon.-Thur.); M/C, VISA.
Power cart: $20/$11. **Pull cart:** $2. **Trail fee:** personal carts not allowed.
Reservation policy: yes, please call 24 hours in advance for your tee-times.
Winter condition: the golf course is open all year long weather permitting.
Terrain: flat, some hills. **Tees:** all grass. **Spikes:** metal spikes permitted.
Services: club rentals, lessons, restaurant, lounge, beer, wine, liquor, pro shop,
driving range. **Comments:** Water hazards and undulating greens make this well
kept golf course a real challenge. Greens can be very difficult to read at times.
The course is a bargain with green fees around the $25 range. Good public track.

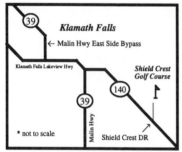

Directions: the golf course is located on the southeast side of town. If you are coming from the north on Hwy 97 take the Alarenda Bypass and proceed through town to Hwy 140. At Highway 140 go east toward Lakeview to the golf course. From Highway 140 go eastbound to Lakeview. The golf course is located 1 mile beyond Merrill, Lakeview Junction.

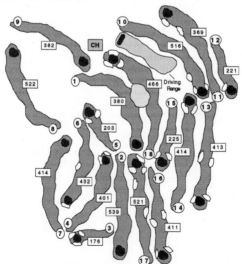

Course Yardage & Par:

C-7005 yards, par 72; M-6687 yards, par 72; W-5410 yards, par 74.

Spring Hill Country Club (private, 18 hole course)
155 Country Club Lane; Albany, OR 97321
Phone: (541) 928-5454. Fax: (541) 924-9166. Internet: none.
Pro: Bill Raschko, PGA. Superintendent: Leonard Jacobs.
Rating/Slope: C 70.5/120; M 69.0/115; W 71.0/123. **Course record:** 63.
Green fees: private club members & guests only; reciprocates.
Power cart: private club. **Pull cart:** private club. **Trail fee:** private club.
Reservation policy: call up to 1 week in advance for tee-times. Members only.
Winter condition: the course is open all year long weather permitting, damp.
Terrain: flat, some hills. **Tees:** all grass. **Spikes:** metal spikes permitted.
Services: club rentals, lessons, restaurant, lounge, beer, wine, liquor, pro shop,
lockers, showers, driving range, putting & chipping greens, club memberships.
Comments: Course has many mature trees that come into play on several holes.
Excellent greens and lush fairways are the trademark of this club. Good track.

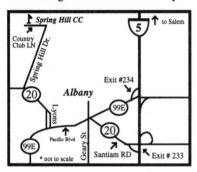

Directions: from I-5 N&S take exit #233
(Santiam Highway 20) and go west to the
Lyons Street (Highway 20) exit. Proceed
through town over the bridge and take
your first right on Springhill Drive. Go to
the Country Club LN turn left to course.

Course Yardage & Par:
C-6432 yards, par 72.
M-6145 yards, par 72.
W-5461 yards, par 73.

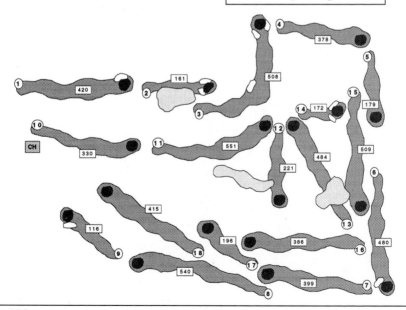

Springfield Country Club (private, 18 hole course)

90333 Sunderman Road; Springfield, OR 97478
Phone: (541) 747-2517. **Fax:** (541) 747-4225. **Internet:** none.
Pro: Fadel Nahle, PGA. **Superintendent:** John Whistler.
Rating/Slope: C 70.2/121; M 68.8/116; W 70.5/115. **Course record:** 63.
Green fees: private club, members & guests of members only.
Power cart: private club. **Pull cart:** private club. **Trail fee:** private club.
Reservation policy: yes, 1 day in advance for members & guests only.
Winter condition: the golf course is open all year long. Damp conditions.
Terrain: relatively hilly. **Tees:** all grass. **Spikes:** metal spikes permitted.
Services: club rentals, lessons, restaurant, lounge, beer, wine, pro shop, lockers,
showers, driving range. **Comments:** Golf course plays longer than the yardage
indicates. Tough greens and several ponds make this golf course a challenge.
A private course that has a golf tradition look and feel. Excellent golf course.

Directions: from I-5 N&S take exit
194 (Highwey 126) and go eastbound
to the 2nd exit (42nd). Turn left on 42nd
and proceed northbound to Marcola
Road. Turn right on Marcola Road and
proceed 5 miles to Sunderman. At
Sunderman turn right to the golf course.

Course Yardage & Par:
C-6341 yards, par 71.
M-5949 yards, par 71.
W-5443 yards, par 73.

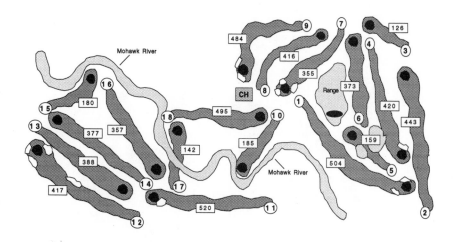

Springwater Golf Course (public, 9 hole course)
25230 South Wallens Road; Estacada, OR 97023
Phone: (503) 630-4586. Fax: none. Internet: none.
Owners: Pat & Vickie O'Meara. Superintendent: Pat O'Meara.
Rating/Slope: M 67.9/120; W 72.8/116. **Course record:** 32.
Green fees: W/D $17/$8.50; W/E & Hol. $21/$10.50; Sr. & Jr. rates (M-F).
Power Cart: $17/$8.50. **Pull Cart:** $2. **Trail fee:** $3 for 9 holes.
Reservation policy: yes, call up to 3 to 5 days in advance for tee times.
Winter condition: the golf course is open all year long. Dry (drains well).
Terrain: relatively hilly. **Tees:** grass. **Spikes:** metal spikes permitted.
Services: club rentals, snack bar, beer, wine, pro shop, putting/chipping greens.
Comments: The golf course is noted for being very playable during the winter months. Two sets of tees will offer you a different look for those wanting to play a full 18 holes. Greens are medium to large with few hazards fronting them.

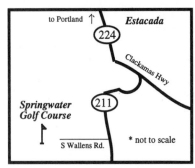

Directions: from Highway 224 exit toward Springwater in Estacada onto Highway 211. From Highway 211 turn right on Wallens Road. Cross over Springwater Road. The course is located on the left hand side of Wallens Road. The course is located 4 miles south of Estacada. Look for signs.

Course Yardage & Par:
M-3003 yards, par 36.
W-2479 yards, par 36.
Dual tees for 18 holes:
M-6204 yards, par 72.
W-5355 yards, par 73.

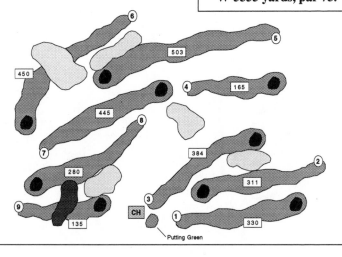

Stewart Meadows (public, 9 hole course)

1801 South Holly Street; Medford, OR 97501
Phone: (541) 770-6554. Fax: none. Internet: none.
Pro: Dan Coughlin. Superintendent: Rod Smith.
Rating/Slope: M 66.1/112; W 67.2/116. **Course record: 65.**
Green fees: $20/$12; Jr. rates, Sr. rates on Thursday's only $12/$7.
Power cart: $9/$5 per person. **Pull cart:** $2/$1. **Trail fee:** not available.
Reservation policy: please call 7 days in advance for your tee times.
Winter condition: the golf course is open all year long weather permitting.
Terrain: flat (easy walking). **Tees:** all grass. **Spikes:** metal spikes permitted.
Services: club rentals, lessons, snack bar, beer, wine, pro shop, driving range, putting & chipping greens. **Comments:** A newer golf course that is beautifully mounded and landscaped. Ponds, bunkers, and a creek makes for a challenging 9 holes of golf. The course will soon sport two set of tees for those wanting to play a different 9 on the second time around. This golf course opened in July of 1994 and is fast becoming a local favorite. Worth a trip if you are in the area.

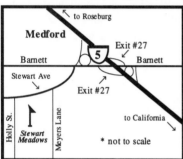

Directions: From I-5 N&S take the Barnett Street exit to South Medford. Cross Barnett Street to Stewart Avenue. Proceed until you reach Holly Street. Turn left on Holly Street. The course is located on the left hand side of Holly Street. Look for signs to the golf course.

Course Yardage & Par:
C-3000 yards, par 36.
M-2858 yards, par 36.
W-2580 yards, par 36.

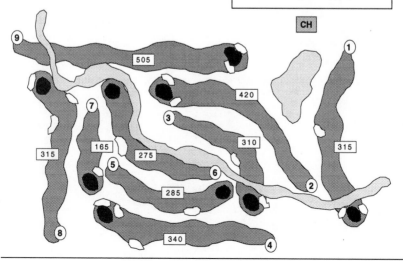

Stewart Park Golf Course (public, 9 hole course)
1005 Stewart Parkway; Roseburg, OR 97470
Phone: (541) 672-4592. Fax: none. Internet: none.
Director of golf: Jim Dowd. Manager: Steven McNelly.
Rating/Slope: M 68.7/112; W 73.5/118. **Course record:** 64.
Green fees: W/D $14/$8.50; W/E $16/$10.50; Sr. rates (M-F); M/C, VISA.
Power cart: $17/$10. **Pull cart:** $2. **Trail fee:** personal carts are not allowed.
Reservation policy: yes, call 1 week in advance for your tee-times.
Winter condition: the golf course is open all year long. Wet at times.
Terrain: flat, some hills. **Tees:** all grass. **Spikes:** metal spikes permitted.
Services: club rentals, snack bar, beer, wine, pro shop, driving range.
Comments: Monthly discounted rates available. Water hazards, bunkers and
newly planted trees make this course a challenge. The terrain is up and down and
gives the golfer a wide variety of lies from the fairway. Great nine hole tract.

Directions: from I-5 N&S take the City
Center exit (#124) and travel westbound.
Turn right on Stewart Parkway to the golf
course. The golf course will be located on
your right hand side. Look for signs that
are posted at your turns.

Course Yardage & Par:
M-2909 yards, par 35.
W-2835 yards, par 37.

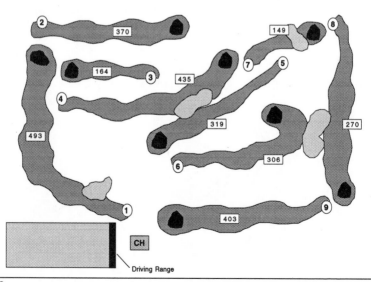

Stoneridge Golf Course (public, 18 hole course)
1523 Satellite Drive; Medford, OR 97504
Phone: (541) 830-GOLF (4653). Fax: none. Internet: none.
General manager: Jim Cochran. Pro: Jim Staal, PGA.
Rating/Slope: T 72.5/132; C 70.6/127; M 68.3/118; W 70.2/120. **Record:** 67.
Green fees: W/D $22/$13; W/E & Holidays $26/$16; ask for special rates.
Power cart: $20/$10. **Pull cart:** $2. **Trail fee:** $10 for personal carts.
Reservation policy: public can call up to 1 week in advance for tee times.
Winter condition: the course is open all year long. Course conditions are good.
Terrain: flat, some moderate hills. **Tees:** grass. **Spikes:** metal spikes permitted.
Services: club rentals, lessons, snack bar, beer, wine, pro shop, driving range.
Comments: beautiful championship golf course. Elevated tees, excellent greens, and lots of character make every hole on this course unique. This course opened in June of 1995 and has been a big hit to all who have played it. Look for the course to expand it's services as time goes on. Good course that is a must play.

Directions: from I-5 N&S take exit #30. Proceed eastbound on Hwy 62. Proceed for 6 miles to Hwy 140 and turn right. Proceed 3 miles to East Antelope Road. turn right. Proceed 1/4 mile to the golf course entrance. Look for signs.

Course Yardage & Par:

T-6738 yards, par 72.
C-6312 yards, par 72.
M-5834 yards, par 72.
W-4986 yards, par 72.

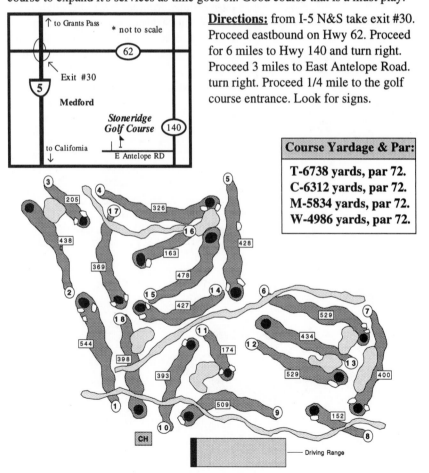

Summerfield Golf & Country Club (semi-private, 9 holes)
10650 SW Summerfield Drive; Tigard, OR 97224
Phone: (503) 620-1200. Fax: none. Internet: none.
Pro: Bill Houston, PGA. Superintendent: none.
Rating/Slope: M 61.4/96; W 65.0/103. **Course record:** 29.
Green fees: $24/$12 all week long; no specail rates; no credit cards.
Power cart: $20/$10. **Pull cart:** $2. **Trail fee:** personal carts are not allowed.
Reservation policy: public times after mens & ladies club play. 2 days ahead.
Winter condition: the golf course is open all year long. Wet conditions.
Terrain: flat, some hills. **Tees:** all grass. **Spikes:** metal spikes permitted.
Services: club rentals, pro shop, lessons, beverages, putting & chipping greens.
Comments: Course is situated among beautiful homes and club house. The golf course is moderately flat so it is very easy to walk. Few hazards come into play off the tee but most of the greens are small in size and fronted by bunkers.

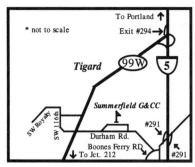

Directions: from I-5 N&S take Highway 99 W exit. Travel south through King City. Turn left on SW Durham. Take the first left at the light on SW Summerfield Drive. Stay right for .5 miles to the golf course which will be located on your right.

Course Yardage & Par:
M-2320 yards, par 33.
W-2231 yards, par 33.
Dual tees for 18 holes:
M-4673 yards, par 66.
W-4452 yards, par 66.

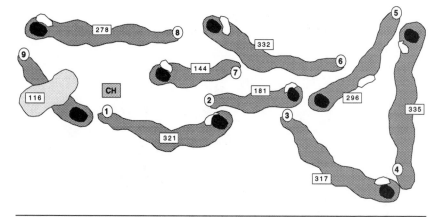

Sunriver Resort (North Woodlands, public, 18 holes)

Highway 97; P.O. Box 3609; Sunriver, OR 97707
Phone: (541) 593-1221, 1-800-962-1769. Fax: (541) 593-3733.
Pro: Jon Noack, PGA. Superintendent: Jim Ramey.
Rating/Slope: C 73.0/131; M 70.2/125; W 70.2/127. **Course record:** 63.
Green fees: $65; lower rates for guests & owners; M/C, VISA, AMEX.
Power cart: $15 per person. **Pull cart:** $5. **Trail fee:** not allowed.
Reservation policy: lodge guests through reservation number, public 2 days.
Winter condition: the golf course is closed from November 1st to April 14th.
Terrain: flat, some hills. **Tees:** all grass. **Spikes:** metal spikes permitted.
Services: club rentals, lessons, snack bar, beer, pro shop, driving range, tennis,
swimming, full resort facility. **Comments:** designed by Robert Trent Jones II.
Rated in *Golf Digest's* top 25 resort courses in America. Excellent golf course
that is a favorite for those vacationing in Central Oregon. Worth a special trip.

Directions: the golf course is located
approximately 15 miles south of Bend,
Oregon off of Highway 97. Look for the
signs to the golf course. Look for signs.

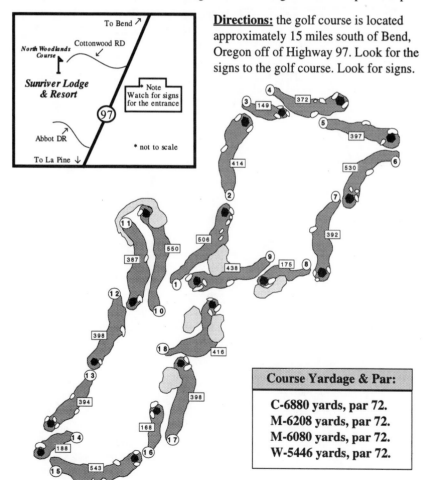

Course Yardage & Par:

C-6880 yards, par 72.
M-6208 yards, par 72.
M-6080 yards, par 72.
W-5446 yards, par 72.

Sunriver Resort (South Meadows, public, 18 holes)
Highway 97; P.O. Box 3609; Sunriver, OR 97707
Phone: (541) 593-1221, 1-800-962-1769. Fax: (541) 593-3733.
Director of Golf Operations: Dave Hall. Superintendent: Jim Ramey.
Rating/Slope: C 72.9/130; M 70.8/125; W 72.1/131 **Course record:** 64.
Green fees: $50/$25; lower rates for guests; M/C, VISA, AMEX.
Power cart: $15 person. **Pull cart:** $5. **Trail fee:** not allowed.
Reservation policy: lodge guests at reservation time, public 2 days in advance.
Winter condition: the golf course is closed from November 1st to April 14th.
Terrain: flat, some hills. **Tees:** all grass. **Spikes:** metal spikes permitted.
Services: club rentals, lessons, snack bar, restaurant, lounge, beer, wine, pro shop, driving range, putting green. **Comments:** Course wanders through lush meadows and tree lined fairways. Fantastic views of Mt. Bachelor throughout the course. These courses are worth a special trip if in the area. Great facility.

<u>Directions:</u> the golf course is located approximately 15 miles south of Bend, Oregon off of Hwy 97. Look for signs.

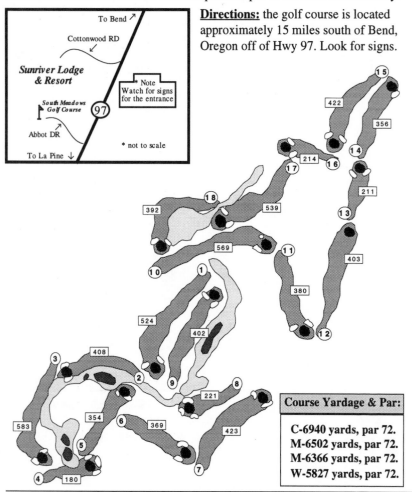

Course Yardage & Par:

C-6940 yards, par 72.
M-6502 yards, par 72.
M-6366 yards, par 72.
W-5827 yards, par 72.

Sunset Bay Golf Course (public, 9 hole course)

11001 Cape Arago Highway; Coos Bay, OR 97420
Phone: (541) 888-9301. Fax: none. Internet: none.
Manager: Rosalie Hyatt. Superintendent: Larry Hyatt.
Rating/Slope: M 68.0/ no slope; W 69.7/ no slope. **Course record:** 31.
Green fees: W/D $16/$9; W/E $17/$10; Jr. rates; M/C, VISA.
Power cart: $22/$12. **Pull cart:** $2/$1. **Trail fee:** personal carts not allowed.
Reservation policy: not needed. Tee-times are on a first come first served basis.
Winter condition: the golf course is open all year long. Dry (drains very well).
Terrain: flat, some hills. **Tees:** all grass. **Spikes:** metal spikes permitted.
Services: club rentals, snack bar, beverages, pro shop, putting/chipping greens.
Comments: Course opened in 1969, and was designed by John Zoller, winner of the 1990 Ross Award for Golf Course architecture. "One of the most interesting courses anywhere" states *Golf Oregon Magazine*. The course is planning to expand to 18 holes in the near future. This course is worth a special trip.

Directions: the golf course is located in the Charleston Recreation Area, 12 miles west of Coos Bay, it adjoins Sunset Bay State Park. From Highway 101 follow the signs to Charleston, State Parks, Ocean Beaches, and the golf course. Look for signs marking your way to the golf course.

Course Yardage & Par:

Yellow/Blue tees: 3020 yards, par 36.
White/Red tees: 2609 yards, par 36.
<u>Dual tees for 18 holes:</u>
Yellow/Blue tees: 6055 yards, par 72.
White/Red tees: 5415 yards, par 72.

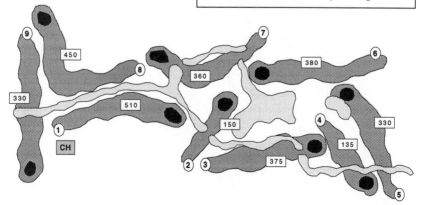

Sunset Grove Golf Club (public, 9 hole course)
41615 NW Osterman Road; Forest Grove, OR 97116
Phone: (503) 357-6044. Fax: none. Internet: none.
Owner: Joan Abarno. Superintendent: Chip Abarno.
Rating/Slope: M 67.6/114; W 67.2/111. **Course record: 63.**
Green fees: W/D $16/$8; W/E $18/$9; Jr. & Sr. rates (weekdays); M/C, VISA.
Power cart: $16/$8. **Pull cart:** $1.50. **Trail fee:** personal carts not allowed.
Reservation policy: yes, call for reservations, they advised them in summer.
Winter condition: the golf course is open all year long. Dry (drains well).
Terrain: flat, easy walking. **Tees:** all grass. **Spikes:** metal spikes permitted.
Services: club rentals, snack bar, beer, wine, pop, pro shop, putting green.
Comments: the golf course is very dry during the winter months so if you are looking for a course to play in wet weather try Sunset Grove. The golf course is wide open and plays to an intermediate level. Greens are fairly large. The golf course is easy to walk and is a favorite for the senior or first time golfer.

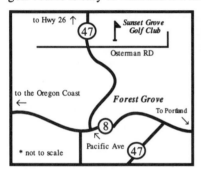

Directions: the golf course is located between Banks and Forest Grove, Ore. From Portland take Highway 26 west to Highway 6, then cut off to Highway 47 south. The golf course is located on the east side of Highway 47. Look for signs.

Course Yardage & Par:
M-2849 yards, par 36.
W-2715 yards, par 37.
Dual tees for 18 holes:
M-5564 yards, par 72.
W-5430 yards, par 74.

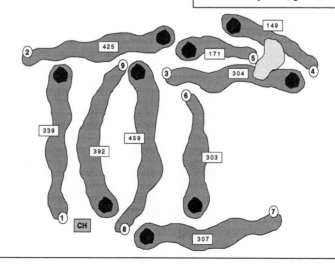

Tokatee Golf Club (public, 18 hole course)
54947 McKenzie Highway; Blue River, OR 97413
Phone: (541) 822-3220, 800 452-6376. Fax: (541) 822-6094.
Mailing address: P.O. Box 989; Eugene, OR 97440
Pro: Dan King, PGA. Superintendent: Ray Telfer.
Rating/Slope: C 72.0/126; M 69.7/119; W 71.2/115. **Course record:** 65.
Green fees: $32/$17 all week long; no special rates; VISA, M/C.
Power cart: $24/$15. **Pull cart:** $3/$2. **Trail fee:** $12 for personal carts.
Reservation policy: yes, call up to 30 days in advance for your tee-times.
Winter condition: the course is closed from November 15th to February 1st.
Terrain: flat, some hills. **Tees:** grass. **Spikes:** metal spikes permitted.
Services: club rentals, coffee shop, beer, pro shop, driving range, lessons.
Comments: the facility has been rated in the top 25 of *Golf Digests* "America's
Best Public Golf Courses" in 1989, 93, 95, 96 and also in 1997. A nice surprise
in Oregon that is a joy to play anytime. This golf course is worth a special trip.

Directions: the golf course is located 47.5
miles east of Eugene, Oregon on Highway
126 (near Blue River). From Highway 126
the golf course is located 7 miles east of
the Blue River exit. Look for signs
marking your way to the golf course.

Course Yardage & Par:
Blue tees: 6842 yards, par 72.
White tees: 6245 yards, par 72.
Red tees: 5651 yards, par 72.

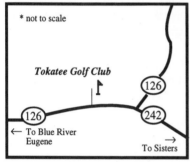

Top O'Scott Golf Course (public, 18 hole course)
12000 SE Stevens Road; Portland, OR 97266
Phone: (503) 654-5050. Fax: (503) 654-0377. Internet: none.
Pro: Scott Nash, PGA. Superintendent: Bob Rose.
Rating/Slope: C M 62.7/103; M 62.1/102; W 61.5/96. **Course record:** 61.
Green fees: W/D \$16/\$9; W/E \$18/\$10; Jr. & Sr. rates; M/C, VISA.
Power cart: \$22/\$11. **Pull cart:** \$2/\$1. **Trail fee:** \$6 for personal carts.
Reservation policy: yes, for weekends, holidays. Please call up to 7 days ahead.
Winter condition: the golf course is open all year long. Damp conditions.
Terrain: flat, some hills. **Tees:** all grass. **Spikes:** metal spikes permitted.
Services: club rentals, lessons, discount pro shop, driving range, putting green.
Comments: Tree lined fairways and tricky greens make this course a challenge.
Beautiful views of the Portland from the east and south. Good course for those
wanting to spend a relaxing day on the links. Much improved from last year.

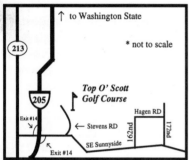

Directions: from I-205 southbound exit
at Sunnyside Road and travel eastbound.
Turn left on Kaiser Hospital, Stevens
Road. The golf course is located across
from the New Hope Church on Stevens
Road. Look for signs marking your way
to the golf course.

Course Yardage & Par:

M-5050 yards, par 67.
W-4605 yards, par 70.

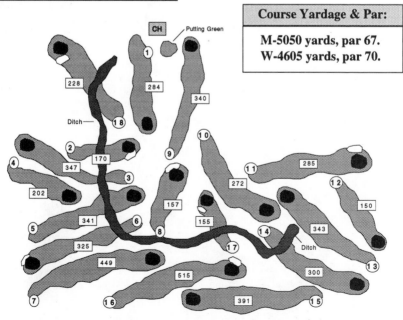

Trysting Tree Golf Club (public, 18 hole course)
34028 Electric Road; Corvallis, OR 97333
Phone: (541) 752-3332. Fax: (541) 754-3550. Internet: none.
Pro: Sean Arey, PGA. Superintendent: Pat Doran.
Rating/Slope: T 73.9/129; C 72.1/128; M 69.9/122; W 71.3/118. **Record:** 64.
Green fees: $27/$15; Oregon College students $14/$9; Jr. rates; no credit cards.
Power cart: $22/$12. **Pull cart:** $3. **Trail fee:** $10 for personal carts.
Reservation policy: yes, call up to 1 week in advance for your tee-times.
Winter condition: the golf course is open all year long. Dry (drains very well).
Terrain: flat, some hills. **Tees:** all grass. **Spikes:** metal spikes permitted.
Services: club rentals, lessons, snack bar, beverages, pro shop, driving range,
putting & chipping greens. **Comments:** Beautiful Scottish links style golf course
with mounds and swales throughout the golf course. Water and bunkers are the
major factor at this course. Be sure not to pass on a chance to play this course.

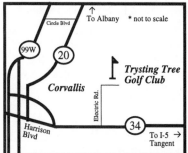

Directions: from I-5 N&S take the exit
for Highway 34 westbound toward the city
of Corvallis. Proceed for 9 miles. Turn
right on Electric Road to the golf course.
The golf course is located on the north
side of the road. Look for signs marking
your way to the golf course.

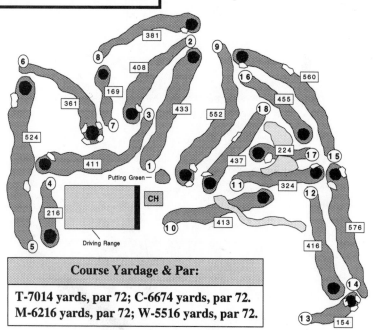

Course Yardage & Par:

T-7014 yards, par 72; C-6674 yards, par 72.
M-6216 yards, par 72; W-5516 yards, par 72.

Tualatin Country Club (private, 18 hole course)
9145 Tualatin Road; Tualatin, OR 97062
Phone: (503) 692-4620. **Fax:** (503) 691-9871. **Internet:** none.
Pro: Jon Peterson, PGA. **Superintendent:** Randy Scholtz.
Rating/Slope: C 72.1/133; M 69.8/125; M 68.9/124; W 71.2/120. **Record:** 63.
Green fees: private club, members & guests of members only.
Power cart: private club. **Pull cart:** private club. **Trail fee:** members only.
Reservation policy: private club members & guests of members only.
Winter condition: the golf course is open all year long. Dry conditions.
Terrain: flat, some hills. **Tees:** all grass. **Spikes:** no metal spikes in summer.
Services: club rentals, lessons, snack bar, beer, wine, clubhouse, pro shop.
Comments: this well conditioned private course is spectacular at every turn. The
fairways are narrow and tree-lined. Greens are medium in size and have bunkers
fronting most of them. This course is a must play if you ever get the chance.

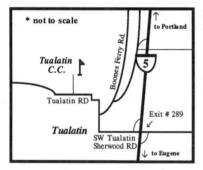

Directions: from I-5N take exit #289
(Tualatin). Turn left over the freeway.
Take the first left on SW Tualatin Sher-
wood RD go .5 miles to Boones Ferry
RD. Turn right. Proceed .3 miles to SW
Tualatin. Turn left on SW Tualatin. Travel
.4 miles to the entrance, turn right.

Course Yardage & Par:
C-6611 yards, par 72; M-6054 yards, par 72. M-5843 yards, par 72; W-5468 yards, par 72.

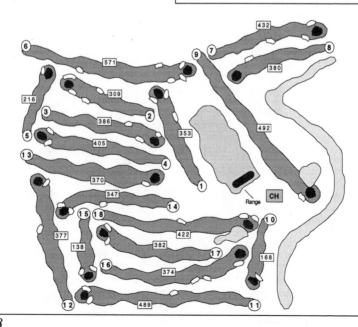

Umatilla Golf Course (public, 18 hole course)

705 Willamette Street; Umatilla, OR 97882
Phone: (541) 922-3006. Fax: (541) 922-5311. Internet: none.
Pro: Todd Demarest, PGA. Superintendent: Joe Matzen.
Rating/Slope: M 69.1/115; W 72.5/119. Course record: 62.
Green fees: W/D $18/$10; W/E $20/$11; Jr. rates; M/C, VISA, DISCOVER.
Power cart: $24/$12. Pull cart: $3/$2 Trail fee: 10/$5 for personal carts.
Reservation policy: weekends yes call ahead. Weekdays first come first served.
Winter condition: the golf course is open all year long. Dry, course drains well.
Terrain: flat (easy walking). Tees: grass. Spikes: no metal spikes permitted.
Services: club rentals, lessons, restaurant, snack bar, lounge, beer, wine, liquor, beverages, pro shop, putting green/chipping greens, lodging at the nearby motel.
Comments: challenging 18 hole layout that offers the golfer wide fairways and large greens. The course is flat and easy to walk. Great golf course for seniors.

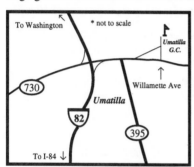

Directions: from I-84 E&W exit at the Irrigon/Umatilla exit. Proceed eastbound for 14.5 miles through the Umatilla city center. The golf course will be located 2 miles ahead. The way to the golf course is well marked with signs along your way. Course is located at the Nendel's Resort.

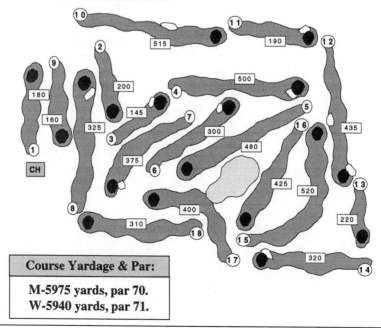

Course Yardage & Par:
M-5975 yards, par 70.
W-5940 yards, par 71.

Valley Golf Club (public, 9 hole course)
345 Hines Boulevard, P.O. Box 96; Hines, OR 97882
Phone: (541) 573-6251. **Fax:** none. **Internet:** none.
Manager: Donald Barnes. **Superintendent:** Joe Rubio.
Rating/Slope: M 69.4/107; W 73.2/115. **Course record:** 33.
Green fees: $17/$11 all week long; no credit cards are accepted.
Power cart: $18/$10. **Pull cart:** $1. **Trail fee:** $5 for personal carts.
Reservation policy: not necessary. Tee-times on a first come first served basis.
Winter condition: the golf course is open all year long. Dry (drains well).
Terrain: flat (easy walking). **Tees:** all grass. **Spikes:** metal spikes permitted.
Services: club rentals, snack bar, beverages, showers, pro shop, putting green.
Comments: Course is well conditioned and easy to walk. The golf course is
fairly long and can play tough when you stray from the fairway. Fairways are on
the large size with wide landing area's. Greens are medium in size and have few
hazards fronting them. Dual tees are available for those wanting to play 18 holes.

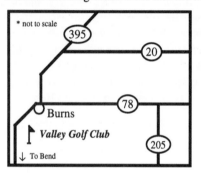

Directions: the golf course is located
between the intersections of Highway 395
and Highway 20, in the town of Hines
Oregon. The golf course is right off of
Highway 395. Look for signs marking
your way to the golf course.

Course Yardage & Par:
M-3190 yards, par 36.
W-3190 yards, par 38.
Duals tees for 18 holes:
M-6405 yards, par 72.
W-6405 yards, par 72.

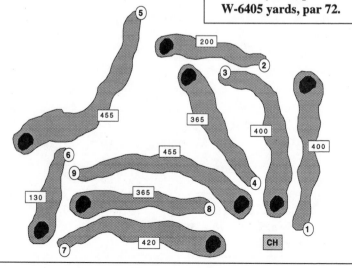

Vernonia Golf Club (public, 9 hole course)

15961 Timber Road E; Vernonia, OR 97064
Phone: (503) 429-6811, 800-644-6535. Fax: (503) 429-6811.
Manager: Fred Fulmer III. Superintendent: John Trent.
Rating/Slope: M 66.8/113; W 68.8/114. **Course record:** 63.
Green fees: W/D $17/$9; W/E $19/$10; Jr./Sr. rates (M-F); M/C, VISA.
Power cart: $20/$10. **Pull cart:** $2. **Trail fee:** $5 for personal carts.
Reservation policy: yes, call 7 days in advance for weekends and holidays.
Winter condition: the golf course is open all year long. Dry (good drainage).
Terrain: flat, some hills. **Tees:** all grass. **Spikes:** metal spikes permitted.
Services: club rentals, lessons, snack bar, beer, wine, pro shop, putting green.
Comments: course was established in 1928. The golf course is situated in a
very scenic, quiet, rural setting along the Nehalem River. It is located only 45
minutes from downtown Portland. Course has dual tees for 18 hole play. Look
for Vernonia to be expanding to 18 holes in the near future.

Directions: from Highway 26 westbound
from Portland to Highway 47 (Vernonia
exit). Proceed for 14 miles. Turn left on
Timber Road. Proceed for 1 mile. The
golf course will be located on your right
hand side. Look for signs at your turns.

Course Yardage & Par:
M-2701 yards, par 35.
W-2547 yards, par 36.
<u>**Dual tees for 18 holes:**</u>
M-5536 yards, par 71.
W-5097 yards, par 72.

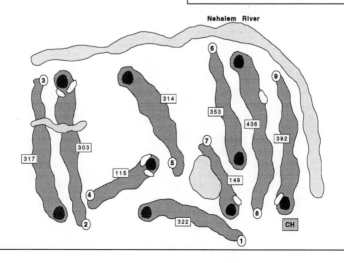

Veterans Administration Domiciliary G.C. (private, 9 holes)
Domiciliary Golf Course; White City, OR 97503
Phone: (541) 826-2111. Fax: none. Internet: none.
Golf Shop Director: Ron Riddle. Superintendent: none.
Rating/Slope: the golf course is not rated. **Course record:** 29.
Green fees: course is for patients and staff of the domiciliary. Play allowed
for outpatients along with their guests as long as they have proper paperwork.
Power cart: no charge. **Pull cart:** no charge. **Trail fee:** no charge.
Reservation policy: Private club members, guests and patients only.
Winter condition: the course is open all year long weather permitting.
Terrain: flat (easy walking). **Tees:** grass. **Spikes:** metal spikes permitted.
Services: all services provided by the Veterans Administration, putting green.
Comments: Golf course is one of the finest recreational standpoints of the
White City Domiciliary Recreation Program. No public play is allowed.

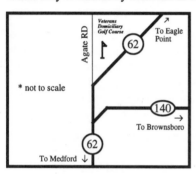

Directions: the golf course is located
northeast of Medford off of Highway 62.

Course Yardage & Par:
White tees: 2018 yards, par 33.
Blue tees: 2018 yards, par 33.

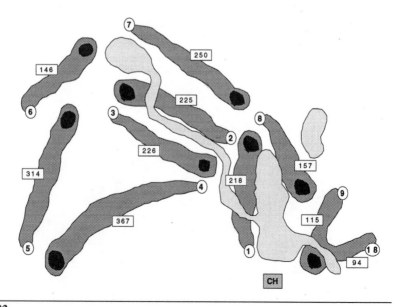

Waverley Country Club (private, 18 hole course)

1100 SE Waverley Drive; Portland, OR 97222
Phone: (503) 654-9509. Fax: (503) 654-4571. Internet: none.
Pro: John Wells, PGA. Superintendent: Richard Schwaubauer.
Rating/Slope: C 71.6/126; M 70.2/122; W 74.1/126. **Course record:** 65.
Green fees: private club; members only; no outside play permitted.
Power cart: yes. **Pull cart:** yes. **Trail fee:** no personal carts are allowed.
Reservation policy: members & guests of members only.
Winter condition: the golf course is open all year long. Dry conditions.
Terrain: flat, some hills. **Tees:** grass. **Spikes:** metal spikes permitted.
Services: private club, restaurant, pro shop, lounge, showers, lockers, driving range (members only), putting & chipping greens, club memberships.
Comments: Course is rich with tradition and character. One of the finest courses in the state of Oregon. Host of many major tournaments throughout the years.

Directions: from Highway 99E (McLoughlin Blvd), take Highway 224 exit and travel westbound to 17th. Turn right (north). Proceed to Waverly Drive. At Waverly Drive turn left to the golf course. Look for a small sign at the turn.

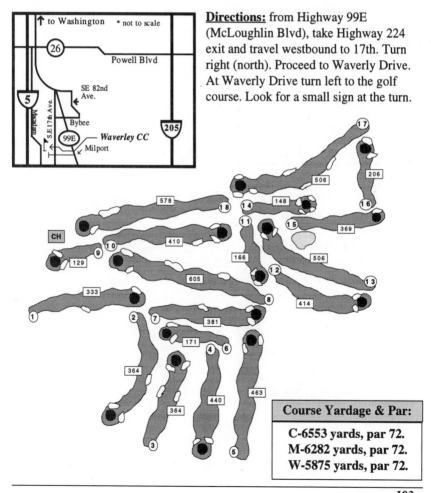

Course Yardage & Par:

C-6553 yards, par 72.
M-6282 yards, par 72.
W-5875 yards, par 72.

Widgi Creek Golf Club (semi-private, 18 hole course)
18707 Century Drive; Bend, OR 97702
Phone: (541) 382-4449. Fax: (541) 385-7094. Internet: none.
Pro: Kelly Walker, PGA. Superintendent: N/A.
Rating/Slope: T 72.5/137; C 70.9/133; M 68.1/125; W 69.2/124. **Record: 65.**
Green fees: W/D $49/$34; W/E $75/$50; off season rates; M/C, VISA.
Power cart: $13/$8 per person. **Pull cart:** $3/$2. **Trail fee:** members only.
Reservation policy: yes, public can call 30 days in advance with credit card.
Winter condition: the golf course is open all year, weather permitting.
Terrain: flat, some hills. **Tees:** all grass. **Spikes:** metal spikes permitted.
Services: club rentals, lessons, snack bar, beer, wine, pro shop, driving range.
Comments: championship course designed by Robert Muir Graves. The golf
course borders the Deschutes National Forest. A challenging, beautiful track. If
you are vacationing in the central Oregon area be sure to visit Widgi Creek.

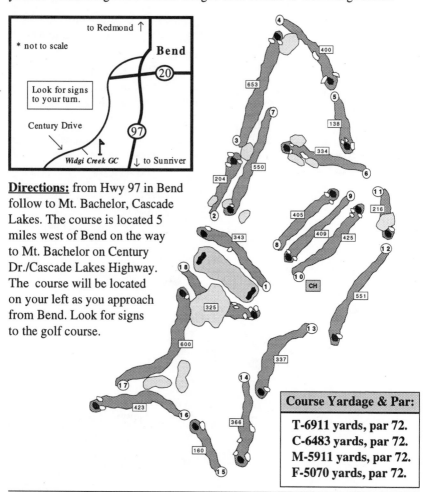

Directions: from Hwy 97 in Bend
follow to Mt. Bachelor, Cascade
Lakes. The course is located 5
miles west of Bend on the way
to Mt. Bachelor on Century
Dr./Cascade Lakes Highway.
The course will be located
on your left as you approach
from Bend. Look for signs
to the golf course.

Course Yardage & Par:

T-6911 yards, par 72.
C-6483 yards, par 72.
M-5911 yards, par 72.
F-5070 yards, par 72.

Wild Horse Golf Course (public, 18 hole course)
72787 Highway 331; Pendleton, OR 97801
Phone: (541) 276-5888. Fax: none. Internet: none.
Pro: to be announced. Superintendent: none.
Rating/Slope: the golf course has yet to be rated. **Course record:** 67.
Green fees: W/D $30/$15; W/E $35/$17.50; M/C, VISA.
Power cart: $22/$11. **Pull cart:** $3. **Trail fee:** not allowed.
Reservation policy: please call in advance for all tee-times.
Winter condition: the golf course open, weather permitting. Dry winter course.
Terrain: flat, some hills. **Tees:** all grass. **Spikes:** metal spikes permitted.
Services: club rentals, lessons, snack bar, restaurant, pro shop, driving range.
Comments: this John Steidel designed layout is a championship caliber course.
The layout features extensive mounding, large undulating greens and well
bunkered fairways laced with water. Worth a trip if in the Pendleton area.

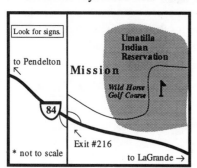

Directions: from I-84 East & West take
exit #216 and head north towards the
Umatilla Indian Reservation. The golf
course is located 1 mile north of I-84 on
the Indian Reservation.

Course Yardage & Par:

T-7000 yards, par 72.
C-6470 yards, par 72.
M-6100 yards, par 72.
F-5610 yards, par 72.

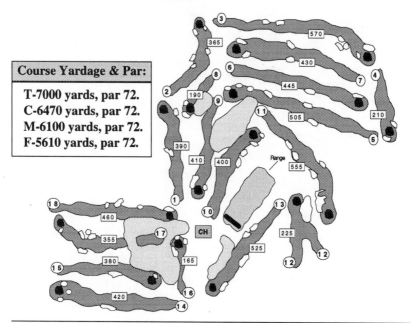

Wildwood Golf Course (public, 18 hole course)
21281 NW Saint Helens Road; Portland, OR 97231
Phone: (503) 621-3402. **Fax:** (503) 621-1056. **Internet:** none.
Owners: Bill & Kay O'Meara. **Superintendent:** Bill O'Meara.
Rating/Slope: M 68.1/111; W 72.4/120. **Course record:** 66.
Green fees: W/D $20/$11; W/E $24/$13. no credit cards.
Power cart: $20/$10. **Pull cart:** $2/$1. **Trail fee:** $3 for personal carts.
Reservation policy: call 7 days in advance for your tee-time reservations.
Winter condition: the golf course is open all year long. Drains fairly well.
Terrain: flat, some hills. **Tees:** grass. **Spikes:** metal spikes permitted.
Services: club rentals, lessons, pro shop, driving range, restaurant, putting green.
Comments: friendly family run course. This golf course sports three creeks
running through it. Great place to host a casual golf tournament or outing.

Directions: The golf course is located right off of Hwy 30, 2 miles west of the Cornelius Pass turnoff. The course will be located on the west side of Hwy 30.

Course Yardage & Par:
M-5756 yards, par 72.
W-4985 yards, par 72.

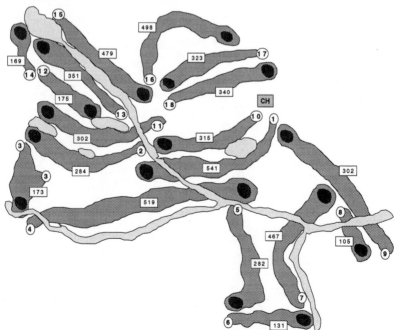

Willamette Valley Country Club (private, 18 hole course)
900 Country Club Drive; Canby, OR 97013
Phone: (503) 266-2102. Fax: (503) 266-4389. Internet: wvccpro@aol.com.
Pro: Pat Akins, PGA. Superintendent: Richard White.
Rating/Slope: C 74.2/132; M 71.2/131; W 71.8/124. **Course record:** 65.
Green fees: private club; reciprocates with other private clubs.
Power cart: private club. **Pull cart:** private. **Trail fee:** private club.
Reservation policy: public tee-times are not allowed. Private members only.
Winter condition: the golf course is open all year long weather permitting, dry.
Terrain: flat. **Tees:** all grass. **Spikes:** no metal spikes April-October.
Services: pro shop, restaurant, lounge, showers, driving range, putting green.
Comments: Course has tree lined fairways and well conditioned greens. Good
private facility. Almost all of the greens are guarded by greenside bunkers. The
course can play very tight at times putting emphasis on accuracy off the tee.

Directions: From Highway 99E turn
westbound on Territorial Road. Proceed
to Maple Street and turn right. Proceed to
the golf course entrance which will be on
your right. Look for a small sign at your
turn to the entrance to the club.

Course Yardage & Par:
C-7008 yards, par 72.
M-6401 yards, par 72.
W-5509 yards, par 72.

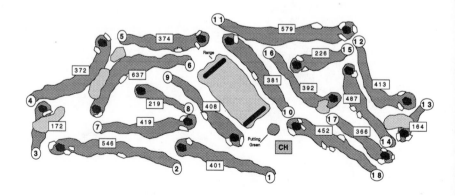

Willow Creek Country Club (semi-private, 9 hole course)
State Route 74; P.O. Box 64; Heppner, OR 97836
Phone: (541) 676-5437. **Fax:** none. **Internet:** none.
Pro: none. **Superintendent:** none.
Rating/Slope: M 56.7/83; W 59.2/85. **Course record:** 26.
Green fees: $12/$7 all week long; no credit cards are allowed.
Power cart: none available. **Pull cart:** $2. **Trail fee:** not allowed.
Reservation policy: not needed. T-times are on a first come first served basis.
Winter condition: the golf course is open all year long. Damp conditions.
Terrain: flat some hills. **Tees:** all grass. **Spikes:** metal spikes permitted.
Services: club rentals, candy, beverages, small pro shop, putting green.
Comments: Short, well kept course that lets you practice your iron play.
Good walking course that does not play very long. Great for the senior golfer.

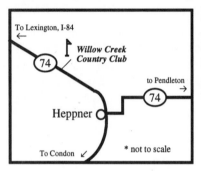

Directions: the golf course is located 1.1 miles NW of Heppner Oregon off of Hwy 74. The golf course is located on the west side of the Highway. Look for signs to the golf course that are posted on the Highway.

Course Yardage & Par:
M-1725 yards, par 30.
W-1725 yards, par 30.
Dual tees for 18 holes:
M-3410 yards, par 60.
W-3410 yards, par 60.

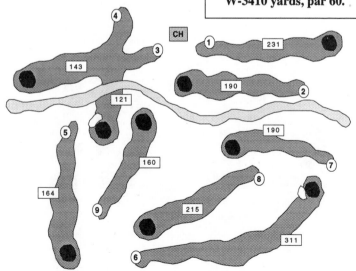

Wilson's Willow Run Executive G. C. (semi-private, 9 holes)

Wilson Road; Route 1, Box 22; Boardman, OR 97818;
Phone: (541) 481-4381. Fax: none. Internet: none.
Manager: Hope Phillips. Superintendent: none.
Rating/Slope: M 55.7/82; W 56.1/79. **Course record:** 57.
Green fees: W/D $8/$5; W/E $10/$6; no credit cards are accepted.
Power cart: $12.50/$7.50. **Pull cart:** $2/$1. **Trail fee:** $3/$2.
Reservation policy: yes, suggested for weekends, holidays only.
Winter condition: open all year. Club house closed December 1st to March 1st.
Terrain: flat (easy walking). **Tees:** all grass. **Spikes:** metal spikes permitted.
Services: club rentals, vending machines, putting green, beginner course.
Comments: Very challenging short "easy" course with water hazards and trees.
Course also features "The Wedge" beginners course and practice area.
($1, complimentary prior to tee time.) Course closed Mondays except holidays.

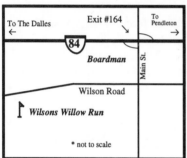

Directions: from I-84 take the Boardman exit #164. Turn left 1 mile to Wilson Road. Turn right and proceed 3 miles to the golf course. The golf course is located at the west end of Wilson Road. Look for signs at your turns.

Course Yardage & Par:
M-1803 yards, par 31.
W-1803 yards, par 32.
<u>Dual for tees 18 holes:</u>
M-3742 yards, par 62.
W-3742 yards, par 64.

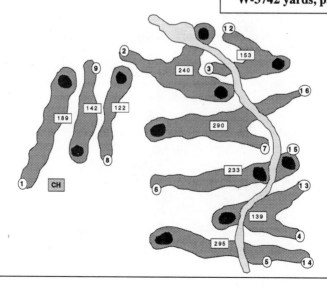

Woodburn Golf Club (public, 9 hole course)
Highway 214 West; Woodburn, OR 97071
Phone: no phone listed. **Fax:** none. **Internet:** none.
Pro: none available. **Superintendent:** none.
Rating/Slope: the golf course is not rated. **Course record:** 31.
Green fees: $2 all day; annual fees $50; husbands & wives $60; no credit cards.
Power cart: none. **Pull cart:** none. **Trail fee:** no charge for personal carts.
Reservation policy: self service. Times are on a first come first served basis
Winter condition: the golf course is open all year long. Very wet conditions.
Terrain: flat (easy walking). **Tees:** all grass. **Spikes:** metal spikes permitted.
Services: very limited services, putting green, picnic table.
Comments: Mens club plays on Wednesday morning. Ladies club plays on
Thursday morning. One of the last courses in the northwest to have sand greens.
The course can be very wet during the winter months. Very rustic golf course.

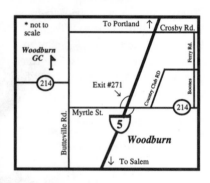

Directions: from I-5 north & south take
the Woodburn exit. Go westbound on
Highway 214 for 1.9 miles. The golf
course will be on your right hand side.

Course Yardage & Par:
M-2592 yards, par 34.
W-2570 yards, par 36.

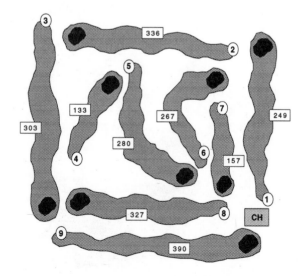

82nd Avenue Range
2806 NE 82nd; Portland, OR 97220
(503) 253-0902. Pro: John Bowen, PGA.
Hours: M-F 9am-10:30pm, Sat./Sun. 7am-10:30pm.
Lights: yes. **Covered:** yes.
Putting & chipping: yes. **Services:** club repair,
lessons, pro shop. **Directions:** I-205 N&S take
airport exit and travel westbound to 82nd. Turn
left on 82nd and proceed to the driving range.
 Map 1; Grid B3

Caddieshack Driving Range
5201 State Street; Salem, OR 97301
(503) 581-7045. Pro: Jim Hynds, PGA.
Hours: 8:30am to dusk. **Lights:** no.
Covered: yes. **Putting & chipping:** yes.
Services: lessons, pro shop, snack bar, rentals.
Directions: from I-5 take the Center St exit and
travel east. At Lancaster turn right and follow to
State St. Turn left on State St and proceed to the
driving range. **Map 1; Grid C3**

Cordon Road Driving Range
4205 Cordon Road NE; Salem, OR 97302
(503) 362-3694. Pro: Mike Dwyer, PGA.
Hours: seasonal hours. **Lights:** no.
Covered: yes. **Putting & chipping:** yes.
Services: lessons, club repair, pro shop, sand
bunker, snacks, putting & chipping green.
Directions: the driving range is located 1/2 mile
north of the Silverton Road and Cordon Road
intersection. **Map 1; Grid C3**

Dino's Driving Range
21661 Beavercreek RD; Oregon City, OR 97045
(503) 632-3986. Owner: Dino Marasigan.
Hours: W/D 9am-dusk; W/E 8am-dusk. **Lights:** no.
Covered: yes. **Putting & chipping:** yes & bunker.
Services: pro shop, four teaching pros, lessons,
food, custom golf clubs, club repair, regripping.
Directions: from I-205 N&S take exit #10 (Park
Place). Head south on Hwy 213. Turn left (east)
at Beavercreek Rd. (third light).The range is located
ahead. **Map 1; Grid B3**

Eagle Driving Range
63977 Imnaha Hwy; Joseph, OR 97946
no phone listed. Pro: N/A
Hours: 7am to dark March-November.
Lights: yes. **Covered:** no.
Putting & chipping: yes, with practice bunker.
Services: lessons.
Directions: the driving range is located 1/2 mile
out of Joseph, Oregon on the north side of the
Imnaha Highway. **Map 3; Grid B4**

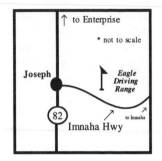

Golden Bear Golf Center @ Sunset
16251 SW Jenkins Road; Beaverton, OR 97006
(503) 626-2244; Manager: Sheri Okazaki.
Hours: W/D 9am-10pm, all year round.
Lights: yes. **Covered:** yes. **Putting/chipping:** yes.
Services: grass tees, mini golf, lessons, pro shop,
deli, club repair, practice bunker. **Directions:** from
Hwy 217 take the Walker Rd. exit. Head west turn
left on Cedar Hills Rd. Proceed to Jenkins turn
right. Go to range.**Map 1; Grid B3**

Grants Pass Golf Center
2450 NW Vine Street; Grant Pass, OR 97526
(541) 479-9500. Pro: none.
Hours: 9am to 8pm (change in winter). **Lights:** yes.
Covered: yes. **Putting & chipping:** yes.
Services: club rentals, lessons, club repair, pro shop.
Directions: from I-5 southbound take the first
Grants Pass exit (last going northbound). Turn right
at the first light. Proceed to Vine St and then turn
right on Vine St. **Map 1; Grid G2**

Jack Creek Driving Range
off of S Bank Chetco Rd.; Brookings, OR 97415
(541) 469-2606. Pro: Bruce Alexander.
Hours: please call for hours summer hours.
Lights: information not available.
Covered: information not available.
Putting & chipping: information not available.
Services: lessons, small pro shop.
Directions: the range is located in the town of
Brookings OR off of S Bank Chetco RD From Hwy
101 turn east. **Map 1; Grid G1**

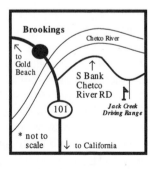

Kik's Driving Range
off of Hwy 730; McNary, OR 97882
(541) 922-2844. Pro: Todd Sprong.
Hours: please call for hours summer hours.
Lights: information not available.
Covered: information not available.
Putting & chipping: information not available.
Services: lessons, small pro shop.
Directions: the range is located in the town of
McNary Oregon off of Hwy 730.
 Map 2; Grid A4

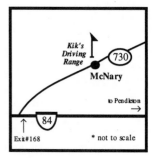

Raymax Golf Center
3707 Eberlein; Klamath Falls, OR 97603
(541) 884-1094. Pro: Hal Greene.
Hours: range open from dawn to dusk.
Lights: no.
Covered: yes.
Putting & chipping: yes.
Services: lessons, pro shop.
Directions: the range is located in Klamath Falls
on Eberlein St. **Map 1; Grid G4**

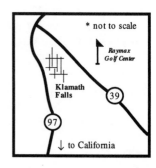

Tualatin Island Greens
20400 SW Cipole Road; Tualatin, OR 97062
(503) 691-8400. Pro: Todd Andrews, PGA.
Hours: 8am-10pm (summer); 8am-9pm (winter).
Lights: yes. **Covered:** yes & heated stalls.
Putting & chipping: yes. **Services:** club repair,
18 hole putting course, snack bar, pro shop, lessons.
Directions: from I-5 N&S exit #289 going west on
Tualatin-Sherwood Road for 3 miles to Cipole Road.
Turn north. **Map 1; Grid B3**

Westside Driving Range
6050 Hwy 22; Independence, OR 97351
(503) 364-3615. Owner: Paul Cheney.
Hours: open daylight hours.
Lights: no. **Covered:** yes.
Putting & chipping: yes.
Services: club repair, lessons, pro shop, sand trap.
Directions: the range is located between Salem
and Independence Oregon right off of Hwy 22.
Look for the signs to the range.
Map 1; Grid C3

A & A Custom Golf
4803 SW 76th; Portland, Oregon; (503) 292-3711
Services: club repair, custom clubs, refinishing.

A Hole in One Golf Shop
2300 NE Division; Bend, Oregon; (541) 388-7537
Services: club repair, custom clubs, club refinishing, swing analysis.

All Seasons Sports
714 Main Street; Klamath Falls, Oregon; (541) 884-3863
Services: retail store.

Bear Clubs Custom Golf
10315 SW Denney Road; Beaverton, Oregon; (503) 520-0204
Services: club repairs, custom clubs, club refinishing.

Caplan Sportsworld
625 SW 4th & Morrison; Portland, Oregon; (503) 226-6467
Services: retail golf store, custom clubs.

Club Crafters
1020 Green Acres Road; STE 2; Eugene, Oregon; (541) 843-2222
Services: club repairs, custom clubs, club refinishing.

Cascade Custom Golf
14980 S Blue Vista Drive; Oregon City, Oregon; (503) 650-9522
Services: club repairs, custom clubs, club refinishing.

Cascade Athletic Supply
245 S Central Avenue; Medford, Oregon; (503) 772-7594
Services: retail golf store.

Club Doctor, The
7846 Battle Creek Road SE; Salem, Oregon; (503) 362-1566
Services: club repair, custom clubs, club refinishing.

Custom Golf by Stu
17110 NE Halsey; Gresham, Oregon; (503) 255-8280
Services: custom clubs.

Dot Golf Center
14624 SE McLoughlin Boulevard; Milwaukie, Oregon; (503) 794-0940
Services: retail golf store, club repair, custom clubs, club refinishing.

Dot Golf Center
8604 SW Hall Boulevard; Beaverton, Oregon; (503) 641-9525
Services: retail golf store, club repair, custom clubs, club refinishing.

Double Eagle Golf Center
8200 SW Scholls Ferry Road; Beaverton, Oregon; (503) 646-5166
Services: club repair, custom clubs, club refinishing, lessons.

Entrepreneurial Golf
PO Box 566; Gresham, Oregon 97030; (503) 666-3152
Services: Golf accessories, prints, tee prizes.

Foltz's Valley Golf Service
5239 Table Rock Road; Central Point, Oregon; (503) 664-3971
Services: club repair, custom clubs, refinishing, custom fitting, used clubs.

Golf USA
3665 SW Cedar Hills Boulevard; Beaverton, Oregon; (503) 526-9218
Services: club repair, custom clubs, refinishing, lessons, nationwide shipping.

Golf USA
2285 Lancaster Drive NE: Salem, Oregon; (503) 375-6203
Services: retail store, swing analyzer.

Golf USA Sport Tech Swing
2061 Roberts Road; Medford, Oregon; (503) 776-1370
Services: lessons.

Golf City
1052 NE 3rd Street; Bend, Oregon; (503) 389-3919
Services: club repair, custom clubs, club refinishing.

Golf Crafters, The
1831 NE Stephens; Roseburg, Oregon; (503) 673-2868
Services: lessons, club repair, custom clubs, retail store.

Golf Den, The
7320 SW Beaverton Hillsdale Highway; Portland, Oregon; (503) 292-6520
Services: club repair, club refinishing, retail merchandise, large pro shop.

Golf Den, The
12433-B NE Glisan; Portland, Oregon; (503) 255-5549
Services: club repair, club refinishing, retail merchandise, large pro shop.

Golf Swing Shop
2061 Roberts Road; Medford, Oregon; (503) 776-3053
Services: lessons.

Golfers Garage
34 Carthage; Eugene, Oregon; (503) 688-3754
Services: club repair, custom clubs, new & used clubs.

Hank Childs Golf Shop
2200 NE 71st; Portland, Oregon; (503) 253-4744
Services: club repair, club refinishing, lessons.

Highline/Mulligans
210 SW Yam Hill Plaza; Portland, Oregon; (503) 295-6702
Services: lessons.

Huff's Golf Shop
5051 NW Garden Valley Road; Roseburg, Oregon; (541) 672-4041
Services: club repair, retail shop, lessons.

International Discount Golf
2806 NE 82nd; Portland, Oregon; (503) 253-0902
Services: retail store, lessons, club fitting, driving range.

International Discount Golf
11493 SE 82nd; Portland, Oregon; (503) 659-4653
Services: retail store, lessons, club fitting.

International Discount Golf
9315 SW Beaverton Hillsdale Highway; Portland, Oregon; (503) 292-5446
Services: retail store, lessons, club fitting.

Jack Beaudoins Golf Shop
1459 NE Burnside; Gresham, Oregon; (503) 666-GOLF
Services: club regripping, repair, lessons, club fitting.

Kangaroo Golf
3988 SE 82nd Avenue; Portland, Oregon; (503) 777-0650
Services: not available.

Las Vegas Discount Golf & Tennis
61249 S Highway 97, Unit A; Bend, Oregon; (541) 383-2944
Services: retail golf store.

Laurel Ridge Golf Company
Grants Pass, Oregon; (541) 476-8929
Services: full service club repairs, custom clubs.

Marvins Golf Town
808 E Main; Klamath Falls, Oregon; (541) 884-1493
Services: club repair, refinishing.

Missing Link, The
1707 N Highway 97; Redmond, Oregon; (541) 923-3426
Services: club repair, custom clubs, club refinishing.

Mulligan's Golf Equipment Liquidators
11040 SW Allen; Beaverton, Oregon; (503) 644-9906
Services: golf closeout merchandise, consignments welcome.

Nevada Bob's
101215 SW Parkway; Portland, Oregon; (503) 297-1808
Services: club repair, custom clubs, club refinishing, retail merchandise.

Nevada Bob's
11211 SE 82nd Avenue; Portland, Oregon; (503) 653-7202
Services: club repair, custom clubs, club refinishing, retail merchandise.

Northwoods
7410 SW Macadam; Portland, Oregon; (503) 245-1910
Services: club repair, custom clubs, club refinishing.

Parfection
1293 NE 3rd; Bend, Oregon; (541) 389-3499
Services: club repair, custom clubs, club refinishing, lessons, retail store.

Partee Time
2310 Washburn Way; Klamath Falls, Oregon; (541) 882-3105
Services: indoor golf facility.

Portland Golf Academy
8103 NE Killingsworth; Portland, Oregon; (503) 253-4653
Services: club repair, custom clubs, club refinishing, lessons.

Portland Golf Outlet
321 SW 4th; Portland, Oregon; (503) 228-7848
Services: custom clubs, hitting net, retail store.

Pro Golf Discount
9160 SW Hall Boulevard; Tigard, Oregon; (503) 646-8673
Services: club repair, custom clubs, club refinishing, retail merchandise.

S-2 Oregon
725 SW 56th Street; Corvallis, Oregon; (541) 752-8649
Services: not available.

Our newest section in *Golfing in Oregon* is called **Weekend Getaways.**
We have received calls from people using the book for suggestions on
weekend trips and my family and I personally enjoy going golfing in the
morning and seeing other attractions in the afternoon. We have designed
this section, therefore, to give you some ideas of short weekend trips you
could take in the area and you can tailor them to your taste! Any further
information you would like on specific lodging availability the Chamber of
Commerce in the destination city would be eager to provide. Some of our
suggestions may be seasonal so it is always best to call ahead.

Gearhart/Seaside: One of the most popular spots on the Oregon coast has
three golf courses to choose from: The Highlands at Gearhart, Gearhart
Golf Links, and Seaside Golf Course. Lodging is available in both
oceanside towns. Besides beachcombing and taking in the magnificent
beauty of the Oregon coast there are many other attractions. Seaside offers
extensive gift shopping, arcades, and dining. Just a short drive south on
Hwy 101 will take you to the quaint town of Cannon Beach. Here you will
find dining, gallery and gift shopping as well as the famous "Haystack
Rock" on the beach. During the summer months Cannon Beach is host to
a world famous sandcastle building contest you won't want to miss.

Grants Pass/Medford: Southwestern Oregon is home to a number of
unique natural attractions which would make for a wonderful afternoon trip
after your round of golf. This area is also has three new golf courses to
play: Dutcher Creek (Grants Pass), Stewart Meadows and Quail Point
(Medford). The other courses available are Bear Creek and Cedar Links.
Both Grants Pass and Medford have plenty of lodging and dining available.
Just a short distance from both cities lies the Oregon Caves National
Monument. The caves are usually open year round with guided tours.
If you enjoy a scenic drive Crater Lake National Park is northeast of both
cities. The 1,962 foot deep lake is an awesome specimen of volcanic
activity from the past. There is a drive you can take that circles the rim
of the crater with viewpoints along the way. A lodge and food services
are available (seasonal). For the real adventurist the Rogue River offers
whitewater rafting trips.

Portland: The thriving metropolis of Portland and its suburbs offer a
myriad of golf courses to play. Portland itself has world class dining and
lodging available. After your round of golf you might enjoy visiting the
International Rose Gardens or take the drive east on I-84 to the Columbia
River Gorge. This scenic area offers extensive hiking trails including one
to Multnomah Falls, the highest waterfall in the state. Mt. Hood is only a
short drive east of Portland as well. The mountain is open for snow skiing

even in the summer months on the glacier at the upper elevation. Timber-
line Lodge, a national historic landmark is also located at Mt. Hood and is
well worth the drive to visit. Portland also offers downtown shopping and
a scenic park on the Willamette River which runs through the city. The city
and surrounding areas offer many museums which concentrate on the
historic Oregon Trail. East of I-5 between Portland and Eugene is the
Oregon wine country where many of the wineries are open for vineyard
tours and wine tasting. Visitor centers provide information on all these
various attractions.

Salishan/Gleneden Beach: The Salishan Resort is excellent for a weekend
getaway on the beautiful Oregon coast. The resort offers an exquisite
restaurant featuring northwest cuisine along with championship golf.

Sisters: Located in central Oregon this area will remind you of the Ponderosa. Black Butte (10 mi west of Sisters) is a full service resort with
horseback riding, 2 championship golf courses on site, fine dining, grocery
store, tennis, swimming and supervised childrens activities. Sisters also has
lodging and dining available. After your golf game there are many things to
interest you. Sisters is designed to look like an old western town with many
small shops to explore. Others might enjoy an afternoon hike up Black
Butte or drive to the Lava fields at the summit of McKenzie Pass which
include a round tower made of the volcanic rock. At the top of the tower
there are observation windows which view each of the many mountain tops
in the area. There is also an interpretive trail through the lava fields. Just a
short drive east of Sisters is Redmond where Eagle Crest Resort is located.
This resort also offers two championship caliber golf courses on site. Other
amenities include tennis, pool and jacuzzi, nature and bike trails, childcare,
a massage, aerobics, and tanning salon, equestrian center, and fine dining.
Also in the area is Crooked River Ranch GC that recently expanded to a full
18 holes.

Sunriver: The Sunriver Resort is also a full service resort offering fine
dining, lodging, swimming, shopping, boutiques, and two championship
golf courses with a third scheduled to open in 1995 called Crosswater. This
private club will reciprocate with Sunriver lodge guests and promises to be a
truly spectacular addition to the central Oregon golf scene. Other attractions
in the area include the High Desert Museum. This features wildlife, an
inter-pretive center, and a replica of the early settlers homes and a sawmill.
Lava Butte (11 miles south of Bend) offers self-guided trails and lava tubes
which you can hike in for up to 1 mile. Bring warm clothes and a flashlight
(or you can rent a Coleman lantern). The lava tubes are quite cool, even in
the summer months.

Welches: Since 1893 The Resort at the Mountain has been catering to the public. First founded near the Oregon Trail, this area is rich in history and natural beauty. Previously known as "Rippling River Resort" the name has been changed to The Resort at the Mountain and extensive re-modeling has taken place. Located at the foot of Mount Hood this is truly an all season resort. Offering 27 challenging holes of golf in an alpine setting is just the beginning for this getaway. The resort also features 160 luxury guest rooms, (some with fireplaces), a complete fitness center, 6 tennis courts, a pool and jacuzzi, two restaurants, hiking, biking, volleyball, basket-ball, croquet, basketball, badmiton, and gift shops. The Mt. Hood and Columbia River Gorge Recreation areas offer guided fishing trips, trout farm fishing for children, river rafting on the Deschutes River, wind surfing, go cart rentals, and much, much, more.

Oregon is a beautiful state with many activities to offer in conjunction with golf. If you desire further information on a specific area or activity the Oregon State Tourism Office will help you.

Call: 1-800-547-7842 (outside Oregon) or 1-800-233-3306 (within Oregon).

Florence: Ocean Dunes Golf Links, Sandpines Golf Links.
Forest Grove: Sunset Grove Golf Club.
Fossil: Kinzua Hills Golf Club.
Gearhart: Gearhart Golf Links, The Highlands at Gearhart.
Gladstone: Rivergreens Golf.
Glenden Beach: Salishan Golf Links.
Gold Beach: Cedar Bend Golf Club.
Gold Hill: Laurel Hill Golf Course.
Grants Pass: Applegate Golf, Colonial Valley Golf Course, Dutcher Creek Golf Course, Grants Pass Golf Center, Grants Pass Golf Club, Hillebrand's Paradise Ranch Resort, Red Mountain Golf Course.
Gresham: Gresham Golf Course, Persimmon Country Club.
Heppner: Willow Creek Country Club.
Hines: Valley Golf Club.
Hillsboro: Kilarney West Golf Club, McKay Creek Golf Course, Meriwether National Golf Club, Orenco Woods Golf Club.
Hood River: Hood River Golf & Country Club, Indian Creek Golf Course.
Independence: Oak Knoll Golf Course, West Side Driving Range.
Island City: La Grande Country Club
John Day: John Day Golf Club.
Joseph: Eagle Driving Range.
Junction City: Shadow Hills Country Club.
Keizer: McNary Golf Club.
King City: King City Golf Course.
Klamath Falls: Harbor Links Golf Course, Raymax Driving Range, Reames Golf & Country Club, Round Lake Resort, Running Y Ranch Resort, Sheild Crest Golf Course.
La Grande: La Grande Country Club.
La Pine: Quail Run Golf Course.
Lakeview: Lakeridge Golf & Country Club.
Lake Oswego: Lake Oswego Golf Course, Oswego Lake Country Club.
Lebanon: Pineway Golf Course.
Lincoln City: Lakeside Golf & Racquet Club.
Lyons: Elkhorn Valley Golf Course.
McMinnville: Bayou Golf Club, Michelbook Country Club.
Madras: Nine Peaks Golf Course.
Manzanita: Manzanita Golf Course.
McNary: Kik's Driving Range.
Medford: Bear Creek Family Golf Center, Cedar Links Golf Club, Quail Point Golf Course, Rogue Valley Country Club, Stewart Meadows, Stoneridge Golf Course.
Milton-Freewater: Milton-Freewater Golf Course.
Mission: Wild Horse Golf Course.

Mollala: Arrowhead Golf Club.
Monroe: Diamond Woods Golf Course
Mount Angel: Evergreen Golf Club.
Mulino: Ranch Hills Golf Club.
Myrtle Creek: Myrtle Creek Golf Course
Myrtle Point: Coquille Valley Elks Golf Club.
Neskowin: Hawk Creek Golf Course, Neskowin Beach Golf Course.
Newport: Agate Beach Golf Course.
North Bend: Kentuck Golf Course
Oakridge: Circle Bar Golf Club.
Ontario: Shadow Butte Municipal Golf Course.
Oregon City: Dino's Driving Range, Oregon City Golf Club.
Pendleton: Pendleton Country Club, Wild Horse Golf Course.
Portland: 82nd Avenue Range, Broadmoor Golf Course, Claremont Golf Club, Columbia Edgewater Country Club, Colwood National Golf Club, Dino's Driving Range, Eastmoreland Golf Course, Glendoveer Golf Course (East & West Courses), Golden Bear Golf Center @ Sunset, Heron Lakes Golf Club (Great Blue Course, Greenback Course), Jim Colbert's Hound Hollow Golf Course & Driving Range, Portland Golf Club, Portland Meadows Golf Course, Progress Downs Municipal Golf Course, Riverside Golf & Country Club, Rock Creek Country Club, Rose City Golf Course, Top O'Scott Golf Course, Waverly Country Club, Wildwood Golf Course,
Prineville: Meadow Lakes Golf Course, Prineville Golf & Country Club.
Redmond: Eagle Crest Resort (Resort Course, Ridge Course), Juniper Golf Course, The Greens at Redmond.
Reedsport: Forest Hills Country Club.
Roseburg: Roseburg Country Club, Stewart Park Golf Course.
Salem: Auburn Center Golf Club, Battle Creek Golf Course, Caddieshack Driving Range, Cordon Road Driving Range, Cottonwood Lakes Golf Course & Driving Range, Creekside Golf Club, Illahe Hills Country Club, McNary Golf Club, Meadowlawn Golf Club, Salem Golf Club, Salemtowne Golf Club.
Seaside: Seaside Golf Course.
Sisters: Aspen Lakes Golf Club, Black Butte Ranch.
Springfield: McKenzie River Golf Course, Springfield Country Club.
Stayton: Santiam Golf Club.
Sunriver: Crosswater, Sunriver Resort (North Woodlands, South Meadows).
Sutherlin: The Club at Sutherlin.
The Dalles: Lone Pine Village Golf, The Dalles Country Club.
Tigard: King City Golf Course, Summerfield Golf & Country Club.
Tillamook: Alderbrook Golf Course, Bay Breeze Golf Course and Driving Range.
Toledo: Olalla Valley Golf Course.
Tygh Valley: Pine Hollow Golf Course.

THIRD EDITION

GOLF COURSES
of the
PACIFIC NORTHWEST

The Complete Regional Golf Guide
by **Jeff Shelley**

In pro shops or book stores near you.

See next page for order information

Fairgreens
M E D I A

a 1997 publication of Fairgreens Media, Inc.
Distributed by MAC Productions

217